What others are saying about Frank Schaeffer's remarkable

Sex, Mom. ⌐~ '

"[Schaeffer's] memoirs have a d-ship. . . . Frank seems to have ent, but his memoirs have a serious purpose. is to expose the insanity and the corruption of what has become a powerful and frightening force in American politics. . . . Frank has been straightforward and entertaining in his campaign to right the political wrongs he regrets committing in the 1970s and '80s. . . . As someone who has made redemption his work, he has, in fact, shown amazing grace."
—Jane Smiley, *Washington Post*

"A penetrating analysis of political extremism, with a moving and at times hilarious account of growing up in one of the Christian right's most influential families. Few writers command Frank Schaeffer's intimate understanding of right-wing radicalism, and even fewer are able to share their insight as entertainingly and with as much moral weight as he has in *Sex, Mom, and God*."
—Max Blumenthal, author of *Republican Gomorrah*

"There is no one today who writes with as much humanity, insight and first-hand knowledge on the Christian experience as Frank Schaeffer, and as always he's at the top of his game in this fascinating and very enlightening book. With devastating insight he shows how the unholy alliance between the morally hypocritical religious right and the Republican Party has materially altered the landscape of American life."
—Vincent Bugliosi,
1 *New York Times* bestselling author of *Helter Skelter*

SEX, MOM, AND GOD

BOOKS BY FRANK SCHAEFFER

Fiction

The Calvin Becker Trilogy

Portofino

Zermatt

Saving Grandma

———————

Baby Jack

Nonfiction

*Keeping Faith: A Father-Son Story About Love
and The United States Marine Corps*
(Coauthored with John Schaeffer)

Faith of Our Sons: A Father's Wartime Diary

Voices from the Front: Letters Home from America's Military Family

*AWOL: The Unexcused Absence of America's Upper Classes from
Military Service—and How It Hurts Our Country*
(Coauthored with Kathy Roth-Douquet)

———————

The God Trilogy

*Crazy for God: How I Grew Up as One of the Elect, Helped Found the
Religious Right, and Lived to Take All (or Almost All) of It Back*

Patience with God: Faith for People Who Don't Like Religion (or Atheism)

*Sex, Mom, and God: How the Bible's Strange Take on Sex Led to
Crazy Politics—and How I Learned to Love Women (and Jesus) Anyway*

Please visit www.frankschaeffer.com

SEX, MOM, AND GOD

How the Bible's Strange Take on Sex
Led to Crazy Politics—and How I Learned to
Love Women (and Jesus) Anyway

FRANK SCHAEFFER

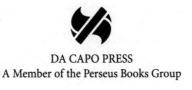

DA CAPO PRESS
A Member of the Perseus Books Group

Set in 11.75 point Minion Pro by the Perseus Books Group

Library of Congress Cataloging-in-Publication Data

Schaeffer, Frank.
    Sex, mom, and God : how the Bible's strange take on sex led to crazy politics, and how I learned to love women (and Jesus) anyway / Frank Schaeffer. — 1st Da Capo Press ed.
        p.   cm.
    Includes index.
    ISBN 978-0-306-81928-5 (alk. paper)
    1. Schaeffer, Frank. 2. Christian biography—United States. 3. Christian biography—Swizerland. 4. Sex—Biblical teaching. 5. Sex—Religious aspects—Christianity. I. Title.
BR1725.S3552A3 2011
270.8'2092—dc22
[B]   2011000929

First Da Capo Press edition 2011
First Da Capo Press paperback edition 2012
ISBN 978-0-306-81985-8 (e-book)
ISBN 978-0-306-82073-1 (paperback)

Published by Da Capo Press
A Member of the Perseus Books Group
www.dacapopress.com

Da Capo Press books are available at special discounts for bulk purchases in the U.S. by corporations, institutions, and other organizations. For more information, please contact the Special Markets Department at the Perseus Books Group, 2300 Chestnut Street, Suite 200, Philadelphia, PA 19103, or call (800) 810-4145, ext. 5000, or e-mail special.markets@perseusbooks.com.

10 9 8 7 6 5 4 3 2 1

CONTENTS

ACKNOWLEDGMENTS

My wife, Genie Schaeffer; my editor, John Radziewicz; my copy editor, Jan Kristiansson; Ashley Makar; and Thom Stark gave me excellent notes on various drafts of this book and made it better. My agent, Jennifer Lyons, always provides good advice. I'm grateful for the book-cover design by Jonathan Sainsbury and for the promotion of my writing by Lissa Warren (head of publicity at Da Capo Press). Collin Tracy (production editor for the Perseus Books Group) helped me get through the final edit process, showing patience and generosity throughout. My friends at Da Capo Press and the Perseus Books Group are good people to work with. Thank you all.

Mom and me (age 7) gardening in 1959

PROLOGUE

One of the things I love most about being with my grandchildren is that they only know me now. So before I explain
how my family helped push the Republican Party into the embrace
of the Religious Right and chronicle my family's complicity in several murders, let me say that my granddaughter Lucy has just
turned two. She, along with my three other grandchildren, is my
second chance now that I've carved out a spiritual identity as dra-
matically eclipsing of my former self as if I'd disappeared into a
witness protection program.

My four grandchildren, Amanda, Benjamin, Lucy, and Jack,
notwithstanding, I'm still prone to label people and ideas as my
mother labeled them. Mom divided everything into Very Important Things, say, Jesus, Virginity, Japanese Flower Arrangements,
Lust, See-through Black Lingerie (to be enjoyed only *after* marriage), and everything else, say, those things that barely registered
on my mother's To-Do List, like home-schooling me. So I'll be cap-
italizing some words oddly in this book, such as Sin, God, Love,

and Girls, and also words like Him when referring to God. I'm not doing this as a theological statement but as a nervous tic, a leftover from my Edith Schaeffer–shaped childhood and also to signal what Loomed Large to my mother and what still Looms Large to me.

Blessedly, Lucy and Jack live only a few hundred feet up the street. I walk to their house every day and collect them for playtime. When it's Lucy's turn, she perches in my arms and talks to me. (Jack is six months old and pulls my nose and laughs a lot but isn't saying much yet.) Lucy likes to be carried when we stroll back to "Ba and Nanna's house." (I'm "Ba" and my wife, Genie, is "Nanna.") Lucy's big brown eyes scan the eighteenth-century clapboard houses of our New England neighborhood to see which of the ubiquitous American flags are wrapped around their above-the-front-door flagpoles "by the wind, Ba," and which are waving free in the ocean breeze.

When we get to my house, Lucy commands me to read *The Tale of Two Bad Mice* by Beatrix Potter. It's a story about two deluded mice, Hunka Munka and Tom Thumb, who mistake a dollhouse dinner laid out in the dollhouse's miniature dining room for real food. When they discover that the lovely looking ham, fish, and pudding can't be eaten, they smash up the plaster "food" in revenge and then spitefully ransack the dollhouse.

When she wrote the book in 1904, Potter couldn't have known that her classic story would someday be an allegory aptly illustrating the delusion suffered by members of the American Religious Right. Some people who helped lead that movement—including me—were very much like Hunka Munka and Tom Thumb. We lived lives informed by beliefs that were not based on fact and that led to deep-seated resentments that couldn't be cured because what we resented never actually happened. We took it as a personal insult that the real world didn't conform to the imagined religious "facts" that we'd been indoctrinated to believe in, and so we did our share of smashing.

My late father, Francis Schaeffer, was a key founder and leader of the Religious Right. My mother, Edith, was herself a spiritual leader, not the mere power behind her man, which she also was. Mom was a formidable and adored religious figure whose books and public speaking, not to mention biblical conditioning of me, directly and indirectly shaped millions of lives. For a time I joined my Dad in pioneering the Evangelical antiabortion Religious Right movement. In the 1970s and early 1980s when I was in my twenties, I evolved into an ambitious, "successful" religious leader/instigator in my own right. And I wasn't just Dad's sidekick; I was also Mom's collaborator in her mission to "reach the world for Jesus."

I changed my mind. I no longer ride around "saving" America for God, nor am I a regular on religious TV and radio these days. Nevertheless—like those two bad mice who later felt remorse and so put a "crooked sixpence" in the dolls' Christmas stocking to pay for the damage they'd caused—I'm determined to acknowledge the destruction I contributed to before Lucy grows old enough to inherit the vandalized "dollhouse" that she'll soon discover lurking beyond her childhood horizon.

Author's Note: Much of the material that is to follow chronicles an intimate journey. Some people's names and other details have been changed. Genie reads my manuscripts, gives me wonderful notes, not to mention her generous permission to "tell all" and put her up on my literary auction block time and again. And I'd like to say this about my mother: At age ninety-six and suffering from short-term memory loss (and sight loss owing to macular degeneration), sadly, Mom won't read this book. But just before Christmas of 2010, we sat down together during a weeklong visit and I told her about my project in detail—including that I was going to "tell the truth and let the chips fall where they may, Mom." With a flash of her old self and a familiar defiant head toss, Mom said, "Go ahead; I don't care what people 'think' and never did!" Given her memory problem, I should add that before it developed and before her eyesight failed, she read my other equally "scandalous" writing, including my novels and nonfiction works, which also drew heavily from memories that to some people might have seemed too private to share. Mom isn't "some people." I once got a letter from one of my mother's followers telling me that, having just read my novel *Portofino* (a work of humor where the mother character, "Elsa Becker," is like my mother in some ways), she was sure it would "kill your mother because of the hatred for Jesus that drips from your SATANIC pen!" Coincidentally, that fan letter (received in the early 1990s before I was using e-mail) arrived in the same post delivery as a note from Mom asking me for another dozen signed hardcover copies of that book so that my mother could send out more to her friends. Mom's follower had signed her letter "Repent!" My mother signed her note "I'm so proud of you." Attempting to unravel the mystery of how my mother managed to have attracted such "fans" and who she really was (and is)—a life-embracing free spirit—nagged me into writing this book. One other thing: No, I *don't* remember every childhood conversation word for word as written here. I have, however, faithfully re-created the content and style of the *sorts* of conversations I *did* actually have. Lastly, in the first chapter readers of some of my other books will run into a few familiar facts. That's because I need to set up this book for those readers who haven't read my memoir *Crazy for God.* But I promise you that if you'll take this journey with me (for better or worse), I'll soon guide you into uncharted territory.

SEX, MOM, AND GOD

CHAPTER 1

Family Planning

M y biblically inspired sex education took a quantum leap in
1960. When I was eight years old, my mother handed me
her diaphragm. I was standing at the window of her hotel room
overlooking the Mediterranean Sea. We were on vacation. I'll explain about the diaphragm once I set the scene by noting that while
the children of lapsed Episcopalians, secular Jews, ordinary pagans,
Hindus, and Frenchmen presumably went peacefully to sleep after
their mothers read them *Goodnight Moon* or *A Tale of Two Bad
Mice*, some of us reared in Evangelical families were tucked into
bed after absorbing rather odd bedtime stories like this one.

"And the LORD spake unto Moses," Mom said, in her most
cheerful singsong bedtime-Bible-story-reading-out-loud voice.
"And the children of Israel took all the women of Midian captives,
and their little ones, and took the spoil of all their cattle, and all
their flocks, and all their goods. . . . And Moses was wroth with the
officers. And Moses said unto them, have ye saved all the women
alive? Behold, these caused the children of Israel to commit trespass against the LORD. Now therefore kill every male among the
little ones, and kill every woman that hath known man by lying

Photo: *Mom (age 1) and her father in China, 1915*

1

with him. But all the women children, that have not known a man by lying with him, keep alive for yourselves."

"But, Mom," the eight-year-old version of me asked, "how did they know *which* women hadn't known a man?"

"Well, Dear, of course they checked," said Mom as she reached over from where she was sitting next to me on my bed and gave my hand a friendly squeeze. Then, with her brightest, most encouraging these-things-are-hard-to-understand-but-trust-me-it's-okay-because-the-Lord-works-in-mysterious-ways-even-if-it-seems-crazy-to-us smile Mom added, "There's a way to tell."

"How?" I asked.

"I've already told you about that precious little barrier called the hymen."

"But why did those women have to die?" I asked.

"Because," Mom said, giving me another radiant smile, "in Numbers 31:9–18 it says that before the battle God told Moses to tell his soldiers to kill all the women who made the children of Israel commit the trespass of following after false gods. You see, Dear, to worship a false god is like going to a prostitute. And besides, anyway, *everyone* is supposed to *wait* for their Wedding Night, Darling, even Midianites. Goodnight, Dear."

"Goodnight, Mom."

Mom completed our bedtime ritual by praying with me. I prayed, too, and she kissed me, turned out my bedside lamp, and left my room. A second later Mom opened the door just wide enough to pop her head back in. Since my room was so small that my narrow bed filled most of it, Mom's face was almost directly over me as she looked down and said, very matter-of-factly, "It is important that when you grow up, you avoid Strange Women."

"I will," I said.

"You know what happened to Solomon because of Strange Women."

"Yes, Mom."

Mom withdrew her head, but just before she clicked the door shut, she added that evening's final instruction. "Marry a virgin, Dear. You don't want your wife to spend the rest of her life comparing you to other men. You should be the *only* man for her."

"Yes, Mom."

"Sleep well."

I'm not saying that this bedtime Bible story exchange was a usual conversation between a typical Evangelical mother and her eight-year-old son in 1960. Edith Schaeffer wasn't typical. I am saying, however, that I know that I'm not the only person trying to get the ringing out of my ears from childhood overexposure to the bizarre collection of Bronze-Age short stories my family called "the Scriptures." I know this because I've received thousands of notes in response to my writing about the impact of religion— even when that impact has been disguised as fiction in my novels like *Portofino, Zermatt,* and *Saving Grandma*—from people who were also raised by parents with a zealous sense of mission and who, like me, once honestly believed that every single word of the Bible was true.

People who say that they believe every word of the Bible (i.e., "Bible-believing" Christians and the more fundamentalist Jews) are not necessarily 100 percent biblical literalists. They believe that everything the Bible *affirms* is true because it is the "inerrant Word of God."* But that's the grown-ups. From a child's perspective peering out at the larger world from deep in the cocoon of a "Bible-believing home," *every word* of the Bible is understood to be true in

---

*By "affirms," I mean the overall message of redemption rather than all the details, like the exact dimension of Noah's Ark or the actual numbers of hours it took God to create the world, which the more diehard fundamentalists take literally, as did my parents in the early days of their ministry.

ways that nothing else is or ever will be even if, years later, that child grows up and changes his or her mind. That former child's grown-up incarnation may be willing to admit Nuance and Paradox, but the emotional "weight" of the absolutely true Word lingers. The actual words in The Word are still the very fabric of a whole private universe inhabiting those raised inside the hermetically sealed tunnel of absolutist faith, "truer" than all the other words he or she will ever hear, say, read, or think put together—truer than any later reasoned evidence. And on top of that the words of the Bible—or even a few notes of an old hymn—cast a shadow of bittersweet nostalgia that defies reason as thoroughly as a whiff of perfume reminds a man of his first lover and evokes a longing that cuts to the heart.

But back to my biblically inspired sex education: It took a quantum leap when my mother handed me that diaphragm. The view beyond the looming diaphragm was framed by the hills and bay of the picturesque fishing village and "Jet Set" hideaway of Portofino, Italy. While contemplating Mom's diaphragm, I was trying to understand how God could have planned everything if Mom and Dad were picking and choosing when to have children. Mom had the answer: "Mommy and Daddy use this wonderful invention, but sometimes God leads me *not* to use it, and then He picks the marvelous egg and individual amazing sperm and the *exact moment* they're conjoined so that the person He's chosen from before the Creation to be born—for instance *you*, my Dear!—may fulfill His Wondrous Plan!"

So God's Foreknowledge included His Foreknowledge of humankind's ability to use rubber in so many interesting ways besides the invention of the tire. Thus, my parents weren't *planning* anything by using contraception but merely doing the Lord's Will by exercising their "Free Will." According to Mom's logic, the Lord knew what would happen, but He wasn't bound by any path

He'd preordained. He could adjust His Plan, thereby changing His Will for your life by issuing factory recalls (killing people) or even changing His Mind (replacing people), but since He knew He'd do that, even when He changed His Mind, that, too, was part of THE PLAN. In that sense even God couldn't outsmart God.

There are many passages in the Bible about God changing His Mind. For example, God sent the flood of the Noah's Ark story when He "repented of" Creation: "The LORD was grieved that he had made man on the earth, and His heart was filled with pain. So the LORD said, 'I will wipe mankind, whom I have created, from the face of the earth—men and animals, and creatures that move along the ground, and birds of the air—for I am grieved that I have made them'" (Genesis 6:6–7). In Exodus, God reserves the right to change His Mind: "Go up to the land flowing with milk and honey," God says to Moses. "But I will not go with you, because you are a stiff-necked people and I might destroy you on the way" (Exodus 33:3).

God's frequent mind-changing notwithstanding, Mom said that God knew everything about everything *before* He made anything to know everything about. God knew and/or planned—depending on how you interpret the interplay of Foreknowledge and Predestination and Free Will—that after The Fall women would conceive at the drop of a solitary sperm. Thus, God made fertility the Chief Punishment of women.

After expelling Eve from the Garden, God said unto the woman, "I will greatly multiply thy sorrow and thy conception; in sorrow thou shalt bring forth children; and thy desire shall be to thy husband, and he shall rule over thee" (Genesis 3:16). That didn't make God mean, though, Mom said, because He also planned to (1) send Jesus to save a very few of His fallen creatures, including a very few women; and (2) pick the sperm and egg that would create Charles Goodyear so that Mr. Goodyear would discover the rubber vulcanization process, which he patented in 1844.

So, according to Mom, God Ordained and Foreknew that a few of us would be forgiven our Sins because we'd adopt Correct Calvinist Theology *and also* that in the mid-1880s German gynecologist C. Haase (using Mr. Goodyear's discovery) would invent a rubber contraceptive device with a handy spring molded into the rim. Therefore, it turned out that God changed His Mind about punishing at least some women by Predestining Protestant women to space their children *and* if they were Reformed Calvinists, too, He'd *also* chosen them to be of The Elect—that is, "elected" (chosen) to go to Heaven.

Thus, my family was fortunate. We were Protestants living *after* the rubber vulcanization process was invented. That meant that Mom was only punished four times—five if you count her miscarriage—unlike Roman Catholic women who, even *after* rubber was invented, still got punished dozens of times because the supposedly infallible popes (filling in for Jesus during His unexpectedly long absence) rejected God's Plan for the Rubber Vulcanization Reprieve.

Anyway, Mom's miscarriage loomed large as an example of God changing His Mind. Luckily for me, my parents had "tried again," as Mom put it, and had me. I was especially lucky because Mom was forty at the time. "I'd never have tried for a fourth child at that age except for the fact I lost your brother and we wanted a son," Mom said. Though, "luckily" is the wrong word. As Mom always said, "Real Christians don't believe in 'luck.' The Lord is in charge, so we *never* use that word because it's a denial of the Sovereignty of God." So, according to Mom, I should rather say that her losing my brother was providential.

I always wondered what my older brother was like or, rather, would have been like. My three sisters were all so much older than me. I would have liked any sibling close enough in age to be a friend rather than more like a second mother. Still, I believed that in Heaven everything we can't understand now would be made clear. For instance, we'd not ever be able to figure out why my older brother was stillborn or even why—when I was two—I'd contracted polio and so had to wear a leg brace. And Mom would explain Dad's "Many Weaknesses" by saying that she was sure she was supposed to learn something from "putting up with your father but will only really understand what it is, someday." All these things would be made "clear later, in Heaven, Dear."

Heaven was a long way off, and meanwhile I would have liked someone my own age to play with. I never blamed God, though, because I always assumed that any problem I had with the way things were was due to the fact that my "knowledge of the big picture" (as Mom called everything of "eternal significance") was incomplete and that "only in Heaven will we fully understand" why, for instance, billions of "unsaved" Chinese, Mormons, Muslims, Jews, Episcopalians, United Methodists, Unitarians, Anglicans, and Roman Catholics—even the "wrong sort of Presbyterians"— were going to Hell with no second chance, let alone why my older brother had died.

Heaven would solve everything. Mom said, "Your bad leg will be perfect in Heaven!" She said that there would be no tears in Heaven. But Mom still cried when she told me about the doctor letting her hold my brother before he "took him away." And Dad was at his most gentle with Mom when she told and retold the story of the stillbirth, how she was in the little Swiss chalet we were living in back then when the "baby came too early" and how she got on her knees and "prayed and wept before the Lord when the contractions started, but His answer was 'no' and He took him."

Mom also said that one good thing was that the miscarriage had helped her better understand her mother. "Mother had something worse happen to her," Mom would say. "Her son died at one year of age when she was in China. They just fed him rice water as 'medicine' because this was long before antibiotics, but the poor little boy died. You see he had dysentery. I had to lose your brother before I really understood why Mother cried so hard, even many years later whenever she spoke of this."

It was a dreadful and awesome thing to know that even if I couldn't "fully understand until we get to Heaven," nevertheless somehow my life was possible because Mom had delivered The Other Baby two months early and he died for me as the doctor "did all he could but failed because God had other ideas—in other words, You, Darling—and besides we weren't in a hospital."

When Mom talked about my older lost brother, she often shed tears. "He had all his fingers and toes," she'd say. "He was so beautiful. His little face was so sweet! I think he would have been my most beautiful child. His fingers looked as if he'd have been a great pianist, so long and graceful! He had a full head of hair just like you did."

My brother was growing up in Heaven instead of with us. Or was he? *Did* babies in Heaven *grow up*? My sister Susan said that they all were "the same age as everyone else is in Heaven is," which, according to her, was thirty-three, the age she said Jesus was when He was resurrected.

"Mom, Susan says my brother is the same age as Jesus," my six-year-old self said.

"Susan can't know that, Dear. We won't know those sorts of things until we get to Heaven."

"But if he's still a baby, who will take care of him?"

"Jesus said that the little children should come to Him so we can be very sure that He is tender with all the little ones."

"But he can't have accepted Jesus because he was too little when he died," my preoccupied seven-year-old self said.

"Yes, but he was also taken *before* the age of accountability, so he hadn't sinned yet."

"Not even by original sin?" the theologically precocious ten-year-old version of me asked.

"We won't understand the balance between Free Will and God's Foreknowledge until . . ."

"We get to Heaven," my thirteen-year-old-smart-ass self muttered while completing Mom's mantra.

"Don't use that tone when talking about the Things of the Lord, Dear! He has a Wondrous Plan for your life, and *you know that*, even if you *are* in a temporary state of youthful rebellion," Mom said.

She was right. I did know that God and I were inextricably entangled, and I still know that, no matter what the fifty-eight-year-old version of me says that I believe or don't believe on my agnostic days. And I still know that God will "lead me" in ways that I'll understand only in Heaven, no matter what I *say* to the contrary, even when I'm in an atheist frame of mind or when I hold forth to other enlightened people (at least "enlightened" in our own minds) speaking in an we're-all-too-smart-to-take-any-thing-at-face-value progressive code that presumes that anyone who disagrees is a backward rube.

Back to Family Planning Day. It unfolded like this: Mom glanced up from reading *Girl of the Limberlost* out loud and said, "We space our children." The "we" she was referring to were all Saved Protestant fundamentalists in general and We Schaeffers in particular. Then Mom whispered, "You see, Dear, *they* don't believe in family planning like *we* do. Those poor Catholics live in such terrible darkness." Mom looked pityingly at the large family sitting next to our family on the Paraggi-Portofino beach. We'd been curious about the twelve children, their ages ranging from one to twenty (or so), attached to the boisterous "Obviously *Very* Roman Catholic Family," as Mom had labeled the overflowing happy tribe lounging on assorted deck chairs.

The Paraggi beach is a narrow strip of sand about three hundred yards long by twenty yards wide, and when we Schaeffers were vacationing there, two hundred or so deck chairs filled the beach. They were arranged in rows so close together that each chair nearly touched the next. The view of the turquoise bay and gnarled pine trees, stark and dramatic as they clung to the rocky cliffs above the water, was magnificent. Vacationers sat under red-and-blue umbrellas emblazoned with the Martini & Rossi and Campari logos in a sort of seaside version of airplane seating. In Italy, going to the beach was a social occasion shared with people who had no sense of personal space. It was inevitable that in such close proximity we'd spend hours comparing others to our family, mostly unfavorably but also somewhat enviously. My sisters Susan and Debby were amusing themselves by trying to figure out the Very Roman Catholic children's ages. Dad, as usual, was ignoring all of us, eschewing deck chairs and lying face down on a towel roasting in the sun while reading back issues of *Newsweek* and the *Sunday School Times.**

Besides having a dead older brother, I had three very much alive big sisters: petite, ineffably kind, intellectually brilliant, and easily-moved-to-tears-by-the-plight-of-The-Lost Debby, seven years older than me; athletically powerful, almost-as-holy-as-

---

*Actually (as best as I remember), on that Diaphragm Vacation Susan was already away from home studying in England. But I've combined the memory of that year's vacation with previous ones when we were all together. Everything is as I remember it, only spread over several summers: The big "Catholic family" was next to us one summer, and the diaphragm revelation happened another year when only Debby was with Mom, Dad, and me.

Mom, and incredibly creative Susan, ten years older than me (who later in life would become an enlightened educator and have children who would found wonderful schools); and as-beautiful-as-Mom, always cheerful, sparkling, and lovely Priscilla, fifteen years older than me, who vomited any time she got upset, which was often because Dad had made her work as his secretary from the time she was thirteen and yelled at her when she mixed up the filing of his letters. (Priscilla got married when I was five, and by the time of the Diaphragm Vacation, she was living in St. Louis with her husband, John, who was in seminary.)

Unlike my sisters, who labored as coworkers in L'Abri from their early teens on, my relationship with my mother was defined by her being either too busy to know that I existed (bedtime stories and Bible stories excepted) and/or so overly solicitous as to virtually crush me in her embrace. You see, my sisters, being much older, had experienced childhood in America and then Switzerland before my parents' ministry became wildly successful. So they had childhoods approximating "normality" or at least as normal a growing up as the daughters of American fundamentalist missionaries could have been. In other words for better or worse my sisters saw a lot more of Mom and Dad than me. By the time I was six or seven L'Abri was swarming. By the time I was twelve my parents might as well have been overbooked rock stars for all I saw of them. While my grown-up sisters tried to follow our mother's example in The Work, I seesawed between wonderfully liberating neglect—no school and the freedom to run wild in the Alps while Mom did the Lord's Work—and Mom's sporadically hovering to an extent that would have put any proverbial "Jewish mother" to shame.

While we were walking up and over the lovely winding footpath that led from the beach to the adjoining Portofino bay, I asked Mom what spacing children meant. She motioned to me to slow my pace. We paused and gazed out at the aquamarine sea as it stretched, glittering, to the horizon. Mom always said that "this view is the most beautiful in the world, except for the view of the Pacific Ocean from Big Sur in California, Dear, that I saw as a young girl." I took a deep breath and was rewarded by what must be the most delicious combination of scents in the world, Big Sur notwithstanding: wild arugula and oregano, Bain de Soleil suntan lotion, gardenia scent wafting from the other side of the old stone wall separating the path from an adjoining estate, a faint hint of garlic and meat frying in olive oil wafting from one of the restaurant kitchens beyond the brow of the hill, balmy salty sea air, pine resin, and, of course, Mom's ubiquitous Chanel N°5.

When Dad and my sisters were out of earshot, Mom explained the basics of contraception. This led to (yet another) discussion of how and why God might have chosen me to be born and not my brother, and that ended with (another declaration) that "we'll never know the answer to that until we're in Heaven." A few minutes later Dad and my sisters strolled off to watch a fishing boat unload. Mom marched me up to her hotel room and, like a magician extracting a rabbit from a hat, pulled her diaphragm out of her toiletry case. "Mommy puts this up inside my Special Place so that when Daddy puts his seeds into me," she said, "this stops them from swimming into Mommy's womb and fertilizing the precious egg God created."

This explanation set my mind on fire with thoughts of *just where that actual diaphragm had been*, which seems an unforeseen consequence, given my mother's insistence that all sex "is wrong outside of marriage." Did my mother really want me zeroing in on Male Vagina Obsession that young? Probably not given that our Puritan ancestors had been "battling the flesh" centuries before we came along and Mom constantly warned her children to beware any temptation that could lead to Sex on the wrong side of the all-important Marriage Bed.

Mom's Puritan forebears (on her mother's side) sailed to America on the second voyage of the *Mayflower*. To gain passage on the *Mayflower*, you had to be an upstanding Believer with impeccable and "correct" theological views. And the essence of Puritan correctness was to brood over the Salvation of your Soul *and* to Worry about whether you were one of The Elect or not.

I was one with my forefathers when it came to The Worry part. The Worry was ever present, no matter what I thought or hoped I believed. I might have chosen God, but the big question was, *had He chosen me?* And one big indicator was if my "Flesh," rather than my "Christ-centered," nonsexualized self, had the upper hand. If it did, then maybe I *hadn't* ever really been Saved or, worse yet, was never elected to begin with!

Mom's ancestors (on her father's side) also sailed to America early in the history of the colonies and were "real Bible-believing Christians," as Mom would often say. Unlike Dad's hard-bitten atheist German and "recently immigrated lower-class sadly *very secular* family," as she always called them, Mom's parents followed in the footsteps of her pious forebears. My mother's great-great-grandparents became wealthy New England bankers, but in the late nineteenth century Mom's parents renounced The World to serve the Lord and sank into the genteel soul-improving penury that's the "gift" given those who "give up everything for the Lord." In other words, my maternal grandparents were "called" as missionaries to China.

My mother, Edith Rachel Merritt Seville, was born November 3, 1914, in Wenzhou, China. She was the fourth child of George and Jessie Seville, who were serving in the China Inland Mission.

Mom's parents gave her the Chinese name Mei Fuh, meaning "beautiful happiness." Mom's sisters were carted off to a mission boarding school, and one of them later joined the American Communist Party. The other married a mental patient who tried to kill her.

After serving as missionaries for many years, Mom's parents left China in 1920 and sailed back to America, along with Mom and her two older sisters. "We had no money, but ours was not a poverty of spirit," Mom often said, then added, "Not only did Mother and Father know and serve the Lord; my lovely parents were educated, refined, and spoke five languages. Their knowledge of art and literature just goes to show that you can be faithful to Christ, believe that *every word* of the Bible is *true*—which it *is!—and* be cultured too! Their only mistake was sending my sisters off to mission schools, and that meant they only saw Mother and Father once a year. The schools were very strict."

Mom was (and is) extraordinarily beautiful. She had a "Mediterranean Italian Jewish look," as my sister Debby once said, jet black hair, large sparkling dark brown eyes, a radiant smile, and a petite hourglass figure. But as if that weren't enough, my mother also possessed so much natural energy as to make all those around her seem sedentary and earthbound.

When Mom was alone with us, she presented Dad to her children as her number one "cross" to bear as well as the "love of my life." It wasn't so much a "love/hate" relationship as a love/pity relationship. Mom was helping Dad improve and helping her children to understand that this was, as it were, her solo ministry within their joint ministry to The Lost. She said that she loved Dad, but also that my father had no sense of humor, a terrible temper, and "no taste in clothes." She would complain that he "never plays with you children," "doesn't read for pleasure," "shouts when he preaches," "hasn't ever bought you children a present even though he always wants *me* to sign every card on the gifts from us both," "can't cook or even boil water," and "made this bruise on my arm when he punched me last night."

But Fran *did* "give up everything for the Lord" and also "stood up to Theological Liberalism," which (for Mom) seemed to outweigh his many "Weaknesses." Mom also said Dad was a passionate lover. "Which," as my sister Susan dryly remarked to me many years later, "was a lot more than we needed to know."

An Edith Schaeffer cult (made up of mostly born-again middle-class white American women) grew up around Mom's books after she began to be published in the late 1960s. I've met countless women who say that they raised their children "according to Edith Schaeffer." Of course, what they mean is that they raised their families according to the "Edith Schaeffer" fantasies they encountered in her books.

Mom went so far as to write several best-sellers with titles like *What Is A Family?* though our actual family was a model of dysfunction. However Mom was no hypocrite. She was just forgiving. The image of Schaeffer family happiness she painted in her books and talks was motivated by her genuine missionary desire to present us as "an example to The Lost." And most of our family's dysfunction was the result of my father's Moods, or as Mom put it, "Fran's Temper" and/or "Fran's Many Weaknesses."

Mom always seemed able to keep the reality of Fran's Many Weaknesses isolated from Dad, as if they existed on their own and weren't really part of the man she had married. Rather, they were caused by some wicked visitor who broke into our home from time to time and made Dad do bad things. So I grew up loving my father but being afraid of him when he became the raging portal for that other visitor. Somehow my mother never wrote off the man she'd married, even though she was openly critical of him in petty ways, not to mention running down that "other visitor," who, with frightening regularity, invaded the good man she loved.

Dad, Francis August Schaeffer, was born on January 30, 1912, and died on May 15, 1984. When Dad died, President Ronald Reagan wrote this note to Mom:

> While words are inadequate to console you on your loss, you can take comfort in knowing that Dr. Schaeffer will be greatly missed by all who knew him and his work. He will long be remembered as one of the great Christian thinkers of our century, with a childlike faith and a profound compassion toward others. It can rarely be said of an individual that his life touched many others and affected them to the better. It will be said of Dr. Schaeffer that his life touched many and brought them to the truth of their Creator. In June of 1982, Francis last wrote to me and enclosed a copy of an address he had just given which described in moving terms that "final reality" which is God. Dr. Schaeffer drew all his strength and spirit from that source and shared that message with a waiting world. Now he has found his final home . . .
>
> *Ronald Reagan,*
> *The White House*
> *May 17, 1984*

Dad is buried in Rochester, Minnesota. He died there following many years of on again, off again treatment at the Mayo Clinic. During those years (1977–1984) I often filled in for him on the big-time American Evangelical circuit. I was already his young sidekick in the antiabortion crusade we'd launched. His illness extruded me to another level of notoriety. If some group or other couldn't get "Schaeffer himself," it would settle for his "up-and-coming" son, who, it was rumored, had "inherited the mantle."

When Dad suffered through his many chemotherapy protocols, or when my father hit bottom during the tumultuous ups and downs of cancer, cast down by "poor blood counts," "platelets" that were "too high" or "too low," and all those other bodily betrayals our family learned about the hard way, I'd be out there keeping the Schaeffer-Saving-America-From-The-Liberals road show going. I'd visit Dad in Minnesota, visit my wife and young children in Massachusetts (where we were living by 1980), and then hit the road—again. I'd do this over and over and spend weeks on end running around North America and speaking to huge audiences that had gathered to hear Dad but got me. For instance, I was the keynote speaker to 24,000 pastors at one year's Southern Baptist Convention in the mid-1980s and to 15,000 religious media leaders at the Religious Broadcasters Convention. By the time I'd spoken to hundreds of groups and hundreds of thousands of people coast to coast, I'd gained a reputation in the Evangelical netherworld as a "hot" rising "star" and "anointed speaker." Then I began to get my own invitations to the very biggest events, and by then no mention was made of Dad. I was "set," except for the fact that I was becoming rapidly disillusioned.

Before those blood counts took their final dive, Dad decided he'd be buried in Rochester, somewhat oddly, since the only thing that brought him to town was cancer and the closest family member (me) lived 1,300 miles away and the rest were in Europe. He was buried in Minnesota notwithstanding the fact that we had a family plot in Philadelphia where Dad's father is buried and another plot in Switzerland where his mother is buried. There were (and still are) seven empty spaces in those plots. Dad lies in splendid isolation in a town that has no associations or history for anyone in our family, other than that he died there.

Rochester gave me the screaming willies from the moment I set foot on Main Street. It struck me as a sort of medical version of Lourdes, filled with the lame and terminally ill from all over the world who had staggered to this particular destination-of-last-resort full of hope and yet redolent of fear. The population (to put it mildly) appeared far from well. And hanging around this strangest place on earth, a nowhere town with more CAT scans and MRIs than parking meters, I, too, soon felt far from well.

The first time I visited, I was sitting in the lobby of a large hotel across from the clinic. I was eating lunch with Dad. An exceedingly pale elderly man who had yellowish skin and who was swathed in several overcoats and many scarves sat down across from us. He was dressed as if in Siberia—even though folks in the Midwest like to heat their buildings as if they're trying to cook food in them. I mean use the *room* to cook *with*. (The restaurant was heated to what felt like 120 degrees.)

Moments into eating his meal the man pitched forward and crashed facedown into a large bowl of split pea soup. I was also about to tuck into the same soup "of the day" but paused with the first spoonful poised halfway to my mouth. He was hustled off into an underground passage that connected the hotel to the clinic. His removal via a gurney was expertly handled by some of the hotel's staff. The waitstaff was well prepared for this eventuality. Gurneys and wheelchairs were parked in tidy rows by the all-you-can-eat (but probably don't want to, given the condition of the egg salad) salad bar, along with the extra oxygen cylinders. The waiters handled the situation as casually as if they were refilling a guest's water glass—rather refilling pewter imitation steins since the "décor" was Midwest/medieval, replete with fake suits of armor and restrooms marked "Maidens" and "Knights."

I didn't eat that soup. And the longer I stayed in town and the more I visited over the years, the more I was sure I had one or more fatal illnesses. After a year or two of virtually monthly visits, I was talked (by Mom) into getting a "full checkup since you're here, Dear, and it's a great opportunity."

I spent five glassy-eyed days in neon Limbo shuttling to various departments for blood "work-ups," scans, and probing. You see I was an "A-List" patient, so I got the full Mayo treatment. There were a number of born-again doctors there who were fans of my parents, so I got no ordinary checkup but, as one doctor proudly told me, "the same level of care that we're giving the King of Saudi Arabia, who's here right now, too." (It was true; I'd seen the Saudi royal family's huge jet incongruously parked in Rochester's tiny airport three days before.)

There was one perk, though, or blessing or whatever you call it: Evangelist Billy Graham was a "lifelong hypochondriac" (as his wife, Ruth Graham, once told me over tea while Billy was getting a CAT scan), and so he was also at Mayo several times over the years. Dad and Billy and I met, or "the Lord drew us together," as Mom put it. Our various meetings took place in the shadow of death and illness (real or imagined), so that made our comparing notes on our joint efforts to Save America seem all the more urgent. We alternated colonoscopies and chemo, checks for bad sunspots and worries over the size of our respective prostrate glands (mine was fine) with our dire predictions about where the Secular Humanists were "taking the country." At other times we compared notes on whether this or that American president Dad and Billy had met with "really knows the Lord personally or is just faking it to get our people's votes."

Dad is still in Rochester, waiting for Mom's body to be shipped from Switzerland to join him. As I write this, she lives across the street from my sister Debby. As for poor old Billy Graham, his future burial arrangements are even less appealing than Mom's.

According to a *Washington Post* story,* a feud erupted in Billy's family over where he and his wife, Ruth, were to be buried. Was it to be in Charlotte, North Carolina, at the Billy Graham Museum erected in the vicinity of the Billy Graham Evangelistic Association headquarters? Or should their remains go to a small private site near their modest family home in Montreat? Franklin Graham, the (then) fifty-six-year-old "heir" to Billy's ministry, insisted that the burial spot be at the $30 million, 40,000-square-foot museum that mimics the farm outside of Charlotte where Billy grew up. Other family members—including (the always sensible) Ruth Graham—wanted to have a quieter final resting place. The *Post* called the family "debate" a struggle "worthy of the Old Testament, pitting brother against brother, son against mother."**

After Ruth's death, Billy was trapped in the middle of the family feud and pondering what to do with her remains. The *Post* said Ruth had signed a notarized document with six witnesses, saying she wanted to be buried near her home. After her death her wishes were ignored, and Billy was talked into doing what Franklin wanted. Ruth was laid to "rest," against her wishes, in what amounts to an amusement park for the greater glory of—what?

Franklin's consultants had worked with the Walt Disney Company to create a large "barn" and "silo" as a reminder of Billy Graham's early childhood. Visitors wishing to visit Ruth's tomb (and/or who wish to become an atheist in just an hour or two) pass through a forty-foot-tall glass entry cut in the shape of a cross

---

*"A Family at Cross-Purposes: Billy Graham's Sons Argue over a Final Resting Place," *Washington Post*, December 13, 2006.
**Ibid.

and are greeted by a mechanical talking cow. From there they walk on paths of "straw" through rooms of exhibits. At the end a stone walkway shaped like a cross takes them to a garden where Ruth lies (as will Billy Graham). The *Post* also reported that tourists have more than one chance to get their names on a mailing list and later be solicited for funds. Maybe Dad got off lightly. Come to think of it, Rochester isn't *that* bad.

Anyway, my mother lives in a beautiful seventeenth-century Swiss chalet just up the road from where I grew up. Last time I checked she was in no hurry to be shipped anywhere. The ceilings are low and rest on heavy beams. The walls are paneled in dark honey-toned pine. The rooms are comfortingly cluttered with a lifetime of memories. Mom is surrounded by her books, art, records, CDs, and old photographs. She eats off lovely china settings that I remember fondly from my early childhood. There are always fresh flowers on the table. My paintings (which I gave Mom years ago as a "thank-you" for her supplying art materials) almost fill her walls floor to ceiling. Every silver teaspoon in her collection is in a little rack on the wall by my mother's kitchen table.

This aesthetic bliss has been achieved by my sister Debby. My mother's old age quality of life is made possible because of my attentive and generous sister and her equally kind husband (and professor of philosophy), Udo. Mom is fortunate to have a daughter like Debby. My sister has cared for our mother in a way that many older people might only dream about. And Debby is not wealthy. The care comes from love alone and is hands-on. For ten years or so Debby and Udo have provided our mother with this wonderful home across the street from their chalet. Debby has struggled to find live-in caregivers for Mom and has also provided her with a life replete with concerts, museum visits, lovely clothes, and reading out loud. Mom doesn't look, smell (sorry, but you know what I mean), or live like "an old person." Debby has made sure Mom has remained herself.

Without Debby and Udo, I think that Mom would have died years ago. Actually, I'm sure of it. Debby has fiercely defended my mother against being "written off" by doctors, nurses, and other people who would not have bothered to care for her so well. Debby and Udo have attended to Mom as if they expected her to live— *and live well*—forever. And my sister Susan has pitched in long distance from England, too, with many long visits. My sister Priscilla (who lives less than three miles away) has had Mom stay with her for several days every week for many years, and her husband, John, helps Mom faithfully. (I live in America. I call and fly over and visit, but it's my sisters and their husbands who "step up.")

During the same approximate period of his life when Dad was visiting Rochester for treatment, inclusive of morbidly interrupted lunches, he was also visiting the White House and talking to (or lunching with) Presidents Ford, Reagan, and Bush Sr. By then Dad had developed a distinctive craggy intellectual look. But when I was a child, he just looked tough.

Dad's voice had a metallic East Coast/Philly/New Jersey edge to it and went up an octave to a jarring screech when he preached. My father grew up helping his father clean out boilers and further contributed to his family's meager budget by selling ice off a horse cart from the age of eleven while also regularly being beaten by his mother for the least offense. If whippings were Dad's formative childhood experience, Dad's formative idea of the Christian life— after he got "saved" in his late teens—was one of mortal combat for church turf via outdoing other Believers when it came to the one-upmanship of fundamentalist biblical correctness.

At Westminster Theological Seminary my father studied with his hero, J. Gresham Machen. He was Dad's "favorite theologian," and years later Dad still kept a poster-sized sepia-tinted photograph of Machen pinned to the inside of his clothes cupboard. Machen had been kicked out of Princeton Seminary when it was "taken over by the Liberals," as Dad called it. In 1937 Dad transferred to Faith Theological Seminary over another theological *split* among Presbyterians and graduated in 1938. This seminary formed after *yet another split* between the Presbyterian Church of America and the Bible Presbyterian Church. My father was the first student to graduate and the first to be ordained in a new superfundamentalist group, the Bible Presbyterian Church (BPC). Then Dad served in Pennsylvania Grove City and Chester and St. Louis, Missouri, as the pastor of various small churches. He soon left the BPC (another *split* over theological purity) and joined the Reformed Presbyterian Church, Evangelical Synod, a forerunner of the superfundamentalist Presbyterian Church in America, also formed by a—*split*.

In 1947 my family moved to Switzerland as missionaries to the Europeans, whom they rarely converted since neither of my parents could speak anything but English. Dad never learned to speak any other language notwithstanding his forty-year sojourn in Europe. So my parents ministered to American tourists and other English-speaking visitors. Then in 1954—after yet more *splits* with the home mission board—Mom and Dad were "led" (another way of saying they had to figure something out when they were kicked out of their mission over a theological dispute) to start their own ministry. My sense is that they did this with the feeling of relief experienced by a longtime renter who—at last—moves into her own house.

My parents theoretically acknowledged that there were other Real Believers, but (many church splits later) there seemed to be no one besides our family that they wholeheartedly approved of. We were *different* and (at least in the early fundamentalist incarnation of our family) sometimes smug in the rightness of our difference. Since our family and my parent's ministry—the work of L'Abri—represented the only truly theologically "sound" configuration of believers this side of Heaven, my sisters stuck around L'Abri even after marriage. Priscilla and her husband, John, returned to us from seminary when I was ten years old, and none of my sisters left home for good until many years later after L'Abri split up along the lines of various personality clashes. My three sisters encouraged their husbands—who had wandered into L'Abri as young men, got "saved," and married a Schaeffer daughter—to join "The Work."

Dad was the mere candle to Mom's sun, the short, somewhat dour-looking James Cagney–type. He was the only child of working-class parents with a hardscrabble life story of modest success extruded from an unlikely beginning. Dad was a man who was "Led By God" to become a pastor but whose natural interests tended to art history, when he was not indulging his taste for full-contact "True Believers" versus "Liberals" theological blood sports. He was also a solitary person, thrust—by both his and Mom's zeal—into a people-oriented ministry where he was swarmed day and night by strangers.

Mom was also in the wrong profession. She should have been a dancer with a Broadway career. This isn't a guess but reflects something she's often told me. My mother had wanted to be a dancer until her missionary parents put a stop to all such "worldly" notions. The strange thing was that Mom told me this several times with a sigh, while *at the very same time* passing on the exact same guilt-induced pietism to me that she'd been indoctrinated with.

As for me, I was outnumbered from the start. I was an American expatriate missionary kid wearing a leg brace (like some sort of ball and chain designed to invite curious stares) being raised in foreigner-hating Switzerland, an Evangelical fundamentalist in a world filled with The Lost, *and* I had three older sisters who were much closer to the Lord than me. On top of that, my sisters and mother shared a secret—Womanhood—that I'd never be able to fathom, though not for lack of trying.

Mainly what I did was sacrifice along with my parents. We had no car, I had no real schooling (until age ten), we ate almost no meat, and this was all a sign of God's Blessing. What we *didn't* have or *didn't* do loomed large and proved (to us anyway) that we were following God's Plan for our lives.

Sacrificing-For-The-Lord was a pride-filled way of life. No owner of a new home, car, or yacht was ever prouder of his or her venal material possessions than we Schaeffers were of *not* achieving our fondest dreams. Mom's father spoke five languages and "could have taught in a secular college, even at Harvard," Mom said. But he *didn't* teach at Harvard; rather, my grandfather taught in a series of small impoverished Bible schools after he returned from China, just like Dad *didn't* pastor a huge church, "even though Fran's a far better preacher than most," as Mom claimed.

What we *didn't* do suited us Schaeffers fine (even if some of us sighed from time to time over missed opportunities). We prided ourselves on how much our family had "given up for the Lord." So Mom *didn't* dance and instead had married a short man after the Lord showed her that together they could Save The Lost, even though "many tall handsome poetic men were interested in me," Mom said. But as Mom also always added with (yet another sigh) when telling me what she'd given up for the Lord, "Worldly success is *not* what counts."

While we Schaeffers were sacrificing everything for the Lord, discipline nevertheless had to be maintained. Both of my parents were resourceful spankers. They used belts, wooden spoons, hairbrushes, and hands. Mom's feeble "spankings" were a family joke, whereas Dad's (mercifully infrequent) whippings raised welts. Susan was beaten more than the rest of us (mostly before my time) and even put in a sort of straightjacket Mom said she'd concocted out of a sheet in which Susan would be tightly wound until she was cocooned head to toe and then left on a bed—in the dark—for hours.

Our "spankings"—a nice catchall term to cover what were actually passionless, "this-hurts-me-more-than-it-hurts-you" beatings—were done in the open and accepted by all of us as normal, as such "discipline" was also accepted as normal by most people during the 1950s. There was no shame in a "firm hand," as my parents' version of child-rearing was called. Mom and Dad often even used to tell "amusing" stories about how they had punished Susan (who was far and away our family's most "difficult child," as Mom always said) for misbehaving in church as a little girl of five, when Dad was still a pastor in the States. When Mom failed to stop Susan from talking during his sermons, Dad would stop preaching, march into the congregation, pick up Susan, and head to the church basement, where he'd thrash her with a wooden spoon and then return to the pulpit. Mom always said how pleased the congregation was to have such a fine disciplinarian leading them as their pastor, and she talked about the churchgoers' amusement at the "cute" sound of Susan's wailing during these little demonstrations.

Life was not all spankings, however. Most of the time our family thrived on a somewhat hysterical diet of "miracles" that provided a constant high. In the 1950s, when my parents' L'Abri Fellowship ministry was just being established, Mom and Dad never asked donors for money, and yet—*miraculously*—the Lord "moved people's hearts" and we were sent gifts to "meet our needs." So we *knew* that From Before The Creation Of The Universe God had planned that in 1954 the Schaeffer Family would found the American mission of L'Abri, located in Huémoz, Switzerland, conveniently near the ski slopes of Villars and the tearooms of Montreux (*and* only five hours by train from Portofino, Italy), with stunning views of the towering mountains in every direction, which He'd *created expressly* for our pleasure. Mom said that our job, and thus the *reason* for both L'Abri's and our existence, was to "*prove* the existence of God to an unbelieving world." We Schaeffers did this by praying for the gifts needed to run our mission. God provided the exhilarating life-affirming supernatural "proof" of His being out there somewhere by answering our prayers and sending us just enough money—*no more and no less*—so that His Work might go forth and so that I'd grow up eating cheese and various other ingredient-stretching casseroles to sustain my life *while* praying for red (or any) meat!

Then, just as God chose me over my brother, not to mention had previously sent Jesus to save some prechosen Elect Sinners *and* sent Mr. Goodyear and C. Haase to reprieve Protestant Women, the Lord answered my prayers for protein. As a side effect of sending juicy quantities of porterhouse steaks my way, the Lord also changed the course of American history.

You see, in the late 1960s Mom and Dad published the first of many best-selling books. My parents became famous Evangelical leaders, and they were unexpectedly awash in book royalties and speaking invitations. When they toured Evangelical colleges and churches all over North America, I often accompanied them and *ate meat at last* while Mom and Dad—unbeknown to them at the time—were being elevated to Evangelical Protestant sainthood. This meant that a few years later when Dad took a "stand" on the issue of abortion, a powerful movement formed almost instantly inspired by his leadership, and the Evangelical-led "pro-life" movement (and the Religious Right) was born.

My father is still a hero to many Religious Right leaders, such as Dave Andrusko (editor of the *National Right to Life News*). In his review of two books on the history of the antiabortion movement, Andrusko notes that the antiabortion movement "attracted people by building on the foundation established by theologian Francis Schaeffer. . . . It is difficult to exaggerate the importance of [Schaeffer's] book *Whatever Happened to the Human Race?* and [the 1970s] twenty-city film and lecture tour [undertaken] to awaken the evangelical community."* And this quote by Joel Belz, founder of *World* magazine, pretty much sums up the Evangelical establishment's view of my father: "Go to any evangelical Christian gathering and ask twenty people the simple question: 'What single person has most affected your thinking and your worldview?' If Francis Schaeffer doesn't lead the list of answers, and probably by a significant margin, I'd ask for a recount."**

Before fame, steak, and political influence came our way, my parents' ministry grew. While we were still struggling to make ends meet, we nevertheless added several more chalets to the work of L'Abri. Mom decided that our family's chalet would, from then on, house only the Girls' dorms—the miniscule rooms we stuffed bunk beds into and filled with lovely, nubile, twenty-something females seeking Jesus and Godly Husbands and not necessarily in that order. The young men guests would thenceforth be housed across the road.

---

*Dave Andrusko while reviewing *Articles of Faith: A Frontline History of the Abortion Wars* by Cynthia Gorney (New York: Simon and Schuster, 1997) and *Wrath of Angels: The American Abortion War* by James Risen and Judy Thomas (New York: Basic Books, 1997) in *First Things* 78 (November 1998): 32–36.
**Endorsements of Dad and his books as quoted on Amazon.com, www.amazon .com/How-Should-We-Then-Live/dp/1581345364/ref=sr_1_1?s=books&ie =UTF8&qid=1285237692&sr=1–1.

By the time I was eight or nine, Dad and I were vastly outnumbered in our house. By then it amounted to a cloistered women's retreat. Our officially male-dominated patriarchal theology (of the type that later had such sway over the Religious Right) seemed to have little influence over the four Schaeffer women when it came to *actual* daily life at L'Abri. Dad would prepare sermons while closeted in his bedroom, cowering behind a wall of sound as he played classical music full blast from dawn to dusk to shut out the noise made by the many young women we had living in our chalet.

Dad did assert himself occasionally. He yelled at Mom, and once in a while he socked her on the arm or slapped her. Oddly, this abuse—I'd place it (morally speaking) somewhere between inexcusable wife-beating and a type of involuntary outburst—left Mom even more in control. Dad would grovel in abject repentance for several weeks after the delivery of a sock to her upper arm or a swift slap to her face. The rest of the time he pretty much did as instructed by my mother: preached, gave weekly lectures, and led discussions with the students. Mom directed everything else, from interpreting the "Lord's Will" for our family (code for when to buy a new chalet and expand The Work), to raising me (endless Talks on Sex and how to be a "Christlike" young man, combined with sporadic ineffectual attempts to teach me to read), to running L'Abri day to day (who stayed where and for how long), to planning and financing our wonderful annual summer and winter vacations, respectively, in Portofino and Zermatt.

Being a missionary in the Swiss Alps is good work if you can get it. The view is wonderful, and the drinking water is clean. And we didn't talk much about our lovely vacations lest, as Mom said, "people get the wrong idea and stop giving." But in one regard we *were* typical American Evangelicals: The Evangelical ghetto is a network of personality cults operating, as far as nepotistic leadership and succession goes, something like North Korea. We were all "in The Work." And that's even before (as a young man of twenty) I became my dad's sidekick.

Since the children of professional Christians are raised in what amounts to cocoons and echo chambers, they are often—literally— unequipped to do anything *except* carry on the family business. And since Protestantism is built on one big church split (the Refor- mation) and then another one and so on, there's always room for yet another "prophetic voice" to be "raised up" to *finally* do some "new improved" version of Christianity *correctly*—at last! And so going into the L'Abri-and-beyond ministry with my father and then starting my own offshoot "ministry"—Schaeffer V Produc- tions, through which I produced, wrote, and directed Dad's two major film series, which was the last step in making him famous in the Evangelical world—were par for the professional-Christian- family course.

I wasted ten years or so of my life chasing "success" in Evangelical and other right-wing circles. Other than collecting material for fu- ture novels (and memoirs), I regret every moment I spent selling myths to the deluded, or I should say that I regret selling myths to myself and then passing them on to people as deluded as I was. Then I escaped, or maybe not. I'm still writing about those experiences.

As for Mom, she radiated the dynamic presence of ten powerful women and the fierce energy of one hundred Amazons. This, too, is not unusual in many Evangelical groups where officially the pul- pit may be closed to women but unofficially many a church, Bible study, and congregation are actually run by wonderfully powerful "Prayer-Warrior" women. The male pastor is just a necessary fig- urehead kept there by smart, sincere women whose only creative outlet is their religion because religion is all they were ever allowed to "do" with a clear conscience, other than have babies.

Anyway, for all those reasons or none, Mom acted as Dad's equal (or even as his spiritual superior) in ways that didn't explicitly contradict Bible-based beliefs about the limited role of women—she'd never preach on Sunday in church—but nevertheless left her in more or less the position of our most senior "bishop" to Dad's "pope." Thus, Mom practiced her brand of Godly Womanhood, even feminism.

Mom was the queen bee of our chalet, bruised arms notwithstanding. She presided over our household by glowing brightly for Jesus and exuding kindness for everyone she met, whoever they were. This kindness was genuine. Mom *loved* people the way hummingbirds are drawn to flowers. She fed them—both literally and spiritually—and in turn was fed.

My mother also was not a "respecter of persons" (to use the biblical catchphrase for not kowtowing to the high and mighty), and she paid warm attention to hotel maids, cab drivers, porters, and the dispossessed, including the many gay visitors to L'Abri, and to pregnant unmarried young women who might have been ostracized by other religiously zealous folks. And in consequence of Mom's genuine compassion and decency, by the early 1960s L'Abri was teeming with young men and women from all races and backgrounds. The women (who usually outnumbered the men about two to one) were looking to Mom to show them how to become "Godly Women," how to eat the royal jelly of insider biblical knowledge, and (besides learning how to be Christlike) how to cajole God into fulfilling their dreams for a mate by helping them snare a "Christ-centered" husband.

"Mom's Girls" (as I thought of the mostly university student-aged females staying in our chalet) watched my mother closely and when not observing her every move—from cooking to teaching Bible studies—asked my mother many questions and attended her extraordinarily long and unusually sexually explicit Talks For

Girls. Mom would let me attend these (otherwise) female-only Talks, at least when I was a young, "harmless" child. The parts in the Talks on marriage resonated! Maybe my mother thought that I was too young to "get" the import of her detailed descriptions of the right kind of lingerie to wear on one's Wedding Night, and the wonders of euphemistically described foreplay, but if so, Mom had underestimated her abilities as a spellbinding speaker and also my precocious interest in All Things Sexual. By eight or nine I was thinking like a somewhat horny twelve-year-old, and by ten I could have taken a premed exam on reproductive female anatomy, and if verbal answers were accepted (I could barely read or write given the "success" of my homeschool experience combined with a case of undiagnosed dyslexia), I would have passed the test.

Mom's advice to women turned out mostly to be about how to become like Edith Schaeffer. Mom passed on these tips: (1) Pack a sheer black negligee when you go to "wherever God calls you" to be a missionary in order to keep your husband happy; (2) prepare wonderful high teas the better to entice people to come to Jesus; (3) pray a lot for guidance that "the Lord might show you His Will for your life, especially who to marry"; (4) *wait* for the Wedding Night; and (5) "always remember that there's no reason that Real Christians can't look like Vogue models!"

Reading between the lines, Mom's brand of Godly (well-dressed) feminism boiled down to using and then teaching other women to use techniques for manipulating The Man In Your Life into doing what you wanted him to do, "as God leads you." She advocated "The Wife's Method," a kind of shaped charge of subversive subservience. He'd *think* he was the Patriarch In Charge, but through stealth-prayer and guilt-inducing piety, "The Wife" could direct "The Husband" to be all he could be (for God, of course) in ways that he had never envisioned, but in ways that you (The Wife) understood because women are closer to God than men are.

So far, so typical. What was unusual about the Schaeffer family was Mom's extroverted sexuality. I think that Mom indulged her Facts Of Life "frankness" when giving her Talks For Girls (let alone when she spoke to her children in private) as a way to prove—at least to herself—that she was sophisticated *despite* being a fundamentalist missionary. I also think that Mom—bless her—LIKED Sex. For Mom, telling her Female Followers about What To Wear On Your Wedding Night (and thereafter to "keep him interested") and even speaking about Dad's sexual appetite, not to mention the merits of black see-through negligees "even if you are called to serve Christ in Africa and that's all you pack besides antibiotics and a mosquito net," were a sort of necessary self-revelation. Mom *needed* to prove that she wasn't your average fuddy-duddy.

Mom was not alone in struggling to make sure people knew that just because she believed in Jesus and was a fundamentalist (in the sense that she held to a literal six-day creation, a universal flood, and so forth) didn't make her crazy. Believing in invisible things breeds an inferiority complex among people competing with science for hearts and minds. Many religious fundamentalists feel under siege by the secular world and harbor a deeply paranoid sense of victimhood. I think of those who turn their sense of victimhood into material and political success and their claims of persecution into strategies of achieving power as Jesus Victims. I don't mean they are victims *of* Jesus; rather, they claim to be victims *for the sake of* Jesus, accruing power through the rhetoric of sacrifice and persecution and grasping at conspiracy theories about how the nefarious "World" and all "Those Liberals" are out to do them in. It is this Jesus Victim note of self-pity that ties together "These People," as some smug secularists might label all conservative religious believers.

CHAPTER 2

Magic Menstrual Mummies

I'd never heard of pheromones when I was ten. All I knew was that each month the large wicker basket in the bathroom on the middle floor of our chalet filled with softball-sized, tightly wound wads of toilet paper. These tissue bundles were evidence that—in biblical terms—the time of Our Girls' Monthly Uncleanness was once again upon them. This was back in the days when a sanitary napkin was a fluffy and formidable thing—about the size and shape of a canoe. I knew God didn't like the Menstrual Mummies because I'd heard Mom read Leviticus 15:19 in a Bible study: "When a woman has a discharge, and the discharge in her body is blood, she shall be in her menstrual impurity for seven days, and whoever touches her shall be unclean until the evening. And everything on which she lies during her menstrual impurity shall be unclean. Everything also on which she sits shall be unclean. And whoever touches her bed shall wash his clothes and bathe himself in water and be unclean until the evening. And whoever touches anything on which she sits shall wash his clothes and bathe himself

PHOTO: *Mom (center) with her sisters on her wedding day in 1935* in water and be unclean until the evening. Whether it is the bed or anything on which she sits, when he touches it he shall be unclean until the evening."

So I never touched the Menstrual Mummies—except once. I unwrapped the tissue-tethered Unclean Thing and took a smear of blood from it to study with a small microscope that a kindly L'Abri student had given me. I wanted to see the egg that Mom said was "washed out each month unless it gets fertilized by the marvelous seed." I didn't see an egg, but I did observe several doughnut-shaped red blood cells after I dabbed a little blood on a handy glass slide and stained it, as per the student's instructions.

About forty years after investigating the Menstrual Mummies in the wastepaper basket, I read an article in the *New York Times* science section about how humans' sense of smell triggers physical responses. The article cited the example that women who live together—for instance, in college dorms, convents, and girls' boarding schools—tend to menstruate at the same time. I don't know if the theory of menstrual synchrony (based on sensitivity to pheromones through smell) will stand up to the rigors of scientific inquiry, but I do know that our middle-floor chalet bathroom wastepaper basket seemed to fill and empty like some sort of metronome, keeping time with a cosmic rhythm as sure as the tides. Maybe Mom and my sisters reset the hormone "clock" of the female helpers (i.e., the cheerful, though virtual slave laborers working in return for room, board, and spiritual help), who lived in our chalet for several years at a time, as well as setting the clock for the students who stayed with us for six to ten months or so.

The nubile, yet torturously unavailable young women filled our chalet with their pheromone-perfumed presence. *And*, as I learned from Mom's Bible study on Leviticus, they were mon-strously defiled as they plunged into their monthly menstrual freshet. I imagined that God was right there with me, in our middle-floor chalet bathroom, brooding over the evidence of His Big Mistake: Women.

The God-Of-The-Bible is appalled by women. According to the prophet Isaiah, God will mightily punish women who overstep their divinely ordained bounds: "Moreover the Lord saith: Because the daughters of Zion are haughty, the Lord will smite with a scab the crown of the head of the daughters of Zion, and the Lord will lay bare their secret parts" (Isaiah 3:16–17). It seems The-God-Of-The-Bible regretted the female human He created—as an afterthought, after squirrels, sheep, whales, and everything else, according to the Bible's most familiar story: "Now the LORD God had formed out of the ground all the beasts of the field and all the birds of the air. . . . But for Adam no suitable helper was found. So the LORD God caused the man to fall into a deep sleep; and while he was sleeping, he took one of the man's ribs and closed up the place with flesh. Then the LORD God made a woman from the rib he had taken out of the man, and he brought her to the man" (Genesis 2:22).

I'm using this *The-God-Of-The-Bible* "handle" as a way to differentiate between whatever actual deity might be out there and the biblical version and caricature of that Person, Force, or Persons. That said, when The-God-Of-The-Bible hastily made the first woman as a sort of garden-warming present for Adam, He must have carelessly botched her plumbing design. Soon after Creation, the Female Plumbing Problem began to weigh heavily on The-God-Of-The-Bible's Mind. Women's brimming bodily fluids—like shellfish, Canaanites, and the wearing of *both* wool and cotton at the same time—are among the *many things* that got out of hand soon after The-God-Of-The-Bible completed Creation, thus inciting His Divine Regret. So The-God-Of-The-Bible expelled the first man and woman from the Garden; He sent a Great Flood; He killed at least as many unruly beings as the numberless descendants He promised

Abraham. The-God-Of-The-Bible issued countless factory recalls (my dead brother multiplied) and complex revised owner's manual updates, replete with regulations and strict rules about how to *deal with* women, *fix* women, *repair* women, *curb* women, *keep* women *in line*, and, if need be, *kill* women if they didn't keep The-God-Of-The-Bible's *many* Women-Managing Rules.

The-God-Of-The-Bible's Women-Management Plan is particularly focused on controlling bodily fluids. The-God-Of-The-Bible hates wetness! I can't imagine The-God-Of-The-Bible volunteering to feed a baby, let alone doing what mothers (and some fathers and grandfathers) do when they use a spoon to scrape dribbled food off a baby's chin and then absentmindedly lick off the spoon. I wonder if The-God-Of-The-Bible would use His Divine Spit (the way Jesus did to heal a blind man) to clean off dirt from a baby's face. However The-God-Of-The-Bible would behave as a babysitter, I imagine He'd be squeamish if He had to take care of a young woman afflicted with her monthly cycle of menstrual impurity, or for that matter a young man afflicted with wet dreams.

I wonder how a woman is to be righteous in the eyes of The-God-Of-The-Bible when her own reproductive organs, *by His Own design*, defile her body and how a man is to live "correctly" when *his own body's arousal* is his biggest Sin? According to orthodox Jewish rabbinical law, a woman becomes impure when she is aware that blood has come from her womb. Even if menstruation started before she sees evidence of blood, the rabbinical regulations say she's not impure until she notices. But as *soon* as she *notices the least stain*, she becomes Unclean. However, if she finds a stain after say, cutting her finger, she does not become impure since the blood is not from her womb. But if there is a bloodstain of uncertain origin, a woman is told to ask the assistance of her *male* rabbi to "help her" determine what to "do" about her "Female Uncleanness."

There's a lot in the Bible about menstruation, and it's all bad. Blood isn't the problem; just *womb blood* is bad. Blood squirting from countless sheep and cows dying while being slaughtered as sacrifices to The-God-Of-The-Bible is just fine. So is male mutilation: circumcision. Even better for Christians is the blood pouring from Jesus' hands and feet. The Christian believer is encouraged to *drink* it, get to Heaven *through* it, and "claim" it! "Have you been to Jesus for the cleansing power?" ask the words of the old camp meeting hymn. "Are you washed in the blood of the Lamb? Are you fully trusting in His grace this hour? Are you washed in the blood of the Lamb?"

The Bible is full of vengeful bloodshed when the righteous are vindicated by the blood of the wicked. As the Psalmist says, "The righteous shall rejoice when he seeth the vengeance: he shall wash his feet in the blood of the wicked" (Psalm 58:10). That "triumphal" blood runs in God-Of-The-Bible-pleasing crimson rivers throughout the Scriptures—from the Slaughter of Midian right up through the Book of Revelation. Evangelical readings of John the Revelator's visions anticipate the day when Jesus will come back à la the Left Behind novels and kill just about all the people abandoned on earth for their unbelieving ways.* These include the "Incomplete Jews" (i.e., Jews who haven't "accepted Jesus"), all Muslims, and all the other "heathens" of the world—which for most Evangelicals include Hindus, Roman Catholics, and Mormons, not to mention all Liberal Protestants of the sort who "took over" the previously "sound" denominations my parents once belonged to—saving only a "remnant" unto Himself.

---

*Left Behind is a series of sixteen best-selling novels by Tim LaHaye and Jerry Jenkins dealing with Christian End Times prophecies, the eschatological viewpoint of the "end of the world," and the Return of Christ to kill and/or judge all "unbelievers."

Now when it came to remnants—in other words to Us Real Christians—there were Actual Jews and then there were Real Jews. Evangelicals believe that they are also The Chosen People. Some Evangelicals believe that they are the *only* chosen people now. Others think that the Jews are *still* chosen, too. American Evangelicals, following the Puritans' conceit of their special "call," cling to the concept of American exceptionalism, some sort of setting-apart "call" to be special—"chosen"—and lead the world to a better place. In other words, we're better than other people and must show the way or at least force it on others through our nonstop wars, sort of like . . . the Jews of the Old Testament. (The Mormons took this idea to its logical conclusion with a nudge from Joseph Smith. He decided that America had to have *actually been visited* by Jesus and that somehow certain "good" tribes of Native Americans were linked to the Jews.)*

Evangelicals brood over the Jews. Jesus was a Jew, but then He started a whole "new" religion that instantly was in conflict with the Jews but . . . *was made up mostly of Jews*, at the beginning of the Church. So Jews were a big deal to the Schaeffer family. We liked Jews and feared them and felt sorry for them. Conflicted is the word. And there is no way to get on the inside of the who-is-chosen question without unpacking the quirky relationship Evangelicals have with Jews, both embracing them *and* condemning them to eternal damnation in what has to be one of the odder relationships ever concocted—sort of like those news stories that crop up once in a while about how a cat befriends a hamster.

---

*The Book of Mormon says "Lamanites," dark-skinned indigenous Americans, fought light-skinned "Nephites." Archaeologists and geneticists do not endorse the existence of Lamanites.

Many American Evangelicals believe that to "be a Real Christian" means that you must give your full support to the extremist elements in the state of Israel. Many Evangelicals believe that God loves some people lots more than others and that He loves Jews most of all. For instance, John Hagee, megachurch pastor and founder of Christians United for Israel, says, "For twenty five almost twenty six years now, I have been pounding the Evangelical community over television. The Bible is a very pro-Israel book. If a Christian admits 'I believe the Bible,' I can make him a pro-Israel supporter or they will have to denounce their faith. So I have Christians over a barrel you might say."*

Few within the Evangelical community have publicly questioned Hagee's approach. But it's more complex than simply having a soft spot for Jews trying to populate "Judea and Samaria" (as they like to call land taken after the Six Day War of 1967). You see, to Us Real Christians, Real Jews were the Good Jews in the Old Testament, and after Jesus arrived (thus "fulfilling the prophecies" of the Old Testament), they were the Jews who *accepted* the Messiah.

Don't get me wrong—Us Real Jews weren't anti-Semites just because we said that the Actual Jews killed Jesus. Like Hagee and company, we *loved* Jews-Born-That-Way-Who-Stayed-That-Way even if their great-great-grandparents had—in a rather imprudent moment—killed God. We didn't blame them for killing God. If you're predestined to fulfill a prophecy, you're going to do it. And so we didn't blame the modern state of Israel's government for its brutality. It, too, was merely "fulfilling prophecy."

Mom often said that the "miraculous return of the Jews to Israel is just one more thing that *proves* the Bible is true." That

---

*John Hagee, The One Jerusalem Blog, January 25, 2007, www.onejerusalem .org/blog/archives/2007/01/audio_exclusive_12.asp.

would not have happened if the Jews *hadn't* killed Jesus, been exiled, suffered the Holocaust—"just what was needed to turn Zionism into a mainstream movement in order to fulfill prophecy," as Dad noted—and returned to Israel in order to pave the way for the Return of Christ. The Jews may have *thought* their return to Palestine was all about them. Of course, Us Real Christians knew better: It was all about *Us*.

Since Us Christians were now The Chosen People (either on our own or in tandem with the Jews, depending on one's theology), as a child, when hearing the word *Jew*, I mentally replaced it with the word *Christian*. Of course, I didn't *actually replace* any words in my Bible's text, mind you, because we believed that the Bible is inerrant, infallible, inspired, perfect, *and* complete, and so one *may* underline meaningful passages and even write notes in the margins (for instance, words like "Praise God this passage really speaks to me!"), but one may NEVER, EVER cross out stuff and/or replace anything! The point was, biblical prophecy applied to Us Real Christians, too. And so did biblical preoccupations about some weird things, say about woman's blood.

Divine Disdain For Womb Fluids is not just an idiosyncrasy of the Jews' Old-Testament-God-Of-The-Bible. Many Christians use "Old Testament God" to distinguish between what they characterize as the vengeful, violent God of the Old Testament and the loving, peaceful God of the New Testament. This is a self-righteous distinction in need of debunking: Divine vengeance runs *throughout* the Bible and throughout Christian history. Many of the Church Fathers (but not all) carried on the misogyny that was ubiquitous in the Greco-Roman world. These Fathers also elaborated on the Scriptures' teachings on women's impurity and turned them into doctrines that bash Sex—even in marriage.

In 241 CE Dionysius, archbishop of Alexandria, wrote to say that "menstruous women ought not to come to the Holy Table, or touch the Holy of Holies, nor to churches, but pray elsewhere." Menstruous women may not receive communion, may not receive baptism, may not visit the Church at Easter. "Corruption" attaches to all sexual intercourse, according to St. Jerome. Marriage and Sex only came *after* The Fall, he said. Jerome went so far as to say that to become human, Jesus had to put up with the "revolting conditions" of Mary's womb! (Or as the Angel Gabriel might have put it: "Rejoice, highly favored *one,* the Lord *is* with you; blessed *are* you among women, except for all the nasty bits of you God made by mistake.")

The-God-Of-The-Bible's aversion to sex-related bodily fluids seemed to contradict Mom's cheerful Sex-After-Marriage-Is-Always-Wonderful philosophy and her talks about "how marvelous" our bodies are, especially the "miracle of life." When I discovered that my Heavenly Maker didn't like my bodily fluids *and* had it in for my foreskin, too, Mom tried to soften the blow: "Real Christians don't have to circumcise," she said. "Since Jesus died for us, we don't have to do this." *That* was a relief! Still, I was worried about retribution for my scientific investigations. So I (obliquely) asked Mom about touching that sanitary pad. I said something like "What happened if a Jew touched a woman's blood, you know by mistake or something if he was just looking for something, or just thought it was chicken blood?"

"Ritual uncleanness is not perceived as worthy of death," Mom-the-ever-merciful said. "It's merely a state in which you can't approach God for a while. You would need to wash yourself, same as when you have a discharge. As Leviticus Chapter 15:17 says, 'When a man has an emission of semen, he must bathe his whole body with water, and he will be unclean till evening. Any clothing or leather that has semen on it must be washed with water, and it will be unclean till evening. When a man lies with a woman, and there is an emission of semen, both must bathe with water, and they will be unclean till evening.'"

"Just with water?" I asked.

"No, Dear, water *and* soap. When you Develop and have the Wet Dreams that God will send you to help you with your Desires, you must tell me and I'll wash your pajamas."

"Even though we're not Jews?"

"Yes, Dear, that's just cleanliness, not the Law."

"But what about that other verse where girls get killed for being Off The Roof?" I said, using Mom's euphemism for her period.

"You must mean Leviticus 20:18," said Mom, and without even opening her Bible, she quoted the passage: "'If a man lies with a woman during her menstrual period and uncovers her nakedness, he has made naked her fountain, and she has uncovered the fountain of her blood. Both of them shall be cut off from among their people.' Do you mean that verse, Dear?"

"Yes. Why would he have to be killed for uncovering her fountain?"

"You don't have to worry because it's about those wicked Canaanites. They used menstrual blood in their rituals when they should've just discarded their used pads in the wastepaper basket or at least washed out their towels or whatever they used. The Mosaic Law aimed to separate the good Hebrews from bad peoples who were dwelling in their midst. That's all, Darling."

"How come bleeding is bad?"

"It isn't 'bad.' God just uses this to remind women that our monthly Falling Off The Roof is a sign that the intimate part of life must be kept sacred. The human Sex Drive was corrupted by The Fall. You know that. The Marriage Bed is undefiled, but there's something that can defile the marriage bed: sexual intercourse when a woman is Off The Roof. So I wish Fran would respect this, but he doesn't because of his Need."

"So should Dad be cut off?"

"No, Dear, we're not under the Law the way the Jews used to be, though Fran *should* pay attention to the passage where the Lord says, 'In you,'—the Lord's talking about wicked men—'they violate women who are set apart during their impurity.' So when I'm Off The Roof, God probably frowns upon Fran's insistence on satisfying his Nightly Need, but because Jesus has fulfilled the Covenant, Fran is covered by The Blood and forgiven."

"Covered in your blood?"

Mom shot the thirteen-year-old version of me an annoyed glance.

"Christ's Blood! And you knew *perfectly well* what I meant!"

"So keeping that stuff in the Old Testament like the Ten Commandments doesn't matter now because no matter what we're forgiven because of Jesus' Blood and we aren't Jews?" asked the doubt-filled sixteen-year-old version of me.

"*No,* Dear, it *all still matters because we're Spiritual Jews*! It's just that some things aren't the same now that Jesus died for us. So we don't put people to death the way we used to or at least not for as many sins. As Paul says in First Corinthians, 'All things are lawful unto me, but all things are not expedient: all things are lawful for me, but I will not be brought under the power of any.'"

"We still keep the parts about men not lying together carnally, don't we?" the eleven-year-old version of me asked, having recently returned from my first term in a British boys' boarding school where group "wanks" were a way of life.

"Yes, Dear, homosexuality is still an abomination because Paul says so."

"But lying with a woman when she's Off The Roof is okay now?"

"It isn't pleasing to the Lord, so I wish Fran would stop, but he doesn't have to be killed because Jesus died for him, too."

"What if Dad did bestiality?" asked the smart-ass fourteen-year-old version of me.

"Why on *earth* would he do *that*?! Really the things you come up with!"

"So who decides what's still a rule?"

"The Holy Spirit leads us."

"What about if He leads somebody to not obey rules you say we're still supposed to keep?"

"It would prove they aren't Real Christians."

"How do you know that the Holy Spirit's leading you and Dad?"

"Because He's blessing the work of L'Abri. This isn't a mere co-incidence. He wouldn't bless us if our theology wasn't right."

Regardless of how right our theology was, my monthly encounter with *material evidence* of that Most Private Place's *actual existence* was thrilling. Holding that pad and putting a little blood on a glass slide, the ten-year-old me became a menstrual-truth-seeker version of Winston Smith, the hero of George Orwell's novel *1984*. Smith and I both faced the ruling oligarchy, "The Party," as Orwell calls it. The Party subjected everyone to snooping; its busybody-imposed "holiness" was a form of conformity very much like that imposed within L'Abri. You either agreed with Mom and Dad, and through them with The-God-Of-The-Bible or you were soon cut off. In our "Party" the slogan might have been, "He who controls the interpretation of the Bible controls the future."

For Winston the moment of truth is when—for one brief instant—he holds *actual contradictory newspaper articles in his hands* that prove that The Party lies. For me I held the *evidence* of *Actual Vagina*. Holding *actual evidence* in his hands of the self-contradicting "Truth" of the government's lies, Smith had his moment of vindication. But Smith didn't have to worry about going to Hell for touching a few contradictory news clippings. I had almost touched the untouchable. And so I had *proof* that nothing could remain hidden forever, even *before* my Wedding Night!

The mummified wads and the slight telltale aroma of menstrual blood filled the bathroom with a mystery as enticing as the best perfume wafting on some languid Mediterranean summer breeze. Here *at last* was The Truth: Women *did* so much more with their bodies than I did! They bled. They produced milk. Their underwear was so much more complex and multilayered. Mom said I'd "develop." So what? All that meant was that I'd grow hair "Down There." With women the whole shape of their bodies changed. Mom had explained sperm production and the "lustful thoughts" I'd start having after puberty. Well, *I was having those thoughts right now,* and all that happened was that a few flaccid inches of pink flesh became erect with greater and greater frequency, something difficult to hide and useless for now. My Wedding Night might as well have been lurking on some distant planet a billion light-years away for all the good it did me.

Women, on the other hand, had their secrets tucked away. How could *they* need anything but *themselves* since THEY were *in and of themselves* the most alluring creatures in the universe?! *They* could get naked in the bathroom and look at A REAL WOMAN any time they wanted to! Even thinking about THEM compelled me to conceal my shame or at least crouch over as I walked to hide the evidence. But nothing on *women*—nipples aside, which sometimes stood up in cold bathing suits—gave *them* away. Did *they* linger at the laundry line for a glimpse of *male* underwear? No! Did *they* work for over an hour during some Bible study to "casually" loll next to the couch so as to slump onto the floor feigning drowsiness in order to angle their head for a look into that dark and wonderful triangular cave between a woman's knees formed by her skirt and thighs? No! And anyway, Our Girls' skirts were most often tucked severely around their thighs and overlapped their knees by several modest inches, so no matter *how* I bent my neck (until it had a painful crick), it was no use.

After I grew up, I discovered that I hadn't been the only person grappling with my Sinful Body and what to "do" about it. Bible-believing Christians aren't alone in struggling with their Sinful Bodies. Jews and Muslims who follow their holy books as absolute sources of moral authority are vigilant about the many, *many* scriptural laws pertaining to women. There are Jewish women who keep the Levitical laws concerning menstruation. And according to Islam, menstrual blood is impure. The Islamic "perspective" on menstruation gets quite detailed when updated to answer modern "moral questions": for example, "what type of 'female sanitary protection' should a woman use?" According to some Islamic scholars, tampons are against the rules. In his commentary on Imam al-Barkawi's "Treatise on Menstruation," the Hanafi jurist Allama Ibn Abidin says that it is offensive (*makruh*) to have cotton inserted in the "internal part" of the vagina because doing so "resembles masturbation."*

There are some secondary unintended very strange results in the lives of people living in cultures shaped by these sorts of "teachings." And the results speak for themselves, as illustrated by this quote from a *San Francisco Chronicle* article:

Western forces fighting in southern Afghanistan had a problem. Too often, soldiers on patrol passed an older man walking hand-

---

*See Majmu'a Rasa'il Ibn Abidin, 1/84–85, www.shariahprogram.ca/islam -qa-women/tampons-permissible-marriage.shtml.

in-hand with a pretty young boy. . . . For centuries, Afghan men have taken boys, roughly 9 to 15 years old, as lovers. Some research suggests that half the Pashtun tribal members in Kandahar and other southern towns are bacha baz, the term for an older man with a boy lover. Literally it means "boy player." The men like to boast about it. . . .

Sociologists and anthropologists say the problem results from perverse interpretation of Islamic law. Women are simply unapproachable. Afghan men cannot talk to an unrelated woman until after proposing marriage. Before then, they can't even look at a woman, except perhaps her feet. Otherwise she is covered, head to ankle. "How can you fall in love if you can't see her face," 29-year-old Mohammed Daud told reporters. "We can see the boys, so we can tell which are beautiful." . . .

A favored Afghan expression goes: "Women are for children, boys are for pleasure." Fundamentalist imams, exaggerating a biblical passage on menstruation, teach that women are "unclean" and therefore distasteful. One married man [interviewed by the reporter on this subject] even asked . . . "how his wife could become pregnant. . . . " When that was explained, he "reacted with disgust" and asked, "How could one feel desire to be with a woman, who God has made unclean?" That helps explain why women are hidden away—and stoned to death if they are perceived to have misbehaved. Islamic law also forbids homosexuality. But the pedophiles explain that away. It's not homosexuality, they aver, because they aren't in love with their boys.*

---

*Joel Brinkley, "Afghanistan's Dirty Little Secret," *San Francisco Chronicle*, August 29, 2010, http://articles.sfgate.com/2010–08–29/opinion/22949948_1 _karzai-family-afghan-men-president-hamid-karzai.

This report was made all the more poignant for me in light of my son John's deployment (twice) to Afghanistan while he was a marine.* And thus when, a few years later, I read this *Chronicle* article, my thought was (and not for the first or last time), what was John defending? I'm not just talking about "defending democracy" (let alone a loopy bogus colonial "nation-building" mantra). I was thinking about my son supposedly trying to bring "civilization" to a country with a particular form of "backwardness" that is embarrassingly close in kind to our *own backwardness* and rooted in the same horrible religious ideas.

The words "Women are simply unapproachable. Afghan men cannot talk to an unrelated woman until after proposing marriage" express an attitude so very like my own childhood ideas about women, Sex, and marriage. How very similar our Schaeffer/ Evangelical-style sexual dysfunction was to the root cause of the Afghan abuse of boys and women, both of which follow from prejudices about women and Sex cultivated by Jews, Christians, and Muslims alike, that is, by "people of the book."

Since the 1970s the American culture wars have revolved around a fear of Sex and women no less insane and destructive than any horror story to come out of Afghanistan. The issues of gay rights, abortion, premarital sex, virginity, abstinence, and the "God-given role" of women (make babies, love Jesus, and shut up) have dominated our political/social debates. Why? Because sexual politics (American style) illustrates how deranged societies become when ideas about Sex are based on literal interpretations of the biblical "account" of the "facts" of existence.

---

*I tell this story in *Faith of Our Sons: A Father's Wartime Diary* (New York: Carroll and Graf, 2004), and I draw on my experiences in my novel *Baby Jack* (New York: Carroll and Graf, 2006).

Extremism, even extreme prudery, begets extremism. Dysfunction begets dysfunction. Wait-until-marriage and women-are-unclean beliefs have generated an insane counterreaction that takes the form of an off-the-wall sexual license, a bizarre mirror image of our prudish North American version of the antiwoman biblical extreme.

In reaction to the fear and loathing of Sex, women, and intimacy that resulted from the biblical teachings against premarital Sex, let alone against women's vile uncleanness, a rebellion took place. This rebellion against fear and antisexual prejudice was ushered in by the "free love" prophets-for-profit like Hugh Hefner. But what started in the 1950s and 1960s as an attempt to balance sexual fear with sanity tumbled into yet another example of dysfunctional American extremism. This happened because the practitioners of three American belief systems (that are so intense they might as well be religions) unwittingly colluded: Progressives (absolutist believers in unregulated Free Speech), conservatives (absolutist believers in unregulated Free Enterprise), and conservative Christians (absolutist believers in the uncleanness of Sex between anyone not married in a heterosexual "traditional" marriage) created a sordid monster—Porn-Gone-Nuts.

The pleasant Greco-Roman/Pagan sexual aesthetic offered in the first generation of 1960s centerfold-type erotica (much of which was lovely) became—in the context of our extremist unregulated capitalist culture in which if something sells, it must be good—a brutal lowest-common-denominator version of Sex. This "sexuality"—once again—leaves women out in the cold as American society slides into an uncharted lowest-common-denominator porn universe gone viral. Add in the invasive Internet, and we have, as they say, a whole new day.

In an Alternet interview with author Gail Dines (a professor of sociology and women's studies at Boston's Wheelock College,

where she researches the "hypersexualization" of our culture),*
she notes that the extremes of today's mainstream pornography
have, in her words, "greatly undermined our ability to have meaningful sexual partnerships." In *Pornland: How Porn Has Hijacked
Our Sexuality*,** Dines traces the history of the porn industry
from *Playboy* and *Penthouse* to today's "entertainment," which resembles the sexual assault of women and is closer in spirit to an
Afghan stoning of a hapless female by ignorant peasants (or the
rape of little boys by Afghan men forbidden relationships with
off-limits women or other men) than to anything resembling
Love or Sex as most people understand either word.

Offering an example of what has to be called brutal sexual extremism, Dines quotes sell-copy text of a type that's all too common on porn Web sites these days: "Do you know what we say to
things like romance and foreplay? We say fuck off! This is not
another site with half-erect weenies trying to impress bold sluts.
We take gorgeous young bitches and do what every man would
REALLY like to do. We make them gag till their makeup starts
running, and then they get all other holes sore—vaginal, anal,
double penetrations, anything brutal involving a cock and an ori-
fice. And then we give them the sticky bath." This quote and the
video images it's selling are typical of "mainstream" porn available online and are viewed by boys and girls the same age I was—
ten or eleven—when the discovery of Sex was something secret,
feared, and off limits but hardly brutal.

As multiple studies confirm, about 65 percent of young boys
are exposed to Internet porn beginning at the average age of

---

*Sonali Kolhatkar, "Should We Worry Whether Porn Has Hijacked Our Sexual-
ity?" Alternet, September 11,2010, www.alternet.org/media/148142/should_we
_worry_whether_porn_has_hijacked_our_sexuality/?page=entire.
**Gail Dines, *Pornland: How Porn Has Hijacked Our Sexuality* (Boston: Bea-
con Press, June 2010).

eleven.* The problem isn't Sex—it is unconstrained capitalism combined with the "Free Speech"–enabled reaction to nutty religion that is appealing to the lowest common denominator in a society where "The Market Rules!" is the eleventh commandment.

What sort of culture stands back and does no more than wring its hands over the fact that many children's first "experience" of Sex is swilling deeply at a trough of violent and demeaning viral infection? Answer: a biblically rooted capitalist society filled with a large group of people raised somewhat as I was who are reeling from the aftershock of Judeo-Christian prudery and want to somehow open the door to forbidden mystery while at the same time having inherited (if unconsciously) the women-are-scary-and-unclean biblical bigotry. Today's misogynist porn does not have its biggest markets in the (relatively progressive) cultures of our big cities. No, it makes its big sales with churchgoing "family men" in the Midwest and South.**

All porn is not as brutal as Dines paints it. There is still a lot of pleasantly titillating erotica created by women and men for couples that is closer in spirit to Renaissance art than to lynch-mob brutality. There is also a lot of amateur porn produced by people because they enjoy it. That said, to care about a child today is also to mourn the loss of an incremental sexual awakening that should be that child's rite of passage, just as it should be a civil

---

*"Boys Who See Porn More Likely to Harass Girls," *Sunday Times*, January 24, 2010, www.timesonline.co.uk/tol/news/uk/crime/article6999874.ece. According to this article, "Boys exposed to porn are more likely to indulge in casual sex and less likely to form successful relationships when they grow older, according to research carried out in a dozen countries," and "the average age at which they first saw porn has dropped from 15 to 11 in less than a decade. The average amount of time they watch porn on the internet is 90 minutes a week."

**Benjamin Edelman, "Markets Red Light States: Who Buys Online Adult Entertainment?" *Journal of Economic Perspectives* 23, no. 1 (Winter 2009): 209–220.

right of every young man or woman to be free of brutal, mind-numbing (and possibly mind-altering) sludge.

About thirty years after I stood, quivering with curiosity, peering into that wastepaper basket full of sanitary pads, my grown-up (and terrified) self crouched next to my wife, Genie, at three in the morning. She was hemorrhaging.

I'd watched my three children being born. I'd seen a doctor cut her to make the passage wider when Jessica—our firstborn—was tearing her mother's flesh as she made her way into the world. Now on this night, after a year when Genie's increasingly long periods became one long trial, it was as if something inside of her had broken loose. Even bath towels couldn't soak up all the blood. I'd been squatting on the bathroom floor at her feet, watching her bleed dreadful clots that looked like slices of raw liver. I was zeroing in on them because one possibility we considered was that, long periods or not, Genie was somehow having a miscarriage. So (illogically) I studied those clots looking for little hands or feet, wildly imagining a small face staring back at me. Was *this* how Mom's miscarriage had started: with a river of blood?

Was that a tiny foot?

This was nuts, but it was three in the morning, and MY WIFE might be dying!

Then we were in the hospital.

Then the bleeding slowed.

Genie was waxy pale, waiting to be examined by a gynecologist. There was a smear of blood on her cheek that I washed off with a paper towel. I was gingerly perching on a stainless steel stool close to a short table with stirrups. I was holding her hand while our first meeting replayed in my brain like a loop of film.

Fall of 1969, a frosty night of bright stars. I hear the door open, and I poke my head around the corner. Regina Ann Walsh is stand-

*ing tall and lovely under our old Venetian wrought-iron and glass
lantern. High cheekbones, full lips, and almond-shaped, almost
Asian hazel eyes, slightly slanted at the corners, some sort of appari-
tion of unattainable perfection. Genie's eyes are framed by her long
auburn hair falling to her waist, points of pelvic bone defining her
hips, belly tight under those second-skin slacks, high glossy boots up
to her knees, generous breasts, and that gorgeous face defining a
moment that remains, for me, holy. With a smile Genie acknowl-
edges me. I hastily set an extra place at my table. . . . Genie men-
tions that she wants to hear the just-released new Beatles album,
Abbey Road. I happen to have the album downstairs in my studio. . . . "Here comes the sun, here comes the sun . . . And I say it's
alright . . . Little darling it's been a long cold lonely winter."*

Next to me was a plastic bag hand-labeled "Rape Kit." We'd been
stowed in a gynecology examination cubicle reserved for female
emergencies like ours—and, apparently, for gathering evidence
from rape victims. I surreptitiously studied that clear plastic bag
without mentioning it to Genie. There was a fine-tooth comb for
combing through a woman's pubic hair to snag a rapist's pubic
hairs. There was a test tube with a Q-tip-type swab in it to absorb
fluids from the next rape victim. There was a sharp plastic stick,
something like an overgrown toothpick, used to scrape under the
victim's fingernails to retrieve blood or tissue from the rapist, if the
victim had put up a fight and scratched her attacker. Next to the
rape kit was a Polaroid camera with a handwritten label taped to it
that read "Evidence Camera. Do *NOT* Remove from Rape Room."

The night duty nurses kept us waiting for the doctor, a bleary-
eyed gynecologist (and a stranger to us since Genie's doctor was
several towns away and we'd made a beeline to the nearest emergency room) who smelled faintly of liquor. We'd waited for over
two hours—plenty of time to study everything in the room twenty
times over while Genie grew colder and colder. I asked for another

blanket and eventually was given one that was as thin and useless as tissue paper. Genie was lying in a dingy cubbyhole dedicated to collecting evidence that proved that Vaginas make women targets.

I'd been Genie's lover since we were teens, and by that night her menstrual blood was merely another drop in the ocean of bodily fluids we'd exchanged. What had once been a very big and titillating event—evidence of women bleeding—was, after twenty years of marriage, a mundane reality to me. Life was no longer all about Forbidden Lust. Moreover, by then my loyalty was to Genie and through her to all women. Whenever I encountered Bible verses that belittled and brutalized women, I took it personally.

CHAPTER 3

Sex with the Ice Sculpture

I laboriously carved my Ice Woman out of the deep, wet snow that lay thick in the woods above our chalet. I worked with as much dedicated concentration as a ten-year-old artist can muster, hunched over my creation, only glancing at the pine trees above me from time to time. Their branches were weighed down so heavily that the snow formed an almost straight white sheath that made the trees appear strangely narrow. Through the trees I could glimpse the high peaks of the Dents du Midi, mighty, dazzling white, and towering over my small frozen world. The snowing stopped and the sky cleared just as I completed my attempt to reenact God-Of-The-Bible's whittling of Eve from Adam's rib.

My act of creation soon taught me never, *ever* again to attempt sex with an ice sculpture. I was not the first Germanic artist with theological/sexual preoccupations to make my art the object of personal Lust. I carved my ice lover inspired by Gustav Klimt's erotic drawings of his lovely models sketched in sexually fraught positions. I'd seen these women in one of Dad's art books back in

PHOTO: *Mom—the well-dressed young pastor's wife, 1937*

57

the days when art books and/or grainy black-and-white surreptitiously collected newspaper underwear advertisements were my treasured porn.

Klimt would have understood my need for a lover. In the late nineteenth and early twentieth centuries, Klimt's models graced his studio/harem and found their way into his beautifully explicit erotic drawings. Klimt fathered fourteen children with his subjects *and* didn't suffer frostbite since his method of combining art with pleasure was more practical than mine.

In addition to Klimt's drawings, there were Lucas Cranach nudes, including *Adam and Eve*, in one of Dad's art books. Cranach was a "Reformation painter," as Dad called him. Cranach was also a close friend of Martin Luther, and his nudes are proof that whatever else Luther was, he was no prude and would have been excoriated by American-style Evangelicals for encouraging his friend to produce the soft-core porn of that day.

Dad liked Cranach and kept books of his art handy. And I did my best to bestow my ice lover with a guileless sexuality that the horny leaders of the Reformation, not to mention the later Romantic Movement painter Klimt, would have admired. Speaking of horny Protestants, I think that Cranach and his sexually avid mentor, Luther, would have liked my ice lover and maybe even would have approved of my actions or, in Luther's case, given "intercourse" with her a try. Luther was enthusiastically sexual. He and his lover had long been "associated" (openly sleeping together) before they married. Luther was a regular visitor to Cranach's home, where Katharine, Luther's future wife (who was a renegade nun under Luther's "supervision"), lived. Whatever some of the Church Fathers had once said about even married couples ideally living like "brother and sister," the restoration of the place of Sex as something wholesome in Luther's vision of correct biblical interpretation was one of his triumphs.

Anyway, my Cranach-derived/Lutheran/Klimtian art had a downside: It was an installation/sculpture and therefore required me to participate in an artistic "happening" in a way that compromised both this artist's dignity and physical well-being. (I've had a bias against art installations ever since and have stuck to painting.)

My Ice Woman was large-breasted and wide-hipped. Her mitten-print-mottled icy thighs lay like fallen marble columns leading to the main event nestled between her legs, that place—*The Place*—on, and mysteriously *in*, all women's bodies and upon which my mind and (if the Bible is any guide) The-God-Of-The-Bible's Mind was focused. My ice lover's legs were spread wide, and her breasts were crowned with pebble nipples. She had a thatch of moss for pubic hair.

I revealed my creation to someone I'll call Seth, the eleven-year-old son of a fellow missionary family (whose parents later quit L'Abri over a difference of opinion concerning predictions about the exact timing of the Return of Christ). Seth had watched me carve my ice lover, with a borrowed serving spoon and Mom's good, never-to-be-taken-out-of-the-house bread knife. He declared my woman "real-looking, except she should be pink like a girl." After offering this critique, Seth said, "I'm not gonna do it," then added, "but I won't tell if you do."

I began successfully enough, trousers down, snow parka pulled up, mittens off (the better to fondle with), and the rest of me assuming the so-called (and Schaeffer-family-appropriate) missionary position. But all-too-brief foreplay and a frantic (and unnerving) attempt at copulation, following Actual Penetration, ended in a debacle.

Dad always said, "Quit while you're ahead" in reference to all manner of overlong persistence. Unfortunately, I didn't apply this advice, as the first shock of my encounter redefined the term "she's frigid." I just kept going and going like some demented sexualized

Energizer Bunny. And this was *after* what my mother euphemistically referred to as my "Little Thing" lost its joyful at-last-I'm-
going-to-have-*Real*-Sex!-but-it's-okay-because-this-isn't-a-real-
Girl-so-it-isn't-fornication erection. My Little Thing also lost its
ability to *feel anything at all* and was—to my consternation—
reduced to a pitifully chafed, apparently lifeless Even Littler Thing.

Eventually, I gave up and rocked back on my knees. Seth squat-
ted to examine my nub close up, then stood, placed his hands on
his hips, and declared, "It sort of looks like a blue acorn."

"It's frozen," I groaned.

"And your nuts have disappeared, too," Seth added.

"I've killed it," I moaned.

In the upstairs bathroom of my parents' chalet, I tremblingly
dipped the remnant into Dad's father's (heirloom Spanish-
American War memento) navy shaving mug filled with hot water.
Seth watched with great interest to see "if it'll come off when you
unfreeze it." Meanwhile, on Evangelical autopilot, I silently began
to pray that God would heal me. But I was scarcely into my pon-
derous "Dear Heavenly Father" opening (of the formal kind reserved for the *most serious prayers*), when I stopped: Maybe it
wasn't such a good idea to attract more Divine attention to my
situation.

I was feeling "cut off from God's love." That's what happens,
Mom always said, when you are "far from the Lord's Will." Cut off
or not, I knew that God sees, knows, and records everything we
do, so it wasn't as if I could hide. I knew that God *knew*—even before the Creation of the Universe—that at *that precise moment*
in January of 1962 I'd be standing in the upstairs bathroom of
Chalet Les Mélèzes in the village of Huémoz, Vaud, Switzerland
with a frozen penis. Everything that happened in the universe, including who was created to be damned to Hell and who was foreordained to be of The Elect, or who would make unto himself a

graven image of snow and go unto her as if "unto an harlot," was already set in cosmic granite.

Every crystallized cell of my blue acorn was known to God. But still, there was no point in making my defiled self even better-known among legions of Heavenly Hosts. I didn't think my problem was worth storming into the Throne Room and risk drawing the attentive eyes of those cherubim and seraphim to my Sin. I figured it was best to just let the four and twenty elders get on with falling at the feet of the Lord, proclaiming what He already knows, again and again and again and again: "Thou art worthy, O Lord, to receive glory and honor and power: for thou hast created all things, and for thy pleasure they are and were created" (Revelation 4:11). No need to disrupt the praise with a plea for help that would go something like this: "Dear Heavenly Father, I just thank Thee for sending Your Son to die for me. Be that as it may, since I've been about nine years old I've wanted to try intercourse. I saw a village boy try it on a sheep, but she bit him. And anyway in the Bible it says, 'Anyone who has sexual relations with an animal must be put to death.' So it wasn't sheep, Lord, just snow. So I was just wondering Lord, if You'd reach out and touchest me, O Lord, and do for my Little Thing what Thou didst for Lazarus before I have to try and figure out how to explain this Blue Acorn Situation to Mom. In Jesus' Name I pray, Amen."

I knew full well that God knew what I *would* have prayed because He always knows what's "on your heart," especially if it's Lustful. As Jesus told his followers, "You have heard that it was said, 'Do not commit adultery,' but I tell you that anyone who looks at a woman lustfully has already committed adultery with her in his heart" (Matthew 5:28).

Since I wasn't married, my attempt at fornication certainly wasn't adultery, but it *was* Lust. After she read that *very passage* (for about the hundredth time) about Lust in your heart counting *as much as actually doing it,* Mom said, "Some misguided wives' give 'permission' when they say to their husbands, 'Look; just don't touch.' But, Darling, God *knows* and it's as if they *did it* when they lusted." Then, shifting from her authoritative Talk For Girls tone to that overly intimate voice, Mom continued, "Which is *one reason* why Fran and I have sexual intercourse *every single night* as I've told you, so that he never has any reason to commit adultery—even in his heart. Though, I'm afraid, he *does* cast what I know are Lustful Glances when he lingers outside that awful nightclub on the Rue de Bourg in Lausanne and looks at the pictures of what they're offering inside that worldly place."

Mom was a much nicer person than her God. There are many biblical regulations, about everything from beard-trimming to menstruating, of what The-God-Of-The-Bible wants us to do or not do, along with rigid laws and Severe Punishment (mostly death) for the least transgression. Mom worked diligently to recast her personal-hygiene-obsessed God in the best light. Rigid Bible-believers would reject my mother's way of benignly dressing up The-God-Of-The-Bible's Word to appear more kindly and palatable, not to mention sane, than the text warrants. Mom struggled to make her "God" kindly. But it's tough to rehabilitate the judgmental misanthropic Spirit of Divine Pettiness who commands no beard trimming, "lest the land vomit you also out when you defile it," as The-God-Of-The-Bible says. "For whoever commits any of these abominations, the persons who commit them shall be cut off from among their people" (Leviticus 18:24).

What's more, The-God-Of-The-Bible doesn't seem terribly concerned with being sensible (let alone nice) when issuing His long lists of Dos and Don'ts: *Don't* clip your beard or defile yourself with menstrual blood, but *Do* help yourselves to slaves, and have your way with them: "You may buy male and female slaves from among the nations that are around you. You may also buy from among the strangers who sojourn with you and their clans that are with you, who have been born in your land, and they may be your property. You may bequeath them to your sons after you to inherit as a possession forever. You may make slaves of them, but over your brothers the people of Israel you shall not rule, one over another ruthlessly" (Leviticus 25:40–45).

The only way Mom could have really let this brutish slave-trader/inventor of genocide, "God" off the hook was to repudiate much of the Bible's portrayal of Him. But when it came to theology, Mom was more loyal to her Bible than to any actual God who might have created galaxies and put Love in the hearts of men and women. She went with His "biographers'" version of Him rather than trusting her heart, let alone her otherwise solid common sense.

When it came to honoring the Bible more than a God Who might have actually created the universe, Mom—like all conservative religionists hiding behind their holy books—seemed to ignore the inner witness of Beauty, Humor, Paradox, Complexity, Love, and most of all in terms of what makes us humans, memories of actual experiences. Yet the irony was that *in her manner of life—* rather than her official theology—Mom lived *as if* God were much bigger than the nasty little eccentric portrayed in the Bible.

The "whole Bible is true," Mom claimed, though everything in her life that was kind and decent and compassionate contradicted this platitude. Given her official fundamentalist allegiance to a book *about* God rather than *to* whatever actual God there might be, Mom couldn't openly deny the truth of any of the Bible's words. To her, the fault always had to be with our human "interpretation" of the Word, not with the Word itself, even if The Word painted God as barbaric and stupid.

Though the subject of slave owning didn't come up much in Hué-moz, we at L'Abri *were* keenly concerned with "applying God's Word to our lives." Luckily, or rather providentially, for me, Mom wasn't keeping all the rules. For a start she hadn't had any of my Little Thing cut off, and as for many other rules Mom decided on a case-by-case basis which ones God had liberated her from by personally shedding His Son's Blood instead of killing us all and/or making us keep all the pre-Jesus rules.

Mom didn't own slaves *or* withdraw to a tent and sit there once a month for seven days the way she would have if she were actually following the Bible. And she ignored the Bible (and some of the early Church Fathers') prohibitions against women teaching, too. Nevertheless, Mom often used Bible verses she wasn't literally following to condemn others for doing things she didn't approve of.

Mom would quote bits of Leviticus when putting down Roman Catholics: "And the Lord said to Moses . . . They shall not make bald patches on their heads, nor shave off the edges of their beards, nor make any cuts on their body." Mom referred to this verse when railing against Roman Catholic monks who were tonsured (with "bald patches on their heads") as further proof that Catholics followed "false teachings." Leviticus 20:10 was useful on the home front: "If a man commits adultery with the wife of his neighbor, both the adulterer and the adulteress shall surely be put to death." That proved that Mom *had* to help Dad with his Nightly Need since adultery was still a serious Sin, and far be it from Mom to be a "stumbling block" and complicit in Dad's Many Weaknesses.

Mom's selective application of Scripture to her life and to others' lives was not usually judgmental and moralistic. More often than not, Mom was softening, mitigating, and/or just ignoring (to put it in the terms she used for Dad) God's Many Weaknesses.

As I've said, she and Dad showed more or less limitless compassion to the many gay men and women who, over the years, were made welcome at L'Abri. But the "You shall not lie with a male as with a woman" admonishment worried me. Although I had no desire to lie with a man, Seth and I used to take care of our Needs in a comradely way. Huddled in my "secret chamber" behind the hot water boiler under the chalet stairs, we'd "touch ourselves" *side by side* while ogling a bra-and-panty advertisement and/or Cranach's *Adam and Eve.* The line between who was wanking with another boy merely for good company and who liked other boys "that way" was never clear, even when I was at boarding school in England. I'd join in "group wanks" with a cheery who-can-squirt-the-farthest abandon. I have no idea who was gay or straight, only that *I* was imagining matron (the *very female* school nurse).

If you could prove you were *thinking* of a naked woman *while* wanking shoulder to shoulder with another male *and* staring at Eve, *not* Adam, in Cranach's Reformation porn, would the Elders at the Heavenly City Gate have let you off with a stern warning instead of stoning you to death? Or was the act of dropping your trousers *with* other *boys*—even if you were sincerely *wishing* you were with a Girl, even with a small-breasted, strange-looking Cranach nude— an "abomination unto the Lord," punishable by death, *whatever* your thoughts were about? Then again, since God "sees the heart," and since Lust is *just as bad* as actually Doing It, surely the Girl you were *thinking of* when you wanked alongside boys *proved* to God you weren't a homosexual, no matter whom you were with or who was holding the art book open to the "best page."

Drawing from experience, I can only offer my speculations about the damage Bible-believing views of sexuality can do. I think the many, many biblical exhortations about the body make for a self-loathing that drives people to take it out on others or to flip to the other extreme and head into a one-way Internet porn thicket of ever-more-degrading material while trying to find what they think they've somehow missed out on. Either way, as a sincere (or even a former) Bible-believer, you're doomed to hate your own body because it tricks you into Lust. And since you hate your own body but don't want to kill it just yet, you redirect your hatred to other people's bodies and what they do with them.

What also pisses you off is to stumble again and again on "nonbelievers" who seem happier than you are. You say you hate the Sin, not the Sinner. But since "Sinners" are rarely grateful for this sort of "love" and resent being judged, pretty soon you get into fights with the Sinners and start to rebuke them. Or you push for legislation like anti-gay-marriage initiatives to stop Sinners from entering into the union you believe is "only for a man and a woman," perhaps because you're bitter that the inerrant Word of God has come between you and your body or between you and the many other bodies you'd like to have had Sex with.

You must "stand against all compromise"; you must hate every "deviation" because you are in a constant battle with temptation. Maybe your temptations lead you to question what you say you believe. Above all, your temptations make you wonder if you are "Saved." So you don't open a door to doubt; rather, you just yell all the louder to drown out the nagging thought that you may, after all, be no better than anyone else and may be just as "Lost" as the next guy. Maybe you build a career out of all that yelling and/or "legislative initiatives." But at some point you have a choice: to listen to your reasonable doubts, follow your questions, and perhaps, as I did, embrace the inexplicable fact of *Merciful Paradox*, or deny the reasonable voice of doubt and redouble your efforts to "keep faith."

Those who fight to "defend the faith" in its fundamentalist harsh incarnation, as Evangelical "professional Christians" often do, have a special need-based interest in making sure *other people* live by the letter of the Bible's "inerrant" Word. As modernity has threatened the belief system of conservative Christians, their resentment has grown into alienation. Rather than rethink their beliefs, many Christian leaders seem hell-bent on forcing the world to conform to their fears.

If professional Christians earn their living *and* derive their meaning from their roles as religious leaders—not to mention enjoy their power over other people—then they have all the more motivation to deny their doubts (and their bodies and perhaps their sexual orientation) and to call for others to conform to their beliefs. But note I say "conform to their beliefs" rather than conform to their *example.*

And therein is the problem: Theory and practice have diverged. Many Evangelical leaders of antigay initiatives have turned out to be closeted gay men. Many leaders in Congress harping on "family values" or state governors crusading on platforms of moral rectitude have turned out to be mired in sexual scandals. Many Roman Catholic "celibate" bishops and popes that sniff around in other people's bedrooms *also are* fighting to keep the public misled about what they and/or many of their priests actually have been getting up to in their *own* bedrooms, including child molesting.

There seems to have been a consistent pattern: The louder the protest against "the lack of morals," the more likely it has been that the person doing the protesting and/or trying to make others conform to his or her beliefs was *also* mired in sexual struggles that, if known, would have given a lie to the protester's moralizing. I think that is why sometimes the sons (or daughters) of some religious leaders are harsher and even more extreme in their rants against "the World" than their parents were.

The next generation must shout down its own doubts all the more loudly since the children of religious leaders have seen first-hand that their parents had feet of clay. These children know that in fact their parents' public image and private lives were often wildly different. For instance, having a father who hit my mother made it a little hard for me to take his book about love *The Mark of the Christian*—described by the publisher in the sell copy as "what a true Christian witness looks like in our needy and broken world"—terribly seriously.*

But my flawed father was just famous in the Evangelical ghetto, not famous in the entire world. Imagine the discrepancy between evangelist Billy Graham's semiofficial status as the American Protestant "pope" (and chaplain to presidents) and the reality of his actual human self as seen daily from the Graham children's perspective. I happen to have become close friends with Gigi Graham when we were both in our twenties. (We've since fallen out of touch.) Suffice to say that when her sister Ruth wrote to me after reading my memoir *Crazy for God* to say that she loved the book and that she and the other Graham children were also "sacrificial lambs," I knew just what she meant.

So the story of evangelist Billy Graham's son Franklin Graham strikes scarily close to my own experiences. Long before he was worrying about where to bury his parents, I met Franklin several times while we were both coming of age as the sons of religious leaders. Our first meeting happened when we were both nine and he visited L'Abri with his whole family and stayed for church and Sunday tea. (Franklin looked as if he'd rather have been just about anywhere else.) A few years later, Franklin was poised to follow in his father's footsteps. But just before that he (all-too-briefly) deviated from the usual nepotistic path. Rumors abounded about Franklin's "wild living" and the rejecting of his family's faith. When I was in my early twenties, I remember talking to Franklin's

---

*Frances A. Schaeffer, *The Mark of the Christian* (Chicago: InterVarsity Press, 1976).

mother and his sister Gigi about Franklin's "period of youthful rebellion" and how sad they were that he'd "fallen so far from the
Lord." But later Franklin "repented" and then rejoined the team and
took over his father's ministry.

Franklin's story is typical of the preposterous nepotistic "model"
of Protestant leadership, what might be called entrepreneurial
ministry through the Divine Right of Succession to the Mailing
List If You Can't Find Anything Better To Do. But Franklin also
represents something else: the second generation in an Evangelical
empire being even harsher and more strictly fundamentalist than
the first.

Franklin's father became less political as the years passed. He
also toned down his earlier hellfire Protestant fundamentalism,
allowing, for instance, that Roman Catholics and other non-born-
again people might even be saved. During one of our meetings at
Mayo Clinic, Billy told my father and me that he'd got burned by
getting too close to Nixon and being identified with his policies
and that he did not intend to be seen endorsing a political figure
or cause again. In the 1970s Billy had even point-blank refused to
become part of the antiabortion crusade we waged, no matter
how often Dad and I begged him to join our "call to save babies."
Billy said that we'd become "too political" and "too harsh." (He
was right.)

By contrast, Franklin Graham became one of the shrillest of the
Far Right Republican Party boosters and also a harsh anti-Islamic
activist who capitalized on the post-9/11 political climate of fear
that burgeoned, in many instances, into paranoia about the Muslim
"Other." Franklin disparaged Islam as "a very evil and wicked religion" that does not belong in the United States. And Franklin embraced overt politics. For instance, in an interview with Newsmax
Television, Franklin was asked if he thought there was a "pattern of
hostility to traditional Christianity by the Obama administration."

"I don't know if it's exactly from President Obama," Graham responded, "but I'm certain that some of the men around him are very much opposed to what we stand for and what we believe." Franklin continued, "It seems as though Muslims are getting a pass [from Obama]." In the same interview Franklin was asked about "secular oppression of Christians" in the United States. "No question, it's coming!" Graham said. "I think when you preach that Jesus Christ is the way, the truth and the life, I think we're going to see, one day, people will say this is hate speech!"*

In 2010 Franklin even managed to get his father to sign a pro–Sarah Palin endorsement. There was something about that action that struck scarily close to home for me because in the 1970s and 1980s I was the Schaeffer version of a Franklin Graham, well positioned to succeed my father as a powerful Religious Right leader all the while goading my father into taking political stands he would have avoided otherwise. Tragically, I was the person who pushed my father into the antiabortion movement. The more doubts I had, the farther to the Right I moved ideologically, as if shouting loudly enough and demonizing any who disagreed with me could solve my real problem: the growing realization that the Bible is horribly flawed. And I think there was another factor in my tilt to the Right that might also have been the case with Franklin: Politics is *sexier* than mere evangelism.

The secret wish of every person dedicated to "full-time religious work" is to somehow be (or at least appear to be) *relevant*. In my case it was my politics, not my faith in Jesus, that got me on "secular TV" (for instance, on the *Today Show* to blast "Liberals") back when I was a Religious Right shill. And "taking a stand" gets

---

*David A. Patten, "Franklin Graham: Obama 'Giving Islam a Pass,' Warns of Persecution," Newsmax.com, May 3, 2010, www.newsmax.com/Headline/franklin-graham-islam-obama/2010/05/03/id/357711.

the blood pumping harder than just doing something as mundane as trying to love your neighbor.

I allow that the Franklin Grahams of this world may well have once believed what they preached about politics or may even have been sincere. There were sincere reasons for my antiabortion stand besides my drift rightward as a way to shout down my doubts. All those single pregnant women my parents had sheltered, all those stories about Mom's miscarried baby, and, above all, the fact I'd gotten Genie pregnant and that "unwanted child" had turned out to be our beloved little Jessica played a part. I'd also lived in a fundamentalist community that was blessedly inconsistent in its own theological beliefs about biblical inerrancy. My parents did what few even in the larger world did at the time: destigmatized "illegitimate" pregnancy.

When the *Roe v. Wade* decision was handed down legalizing abortion, something in me connected empathically to the unborn babies and to all those mothers and mothers-to-be I had been raised around, and I rebelled at the idea that pregnancy should be treated as a disease. That's how my "pro-life" gut reaction started anyway, at least as seen by me in 20/20 hindsight. But soon my antiabortion activities were all about wielding power and sticking it to those who were Not Like Us, an expression of my resentment at being stuck with a belief system that can't withstand honest questions. So I spoke out vehemently against any pro-choice advocates who I believed were tampering with The-God-Of-The-Bible's Wondrous Plan for their unborn children. In retrospect, I think my political activism was coming from the same need to be vindicated that seems to have plagued Franklin Graham. It also was related to a more deadly phenomenon: the worldview that incited (TV evangelist) Pat Robertson to blame the Haitians for the 2010 earthquake in their country because they had once made a "pact with Satan."

According to Robertson, the Haitians "told Satan" that if he'd rid them of their French masters, they would worship him. Robertson said this "explained" why Haiti was not only poor but had also just experienced almost total destruction. This statement shocked and infuriated even some of Robertson's fellow Evangelicals. But his explanation was in keeping with the religious view of The Other that I had once embraced or should I say that I had once hid my own doubts behind. No matter how bad Robertson's public relations judgment was in blurting out his belief that the Haitians were to blame for their own destruction, Robertson's outrageous statements are symptomatic of the tendency—in fact, the *necessity*—for all religious extremists to demonize The Other. They *must* blame the victim since to do otherwise would be to blame their version of God for such tragic events.

What Robertson did when defaming the Haitians is what many religious conservatives do to lesbian, gay, bisexual, and transgender people and what Jerry Falwell did when he claimed that the 9/11 terrorist attacks were divine punishment of America for its tolerance of homosexuality. Falwell's and Robertson's outrageous reaction to The Other was not so far-fetched for Bible-believing fundamentalist Christians steeped in the biblical "prophets'" scathing rants against the sons and daughters of Zion for bringing The-God-Of-The-Bible's wrathful destruction upon themselves.

The history of theology (Christian or otherwise) is the history of people desperately trying to fit the way things *actually are* into the way their holy books *say they should be*. (Think of the billions of words written in tens of thousands of books on religion "explaining" pain and suffering in the light of God's purported goodness.) So some people do what Mom did: spend a lot of time making excuses for The-God-Of-The-Bible. Others contrive their theology to make it seem more enlightened than it is: Roman Catholic medieval dogma is rechristened as "Natural Law,"* Creationism is rebaptized as "Intelligent Design," Islam calls the oppression of women the "protection of women," and so forth.

There is another choice: To admit that the best of any religious tradition depends on the choices its adherents make on how to live *despite* what their holy books "say," not because of them. "But where would that leave me?" my former self would have asked. "I'd be adrift in an ocean of uncertainty." Yes, and perhaps that's the only honest place to be. Another name for uncertainty is humility. No one ever blew up a mosque, church, or abortion clinic after yelling, "I could be wrong."

---

*Natural law refers to the use of reason to analyze morality. Some Church Fathers in the West incorporated natural law theory into Christian theology. Recently, conservative Roman Catholic intellectuals have used natural law to support their theological Far Right ideas. Here is a good definition by Elizabeth Anscombe, one of the leading Roman Catholic intellectuals of the twentieth century: "Any type of wrong action is 'against the natural law': stealing is, framing someone is, oppressing people is. 'Natural law' is simply a way of speaking about the whole of morality, used by Catholic thinkers because they believe the general precepts of morality are laws promulgated by God our Creator in the enlightened human understanding when it is thinking in general terms about what are good and what are bad actions. That is to say, the discoveries of reflection and reasoning when we think straight about these things are God's legislation to us (whether we realize this or not)." G. E. M. Anscombe, "Contraception and Chastity" (London: Catholic Truth Society, 1975).

CHAPTER 4

The-God-Of-The-Bible's Unauthorized Biography

M om was sitting on my bed next to the eight-year-old version
of me, reading the story of King David's Sin to me (again),
when she looked up from her Bible and cheerfully declared, "Your
father demands sexual intercourse *every single night* and has since
the day we married because he doesn't want to end up like King
David!" I got that sinking feeling. I knew Mom was about to launch
onto her favorite topic (besides Sex): how examples of Sin in the
Bible help us all "better understand Fran's Many Weaknesses."

"Uh," I said noncommittally, while trying not to sound too
interested.

"You see, Dear, King David and Fran share a Very Strong Drive
in That Area. At least Fran recognizes his Need." Mom paused,
smiled sweetly, then added in a brisk upbeat tone, "But *I* don't want

PHOTO: *Mom and Dad, 1947*

you to get the wrong impression; it's not that *I* don't enjoy being with Fran in That Way. Within a Christ-centered marriage the union of a married man and his wife is a wonderful gift. It's just that because Fran has a Daily Need, I have to go with him on *every single speaking trip*. I hate leaving you alone so often, even in a good cause."

To an outsider, Mom's constant citing of Bible passages like King David's Sin to "explain" Dad's failings might have seemed like a snide rebuke. Actually, it was Mom's way of defending Dad. She was placing his Sins on a high pedestal right up there with the failings of the biblical heroes. Mom was excusing Dad by saying in effect, "Even King David, that the Bible says God loved most of all, sinned terribly. He was forgiven and I forgive Fran, too. Moreover, if *even King David* was awful sometimes, how can Fran be perfect?"

I don't know if the good cause Mom referred to was traveling to teach Bible studies (from Holland to Italy to England and France), enjoying the "union of a married man and his wife," or keeping Dad from straying by meeting his "Daily Need." Since the Bible is full of Sex, and since Mom *wanted* (had?) to talk about Sex, Dad, and God—a lot—my mother could use our Bible studies as the excuse to "share" the Facts Of Life *and* exonerate Dad in the context of putting him in the company of biblical heroes who had "sinned too, Dear."

One thing I do know is that every time Mom left home, she'd leave a note and small gift for each bedtime she'd be away. My parents' speaking trips sometimes lasted up to a month. I remember the sense of being enveloped in her love as Debby or Susan would read the daily note to me as I'd unwrap that day's gift. (I collected a whole shelf full of excellent model car Dinky Toys in this way.)

I also look back on my mother's tremendous warmth and kindness as her love spilled into the lives of the next generation. My mother showed unbounded love to my daughter, Jessica, and son Francis when Genie and I were living in "Noni's" home (as her grandchildren call Mom). From birth until Jessica was ten and Francis seven, Noni played an outsized role in their lives. We lived with my parents in their chalet's basement apartment for the first five years of our marriage, then we moved into our own place across the street. (When Jessica was ten and Francis was seven, Genie and I moved to the States and our children's daily encounters with Noni ended.)

My mother's influence in Jessica's and Francis's lives was significant. She patiently compensated for Genie's and my being so young. As Genie says, "Noni was the best mother-in-law a young married woman could ever have had. She never 'advised,' rather was just always there to help and, when asked, gave the wisest relationship advice I've ever heard." And Jessica and Francis loved visiting Noni; as Jessica described it, "Going upstairs to Noni was a moment each day when I felt as if I was stepping into bright sunlight." Francis has always compared all ice cream to Noni's Sunday ice cream and chocolate sauce. "She always let me help her make it," he says; "it was the best ice cream I've ever tasted."

When Mom was home, she always had handy a Bible story that, with just the slightest nudge, could illustrate my father's Sins— from his Strong Drive In That Area (King David) to his sometimes violent Moods (King Saul). *And* the cross she had to bear because of his "unfortunate working-class background" (reminiscent of Esau and the Bible's other "rough-mannered men") was handily illustrated by the Apostle Peter, along with the other confused and uneducated working-class fishermen Jesus called to follow Him and to whom He had to *explain everything,* just like Mom constantly had to instruct Dad.

Mom often said, "Shall we consider King David?"

"Yes, Mom," I'd answer, knowing full well that we were *going* to consider King David with or without my permission.

"The story is in the book of Second Samuel," Mom said, flipping open her well-worn and heavily underlined Bible. She started to read in her impeccably clear, lilting, Bible-reading voice, enunciating each word c-r-i-s-p-l-y and pronouncing the biblical names perfectly: "Then it happened in the spring, at the time when kings go out to battle, that David sent Joab and his servants with him and all Israel, and they destroyed the sons of Ammon and besieged Rabbah. But David stayed at Jerusalem." Mom paused to comment, switching from her Bible-reading voice to a more intimate, conspiratorial, tone: "You see, Dear, David wasn't where he belonged. If David had been out on the battlefield killing the enemies of God where the King was *supposed* to be in the springtime, instead of turning his palace into a peep show, this never would have happened."

"What's a peep show?"

"We'll get to that later. The point now is that David was battling a midlife crisis, too. He wasn't in Paris, where Fran dragged me that time. But like your father, David wasn't where God wanted him either, which is always that first tragic step of backsliding, as Fran knows. Do you understand?"

"Yes, Mom."

Mom reached out, took my hand in hers, and then continued to read.

"Now when evening came David arose from his bed and walked around on the roof of the king's house, and from the roof he saw a woman bathing; and the woman was very beautiful in appearance. So David sent and inquired about the woman. And one said, 'Is this not Bathsheba, the daughter of Eliam, the wife of Uriah the Hittite?' David sent messengers and took her, and when she came to him, he lay with her; and when she had purified herself from her uncleanness, she returned to her house."

Mom closed her Bible with a snap and sighed.

"I should point out," said Mom, shaking her head in a manner that denoted her seen-this-a-thousand-times sadness at the way *some people* carry on, "that Bathsheba shares in David's guilt. A woman has no business bathing in public or for that matter even wearing a two-piece bathing suit. Men hardly need stirring up." Mom sighed deeply. "Of course her guilt was nothing compared to his! I'm sorry to say that David just wanted what we call a 'one-night stand,' but, as usual, Sin had consequences: The woman conceived." Mom leaned toward me, lowered her voice to a just-between-us amused whisper, and said, "David hadn't *planned* on *that* possibility, had he?"

"Was he a Roman Catholic?" I asked.

Mom laughed.

"Contraceptives weren't invented yet, so they were all Catholics back then—in a Jewish sort of way. The only 'method' in those days was for the man to pull out before ejaculation, and that's not reliable. But evidently David didn't even do that," Mom said. "Even if he had, that would have been a Sin, too."

"Why?"

"Because in the Book of Genesis, after God had killed Onan's brother Er, Judah asked Onan to have sexual intercourse with Tamar and impregnate her. Then Onan had sex with Tamar and sinned by coitus interruptus, casting his seed on the ground because he didn't want any offspring he couldn't claim as his own. The Bible says this displeased God."

"How do we know it displeased God?"

"It's pretty obvious: God killed Onan, Dear."

"So King David couldn't pull out because he knew what had happened to Onan?"

"I'll ask your father what the Reformed Presbyterian position on the meaning of the seed-wasting Onan passage is. I'm sure he must have studied it in seminary. I don't know if the Sin was casting seed on the ground in general or just in this one instance. Anyway, Dear, I *do know* that passage explains the origin of the term 'Onanism.'"

"What's that?"

"Just don't! When you get to puberty and start having Those Feelings we've discussed, think of poor old Onan and *wait* for God to send Wet Dreams, though God didn't kill Onan for Touching Himself but for not raising up offspring to honor his dead brother's name. But the point you need to remember is that in Leviticus 15:32, the 'emission of semen' is referring to Touching Yourself. Notice that masturbation would cause a man to become Unclean under the Law of Moses."

"Like having babies makes women Unclean?"

"Sort of, but before the coming of Jesus, the male seed was Unclean; not only was the Onan-type misuse of seed Unclean, but the actual seed was unredeemed."

"What?"

"Children born in the Old Testament were Unclean, so nocturnal emissions were Unclean, too. Now that Jesus has come to redeem everything, even Wet Dreams are no longer Unclean, unless you do it on purpose!"

The "menstrual track" of thought (that I started over forty years ago while peering into those wastepaper baskets) illustrates my cure from brooding on the "Unclean." You see, there came a day when a Vagina was no longer an object that seemed to exist independently of a person but rather was one beloved woman's property and interesting to me not just because it was a Vagina, but also because that particular Vagina belonged to a person I loved, treasured, and respected body and soul.

Once that's how I started to perceive Genie and her lovely body, I had a problem with the fact that The-God-Of-The-Bible sanctions rape. As we've seen, Moses commanded his soldiers to take their enemy's virgins for their pleasure and to "have"—that is, rape—them. Remember, after Moses told his troops to kill all the enemy's men, he said, "But all the young girls who have not known man by lying with him, keep alive for yourselves." Did all those girls then fall in love with the men who they had just watched butcher their mothers and fathers? Did the surviving virgins then marry and bed their captors willingly?

The supposedly "more loving" New Testament doesn't let Christians off the hook. To the contrary, it makes everything far worse. A verse in the book of Second Timothy says that all Scripture is for our edification. This absurdly self-referential circular argument states that the Bible is true because . . . this book says so!

In Second Timothy (3:16) we read, "All scripture is given by inspiration of God, and is profitable for doctrine, for reproof, for correction, for instruction in righteousness." The "all Scripture" being spoken of means the Old Testament, of course, since the New Testament was being written at the time by people who had no idea that their assorted letters and such were going (over a four-hundred-year period) to be edited and then collected into one book—the New Testament—much less appended to the Hebrew Bible.

How scary is this verse? Well, take every vile verse and myth reeking of barbarity in the Bible (and there are hundreds of such passages) and add this: the "All scripture is . . ." ending. For instance, take this New Testament "advice" to women: "I do not permit a woman to teach or to have authority over a man; she must be silent" (1Timothy 2:12). Then add, "*All scripture is given by inspiration of*

God, and is profitable for doctrine, for reproof, for correction, for instruction in righteousness." End of discussion! Be Silent!

Or . . .

"This is what the Lord Almighty says . . . 'Now go and strike Amalek and devote to destruction all that they have. Do not spare them, but kill both man and woman, child and infant, ox and sheep, camel and donkey'" (1 Samuel 15:3). "But Christ has changed all that mean stuff," the hopeful Evangelical says. Not so fast! "*All scripture is given by inspiration of God, and is profitable for doctrine, for reproof, for correction, for instruction in righteousness.*"

Or . . .

"Slaves, submit yourselves to your masters with all respect, not only to the good and gentle but also to the cruel" (1 Peter 2:18). Say again? "*All scripture is given by inspiration of God, and is profitable for doctrine, for reproof, for correction, for instruction in righteousness.*" And by the way, that proslavery teaching is a post-Jesus, "nice God," New Testament verse.

When rape *is* finally (sort of) "condemned" in the Bible, a woman's rights aren't even mentioned. "If a man meets a virgin who is not betrothed, and seizes her and lies with her, and they are found, then the man who lay with her shall give to the father fifty shekels of silver, and she shall be his wife" (Deuteronomy 22:28–29). According to the Bible, the raped woman is forced to marry the rapist and the only person made whole is her "dishonored" father. And part of the man's "punishment" is that *he* is never allowed to divorce the women *he* raped and then had to marry. *She*, of course, has no say.

I'll take lovely, civilized, forgiving, kind, and intelligent women like my mother, sisters, wife, daughter Jessica, daughter-in-law Becky, not to mention my granddaughters, over the idea that the Bible "is all true," let alone all "God's Word." I'll trust the *actual evidence* of just how lovely women *are* as proof of God's goodness and creative ability rather than what is *written about* women by women-haters trying to rope God into their nasty arguments.

I *hated* being in that room with that Rape Kit. The thought that the next rape victim who would lay there, the next woman whose bruises and cuts and broken bones would be photographed, could be my daughter Jessica or my wife was terrifying. Would the next rape victim be shivering as Genie was for over two hours before a doctor showed up? Would anyone comfort her?

Sitting in that hospital examination room, and not for the last time, I found myself wondering why my sweet, forgiving, and kind mother was so much nicer than The-God-Of-The-Bible she said she worshipped. He had been ready to command the wanton slaughter of innocent women, rape, and the murder of babies, whereas Mom agonized during a whole lifetime over *one* tiny un-named child. She'd passed her empathy and reverence for life to me. When (absurdly or not) I'd been scanning those blood clots for signs of a fetus, it was with a sense of looming tragedy. I'd held Genie's hand tightly and wondered why anyone would worship a God who doesn't love women and children.

Years later I began to think that *if* there is a God, and *if* Jesus spoke the truth about how we are to care for others, and *if* my love for Genie is a gift from the Creator, and *if* the Light of Love in my life has taught me anything (besides a compulsion to follow my children and grandchildren into the world and protect them), then maybe the best thing a believer in God can do is to declare that a lot of the Bible is hate-filled blasphemy—*against God.* Maybe the *actual God* who kicked off the evolutionary process that wound up producing people like my mother, my wife, and my luminous grandchildren doesn't endorse The God-Of-The-Bible either.

This possibility undermines most arguments for atheism made by most "professional atheists." The books written by "New Atheists" like Richard Dawkins, Christopher Hitchens, and Sam Harris attack God by attacking religion. But that's not an argument that even begins to address the question of God (or some other outside power's meddling in the formation of the Universe, let alone first causes in cosmology). The New Atheists' arguments make sense only as attacks on religion. There's plenty to attack. But who says religion as practiced today, let alone as "revealed" in holy books, has *anything* to do with an actual Creator? As Vincent Bugliosi writes in his remarkable book *Divinity of Doubt,* "Harris (like Hitchens) seems to believe something that is so wrong it is startling that someone of his intellect wouldn't see it immediately—that gutting religion (as Harris tries to do by his technique of decimating faith that fosters religion)—does not, ipso facto, topple God."*

Mom was always interpreting the Bible and thus correcting Paul, Jesus, Moses, and anyone else who was confused. "It only seems that way, but really" was Mom's operative opening phrase when it came to straightening out all our "misunderstandings" of passages that "so many people don't understand properly." Mom would even whisper corrections of Dad's theology to me during his sermons when she felt Dad had got some point "slightly wrong." She'd purse her lips and shake her head when Dad said something that she didn't wholeheartedly agree with, and I'd know to lean closer to Mom for the whispered theological clarification, beginning with "Daddy should be a bit clearer on this." Or "Fran should really say that in some cases . . ."

The-God-Of-The-Bible suffered by comparison to my mother. Mom just couldn't imitate the loopy extremism oozing from her Holy Book. She never threatened eternal torture for those who did no more than cause some believer to "stumble"—that is, to doubt

---

*Vincent Bugliosi, *Divinity of Doubt: The God Question* (New York: Vanguard Press, 2011), 47.

what he or she had been told in the latest Bible study. All in all, Mom was much more civilized than her Messiah, or maybe some of the reporting on what He's *said to have said* is a case of wishful revisionist editing by His biographers, who were adept at revising history in their favor.

Remember, by the time the writers of the New Testament were remembering forty, fifty, sixty years later what Jesus had said, they were *also* building a self-interested organization based on His life. They were settling disputes and splits among themselves. What better way to strengthen their arguments than to draft The Master—in 20/20 hindsight—into supporting them in various Early Church turf wars and their fights with each other. How better to win theological battles than to "quote" Jesus about the "correct" view of celibacy or how to "deal with" the Jews or how to scare the faithful into *remaining* faithful or how to encourage them to stay faithful in the face of Roman persecution?

I *hope* some of the things Jesus "said"—which have a very different tone from the sublime humane passages that stand the test of both time and the Light of Love in the human heart—are a matter of the Early Church's leaders' wishful thinking! I'm rooting for Jesus based on the compassion and wisdom of His words as they escape from the pages of an otherwise tarnished book. But some of what's been written about Him in the Bible, not to mention some of the out-of-character sayings attributed to Him, are plain goofy.

Jesus "said" He'd be back soon, *very soon*, in time so that some who were with Him would not taste death before his return. We're still waiting. Jesus "told" his disciples: "There be some standing here, which shall not taste of death, till they see the Son of man coming in his kingdom" (Matthew 16:28). "Behold, I come quickly" (Revelation 3:11). It's been almost 2,000 years, and many believers, including my mother, are still waiting for that "quick" return. He got that wrong, or the people recording His "infallible" sayings did.

I'm not the only person who is rooting for Jesus but who also is asking questions about the Bible and challenging the idea that what we know about God is contained therein. Thom Stark begins his book *The Human Faces of God: What Scripture Reveals When It Gets God Wrong (and Why Inerrancy Tries to Hide It)* like this: "In the beginning was the Argument, and the Argument was with God, and the Argument was: God. God was the subject of the Argument, and the Argument was a good one. Who is God? What is God like? What does God require of us?"*

Stark explains, "The doctrine of biblical inerrancy dictates that the Bible, being inspired by God, is without error in everything that it affirms—historically, scientifically, and theologically."** Stark develops a strong argument against this Evangelical/fundamentalist doctrine of inerrancy. Here's Stark's conclusion:

> The scriptures are not infallible. Jesus was not infallible—or, if he was, we have no access to his infallibility. So where is our foundation? Upon what do we build our worldview, our ethics, our politics and our morality? The answer is that there is no foundation. There is no sure ground upon which to build our institutions. And that is a good thing. That is what I call grace.
>
> An infallible Jesus, just like a set of infallible scriptures, is ultimately just a shortcut through our moral and spiritual development. To have a book or a messenger dropped from heaven, the likes of which is beyond the reach of all human criticism, is a dangerous shortcut. It is no wonder humans have always attempted to create these kinds of foundations. And it is a revela-

---

*Thom Stark, *The Human Faces of God: What Scripture Reveals When It Gets God Wrong (and Why Inerrancy Tries to Hide It)* (Eugene, OR: WIPF and Stock, 2010), 168.
**Ibid.

tion of God's character, from my perspective, that cracks have been found in each and every one of those foundations.*

Maybe (if Stark is right) God feels slandered by the Bronze-Age-to-Roman-era "biography" of Him that, it turns out (judging by the insanity that makes up so much of the Bible), wasn't an authorized biography, let alone an inspired one. It seems to me that as far as the best parts of Christianity go, traditions of beauty in art, music, and literature and the humanism expressed in the abolition of slavery movement and so forth, what might be called the good results are proof that enlightened believers have been picking and choosing all along when it comes to what they take seriously in the Bible. For instance, many Christians were abolitionists in the fight against slavery. Since the Bible, at best, cancels itself out on this subject, the clearly proslavery bits in juxtaposition to the enlightened do-unto-others bits, the Bible wasn't the only source of the push for freedom. That enlightenment came from within the hearts of men and women who then cast around for any supporting argument they could find, including some verses taken out of the general context of the proslavery sentiment expressed in the Bible.

To reject portions of the Bible is not necessarily to reject God or even the essence of Christianity. A great deal of the Bible is contradicted by the Love that predates it and, more importantly, survives in you and me. And that Love edits the Bible for us. Call that editing the Holy Spirit, or call it a more evolved sense of ethics and human rights, but most people know what to follow and what to reject when it comes to how they live. Sacrifice *for* others, not sacrifice *of* others, is the message of the "better angels" of spiritual faith.

---

*Ibid., 207.

Or put it this way: I trust the Love that I see in my grand-children's eyes as the true witness of God more than anything written in any book. I also trust my personal experiences of the Love of Jesus more than any words about Jesus.

The fact that religion has time and again been awful is no more here nor there when it comes to God than the fact that humans have damaged everything we've touched is an argument for the liquidation of every human being. Indeed, how could religion be anything *but* a mess? We invented it! That doesn't mean that the longing for meaning that drove us to invent religion isn't a reflection of something real: a Creator Who many of us sense is there but Who is also beyond description.

I think that the best argument for God's existence is that humans long for meaning. A corollary is that the word "beauty," however indefinable, means something real to most people. And then there's that question about the origin of everything, to which, I think, the only sensible answer is a resoundingly agnostic "We'll never know." Meanwhile science truthfully explains our evolution from single-celled organisms. But it doesn't tell me why I *know* Bach's Partita 1 en Si Mineur Double: Presto is more important than a jingle for MacDonald's. And even if brain chemistry unravels this secret, it will reveal only the how, not the why. But you and I know that when the MacDonald's Corporation is long forgotten, chances are Bach's music will have survived. Our longing for God (by whatever name) will also be there as one constant in a future that otherwise may not be recognizable.

All the actors in Mom (and her God's) drama were part of the Heavenly Battle between Satan and God, in which it was Mom's good fortune and tragic misfortune to play the leading role. And yet the supreme irony is that *her manner of life—*generous and caring, sacrificial, intelligent and well read—contrasted so sharply with what she *said* she believed. Mom spent hours collecting moss, wildflowers, bark, branches, twigs, grasses, rocks, shells, and reeds. She then would lay them all out on the table behind the kitchen and arrange flowers in ceramic bowls, vases, and platters of the kind used to grow Bonsai trees in. Mom's arrangements were of a piece with all the Japanese and Chinese prints she collected, mostly reproductions from calendars, along with a few treasured originals her parents had brought with them when they left China. Mom's Chinese artworks were by masters who had painted on silk and handmade paper. Their art was filled with literary allusion and calligraphy, but the primary image was typically a contemplative landscape.

Having been born in China, Mom had a lifelong nostalgic attachment to all things Oriental that showed itself in her affinity for art and people even vaguely connected to China, Japan, or, for that matter, Korea. Never mind that these cultures hated one another and made constant war on one another. To Mom they were all wonderful. If Mom were in a cab with a Chinese driver, she'd launch into childhood reminiscences of China. If a Korean showed up at L'Abri, she'd give that visitor special attention.

My mother's objects of abstract beauty were superb. Mom's poetry wasn't only in her writing, which sometimes took the form of earnest biblical propaganda, but also in her choice of those watercolors and prints serenely depicting fogbound hills and solitary cranes standing in water and in her exquisite arrangements where a piece of driftwood, a handful of luxuriant moss, and a single flower or fern proclaimed a whole inner aesthetic and longing for transcendent meaning. Mom loved plants, their stems, the shapes of their leaves; she cherished the forms nature carved by wind, rain, or carpenter ants out of a piece of wood or stone. Mom offered her spirit to each arrangement; natural textures, graceful lines, and a sensual connection to her inner life spoke clearly about who my mother would have been if she'd been raised by anyone but pietistic missionaries who drastically narrowed her life choices by placing The-God-Of-The-Bible's heavy "call" on her shoulders.

Who was Mom as she might have been if part of her brain had not been crippled by her missionary parents' indoctrination of her, just as the bones in the feet of little girls in China were once deformed by foot-binding? My mother unbound was a minimalist making poems with what she found on the ground. When could I see my mother most clearly? When Mom came back from the woods or garden carrying handfuls of what looked like random odds and ends that other people would have discarded. An hour later Mom would have transformed these scraps into a centerpiece for the dining table that looked as if it had come from some other, more perfect universe.

I think it was that kind of otherworldly poetry that Mom was looking for and why she paid so much attention to the artists who visited L'Abri. In their free lives, in which they were immersed in creating for creating's sake, perhaps she saw a life she'd been robbed of. My mother loved art and loved the idea of loving art. She took us to the Montreux classical music festival. She spent long hours making her flower arrangements. She always agreed to read us "just one more chapter" when the book, like *Oliver Twist*, was good. She lavished art supplies on me and after I became Dad's sidekick constantly asked me when I'd start painting again. All this added up to a lifetime commitment to artistic expression such as I've never seen in anyone else before or since. It was as if my mother tried to make up in her enthusiasm for art the time lost in sacrificing her interests for her "higher call," as if having given up dancing, she could still be an artist vicariously. Mom wanted to haunt those foggy watercolor mountainsides and contemplate a single cypress silhouetted against a pale sky. I think she also ached for someone in her bed who understood her flower arrangements soul to soul. It was my mother who encouraged me to paint—not to mention reveled in my early successes as a painter by attending my shows. After I fled the Religious Right, I returned to her vision when I began to write novels and later to paint again.

Edith Schaeffer *herself* was the greatest illustration of the Divine beauty of Paradox I've encountered. She was a fundamentalist living a double life as a lover of beauty who broke all her own judgmental rules in favor of creativity: She read us real books, swearwords and all; she bought me a Salvador Dali art book that included his hypersexuality and "blasphemy" (as other Evangelicals would have described Dali's work). Mom also lived by a lovely double standard when it came to "those lost Roman Catholics" (as she described them back in her more fundamentalist days) by taking us to see their art and rhapsodizing about it as if the art happened to be somewhere *other* than in a Roman Catholic church.

Mom was just so un-Edith-Schaeffer-like in person! And Mom's embrace of the contradiction within herself, not to mention her mitigating her faith to accommodate her humanity, was quite an accomplishment for One Lone Brave Woman. It was as if my mother were struggling to humanize the 5,000-year-old tradition that had consumed whole races in endless war and had inspired collective intellectual suicide by countless Jews and Christians who denied their brains so that they wouldn't put The-God-Of-The-Bible in a bad light by questioning the book that "described" Him.

My mother deserved better. A lifetime of reaching out to The Lost and sacrificing on their behalf imbued her with a kindly spirit that even in addled old age shone through. Her example was not lost on me. I simply chose to follow the "other" Edith Schaeffer, the one whose heart was elsewhere than in the lifeless theories she paid lip-service to.

Mom's only mistake was that she left unchallenged the theological mind-set she had received from her missionary parents. But when it comes to life wisdom, it turns out Mom was right about so much that's important to me now—Art, Love, Family Life—even if she sometimes justified her conclusions with the wackiest theological myths.

Mom introduced me to a powerful conduit of Love. So I tell God I love Him and am comforted, though I have no idea Who God Is. I know only that Love and Beauty come from beyond the stardust we're all made of. Love outshines the fact of pain in the same way that Bach's Sonatas and Partitas for solo violin, which Mom loved so passionately, outshine all the bad music in the world, though on any given day Bach is outnumbered.

When I was eleven, Mom held my hand tightly as Yehudi Menuhin played the Bach Sonatas and Partitas at a concert in Montreux where my mother had bought her family front-row seats. When the applause died away, Mom turned to me with tears on her cheeks and said, "That music is bigger than death, my Dear."

When I was writing this book and sat with my mother during our lovely weeklong (pre-Christmas 2010) visit (when I also told her about what was in the book), we listened to those same pieces of music again. I reminded Mom of what she'd said all those years ago.

"Mother?"

"Yes, Dear?"

"Do you still believe that music is bigger than death?"

"Yes, I do."

CHAPTER 5

It's Good to
Be the Queen
(and Rushdoony)

A lice and her sister ran our village post office. They lived above it with their mother, who wore hairnets and was a generous supplier of excellent gingersnap cookies. Alice was one of the only villagers who both spoke English and liked my outsider family. And we liked her a lot, too, even though, as Mom said, "Alice isn't saved and is a bit odd."

Alice was in her early thirties when I first met her. She had been a governess in England during the Second World War. Alice would deliver the mail with serious dignity, as if handling state secrets. Should an errant snowball land in her mailbag, a shrill rant about tampering with the mail being a "Swiss federal crime!" would follow. Otherwise, Alice was cheerful and unfailingly kind.

When I was three or four, Alice (when not delivering the mail) started to work part-time for my mother as my nanny. This arrangement lasted only until I was seven or so but was a long

PHOTO: *Mom, Susan, Priscilla, Debby, and me shipboard in 1954* enough association to give me a lifelong fondness for mail carriers—and for transvestites. Alice and I remained friends for over forty years thereafter until her death. Don't get me wrong. Alice was not a transvestite, nor am I. But through Alice I do have a been-there-done-that admiring affinity with cross-dressers.

Alice had short, thick, hiker's legs, and she wore light gray tweed midlength skirts. Her stockings had seams. She had wide hips, a fertility-doll-type generous bottom, and a broad, friendly face dominated by a large fleshy nose and a wide smile. Alice had very large breasts, something like the prow of a mighty ship. When she was marching up the road delivering mail, the strap of her heavy leather mailbag divided and accentuated her formidable cleavage.

When she was bathing me, "Alice's Bosoms" (as Mom called them) would be mere inches away, and Alice's tangy "unfortunate Swiss odor" (as my mother described such scents, back in the days when deodorant was still mostly an American commodity) enveloped me while Alice bent over the tub to wash my hair. When her blouse got wet, I could see the imprint of a huge white lacy bra. When doing my bit as Mom's secret agent for the Lord, I asked Alice if she ever prayed, and she just changed the subject to a discussion of young Prince Charles's virtues.

The big adventure of Alice's life was her stay in England, and the high point of that adventure had been witnessing the coronation of Queen Elizabeth II. Alice gave me several souvenirs of the royal event, including a miniature die-cast metal and beautifully gilded replica of the coronation carriage and eight horses. There were pictures of the Royal Family all over Alice's home. When I'd misbehave, Alice would say, "Prince Charles would not do that," or "Would you do *this* in front of the Queen?"

As noted, Alice was not "saved." Had she been saved when I'd asked about prayer, she would have used that "opportunity" to

launch into what we used to call a "testimony," a blow-by-blow account of the time, day, and place where she had "met the Lord."
Besides not being saved, Alice seemed to be some sort of idolater
of British royalty. And yet Mom was pleased to have Alice help
raise her son. Both of them agreed that table manners were very
important, even if my mother was less fixated than Alice was on
preparing me for the day when I might be invited to tea at Wind-
sor Castle.

Mom didn't know it, but her willingness to trust someone so very
not like us, someone Lost, someone different from us, provided me
with a powerful vaccination against the rejection of The Other. Alice was one reason that, some twenty-five years later, I'd turn my
back on people who would have stoned Alice to death—literally—if
they only could have convinced more Americans to accept their
version of Jesus.

The people that I'd be working with a few years after splashing
in the bath under Alice's watchful eye were Reconstructionist
Evangelicals (a term I'll explain in a moment), who would have
gladly executed Alice for her "perversions." For you see, Alice
would dress me up as the Queen of England.

I'd wear a large white bath towel for a cape, fastened by Mom's
biggest glass-bead brooch, and a crown made of pipe cleaners, wo-
ven together and covered with tinfoil. And the Bible says Alice and
I were worthy of death for this ritual. "A woman must not wear
men's clothing, nor a man wear women's clothing, for the LORD
your God detests anyone who does this" (Deuteronomy 22:5).
Aside from that God-detested towel, I was naked because this
dress-up game happened right after my bath and was part of our
cross-dressing ritual of my processing from the bathroom to my
bedroom, where I'd put on my pajamas. Alice would call me "Your
Majesty" and walk backward in front of me while I marched regally

along our chalet's narrow upstairs hall as she sang "God Save the Queen" in her heavily accented Swiss-French English.

We did this more or less every night for four years or so. (Alice's care of me was limited to late afternoons and bedtimes. The rest of the day I ran free.) During that period of my life my room gradually filled with postcard-photograph "graven images" of the Queen, Prince Charles, and even (for reasons I have now forgotten) Princess Beatrix Wilhelmina Armgard of the Netherlands in direct contravention of this command: "Thou shalt not make unto thee any graven image, or any likeness of any thing that is in heaven above, or that is in the earth beneath, or that is in the water under the earth: Thou shalt not bow down thyself to them, nor serve them: for I the Lord thy God am a jealous God, visiting the iniquity of the fathers upon the children unto the third and fourth generation of them that hate me; And showing mercy unto thousands of them that love me, and keep my commandments" (Exodus 20:4–6).

My bath-time transvestite wardrobe became rather elaborate. By the time I was six, Alice had added to our nightly ritual what she said was "an ermine cape," which seemed very much like smelly rabbit fur but otherwise was quite glamorous. She also would let me wear one of her bras stuffed with facecloths to give me a queenly bosom. Then she began to add lipstick.

Maybe Alice's influence is why I watch *The Birdcage* once a year or so to savor the delicious talents of Nathan Lane, not to mention Hank Azaria as the ever-memorable Agador. And Eddie "I grew up in Europe, where the history comes from" Izzard, a self-described "action transvestite" (the kind who, as he explains, isn't gay and has girlfriends), is the greatest standup comic for many reasons, not to mention he looks good in a skirt. He has the best-informed and most intelligent (and hilarious) routines related to religion of any comic or, for that matter, theologian; all of which The-God-Of-The-Bible hates, too, given that Izzard some-times wears lipstick. But what decent God worth worshipping (who, come to think of it, created Izzard's sense of humor and desire to wear women's clothes) would *not* laugh at his routines?

Izzard (playing both roles):

"Father, bless me, for I have sinned. I did an Original Sin; I poked a badger with a spoon."

"I've never heard of that one before. Five Hail Marys and two Hello Dollys."

"All right. Bless me, for I slept with my neighbor's wife."

"Heard it! I want an *original* sin!"

"Oh, I'm terribly sorry."*

Perhaps my finding myself in the Izzard Camp, rather than the Evangelical Camp, when it comes to how I see most things has something to do with dressing up as the Queen. The odd assortment of formative influences in my life was liberating: God, the Alps, the Old Testament "people of God" who were killing everyone in sight and/or "taking" them and "knowing them" and "going in unto them," Alice and the Queen, my queen bee of a mother, boys boarding school group wanking, a good working knowledge of diaphragms, *and* a household full of young women not related to me who also mothered me, bled in unison, *and* hung their very interesting lingerie on the clothesline to flutter alluringly in the breeze. . . . By age eight I knew that Women Have Plumbing Problems and Ovaries that must be tended as assiduously as one had to attend The Moods that went with these Female Mysteries. I also

---

*Eddie Izzard, "Dress to Kill" San Francisco, Script-Dialogue Transcript, www.script-o-rama.com/movie_scripts/e/eddie-izzard-dress-to-kill-script .html.

had a mother who regaled me with regular dispatches from Female Land of a kind usually reserved for students of gynecology.

I'm lucky that Mom and Dad and the actual life lived in L'Abri were so wonderfully out of step with their official doctrine. There was room for Alice and many other eccentrics busily breaking biblical laws. And I think that my introduction to human diversity, as well as my strange, oversexualized childhood (not to mention my mother reading good books to me by authors who were very different from Us Real Christians), is what eventually opened the door to my being a writer.

Other Evangelical children weren't so fortunate. Many of them were raised in homes without enough humanizing hypocrisy when it came to saying one thing—"We believe the Bible to be entirely true"—but doing another, as in "Let's not stone Alice to death today but go skiing instead."

Since the 1960s there has been a growing tendency among American fundamentalists to denounce all but the most conservative, absolutist readings of Scripture, all the while keeping their children in enclaves (homeschools and Christian schools) to "protect" them from the world. Even the slightly open-minded Bible interpretation that people like my mother and father practiced would be too compromising for today's Evangelicals, who want public life to reflect their "values" and who band together to try and legislatively remake the world in their image.

I believe that the strange contradictory activities of circling the wagons and looking inward *while* lashing outward at Sinners *and* trying to legislate against their "immorality" happened because Evangelicals, along with other religious conservatives, lost the culture wars. Conservative Roman Catholics, Mormons, and Evangelicals couldn't turn back the gay rights movement and the progressive attitudes of most Americans about sex and legalized abortion, so they indulged in vehement anti-gay-marriage or anti-stem-cell-research referendums meant to rebuke, if not hurt and punish, more than to change hearts and minds. When these efforts mostly failed (some "succeeded"), the Jesus Victims doing the loudest talking about "traditional family values based on the Bible" were sure they were being persecuted "for the sake of Christ." Actually, all that was happening was that their absolute certainties were not so convincing to most Americans.

Believing that those who disagree with you are your persecutors leads to fear, and fear leads to hate. What feeds the hate? What feeds the paranoia? What nurtures the "we've lost our culture" victimhood, on the one hand, and hubris about "taking America back for God," on the other hand?

America has a problem: It's filled with people who take the Bible seriously. America has a blessing: It's filled with people who take the Bible seriously. How does this blessing coexist with the curse derived from the same source: the Bible? The answer is that the Bible is a curse or a blessing depending on who is doing the interpreting. Sometimes belief in the Bible leads to building a hospital. Sometimes it leads to justifying perpetual war and empire building. Same book—different interpretation.

If the history of Christianity proves one thing, it's that you can make the Bible "say" anything. When you hear words like "We want to take back America for God!" the twenty-first-century expression of such theocratic ideas can be traced back to some of my old friends: the Reconstructionists. Most Americans have never heard of the Reconstructionists. But they have felt their impact through the Reconstructionists' profound (if indirect) influence over the wider (and vast) Evangelical community. In turn, the Evangelicals shaped the politics of a secular culture that barely understood the Religious Right, let alone the forces within that movement that gave it its edge. The Americans inhabiting the wider (and more secular) culture just saw the results of Reconstructionism without understanding where those results had come from—for instance, how the hell George W. Bush got elected and then reelected!

If you felt victimized by modernity, then the Reconstructionists had the answer in their version of biblical interpretation. Reconstructionists wanted to replace the U.S. Constitution and Bill of Rights with their interpretation of the Bible.

In the Reconstructionists' best of all worlds, Eddie Izzard would have been long since executed for the "crimes" of inappropriate wardrobe, not to mention "blasphemy." If given the chance, they would burn people like my mother at the stake for her "heresy" of explaining away the nastier bits of the Bible or at least not living by its meaner rules.

Most Evangelicals are positively moderate by comparison to the Reconstructionists. But the Reconstructionist movement is a distilled essence of the more mainstream Evangelical version of an exclusionary theology that divides America into the "Real America" (as the Far Right claims only it is) and the rest of us "Sinners." And it was those "Real Americans" who were Bush's base.

The Reconstructionist worldview is ultra-Calvinist but, like all Calvinism,* has its origins in ancient Israel/Palestine, when vengeful and ignorant tribal lore was written down by frightened men (the nastier authors of the Bible) trying to defend their prerogatives

---

*Calvinism (also called the Reformed tradition, the Reformed faith, or Reformed theology) is a theological system. This branch of Christianity is named for French reformer John Calvin. According to Calvin, God is able to save every person upon whom He has mercy and His efforts are not frustrated by the unrighteousness or the inability of humans. The system is based on Five Points: total depravity, unconditional election, limited atonement, irresistible grace, and perseverance of the saints. The doctrine of total depravity says that, as a

to bully women, murder rival tribes, and steal land. (These justifi-
cations may have reflected later thinking: origin myths used as
propaganda to justify political and military actions after the fact,
such as the brutality the Hebrews said God made them inflict on
others and/or their position as the "Chosen People.")

In its modern American incarnation, which hardened into a
twentieth-century movement in the 1960s and became wide-
spread in the 1970s, Reconstructionism was propagated by people
I knew and worked with closely when I, too, was both a Jesus Victim *and* a Jesus Predator claiming God's special favor. The leaders
of the Reconstructionist movement included the late Rousas
Rushdoony (Calvinist theologian, father of modern-era Christian
Reconstructionism, patron saint to gold-hoarding haters of the
Federal Reserve, and creator of the modern Evangelical homeschool movement), his son-in-law Gary North (an economist and
publisher), and David Chilton (Calvinist pastor and author).

No, the Reconstructionists are not about to take over America,
the world, or even most American Evangelical institutions. But
their influence has been like a drop of radicalizing flavoring added
to a bottle of water. Though most Evangelicals, let alone the general public, don't know the names of the leading Reconstructionist

---

consequence of the fall of humanity into sin, every person born into the world
is enslaved to the service of sin. The doctrine of unconditional election main-
tains that God chose from eternity those whom He will bring to Himself. The
doctrine of limited atonement asserts that Jesus' substitutionary atonement
was definite and certain in its design and accomplishment. This implies that
only the sins of the elect were atoned for by Jesus' death. The doctrine of irresistible grace says that the saving grace of God is effectually applied to those
whom He has determined to save (that is, the elect) and, in God's timing, over-
comes their resistance to obeying the call of the gospel. The doctrine of perseverance (or preservation) of the saints asserts that since God is sovereign, His
will cannot be frustrated by humans or anything else.

thinkers, they helped create the world we live in—where a radical-ized, angry Religious Right has changed the face of American politics. Writer Chris Hedges has called this the rise of "Christian Fascism," where "those that speak in the language of fact . . . are hated and feared."* Anyone who wants to understand American politics had better get acquainted with the Reconstructionists.

Reconstructionism, also called Theonomism,** seeks to reconstruct "our fallen society." Its worldview is best represented by the publications of the Chalcedon Foundation, (which has been classified as an antigay hate group by the Southern Poverty Law Center). According to the Chalcedon Foundation Web site, the mission of the movement is to apply "the whole Word of God" to all aspects of human life: "It is not only our duty as individuals, families and churches to be Christian, but it is also the duty of the state, the school, the arts and sciences, law, economics, and every other sphere to be under Christ the King. Nothing is exempt from His dominion. We must live by His Word, not our own."***

Until Rushdoony, founder and late president of the Chalcedon Foundation, began writing in the 1960s, most American fundamentalists (including my parents) didn't try to apply biblical laws about capital punishment for homosexuality to the United States. Even the most conservative Evangelicals said they were "New Testament Christians." In other words, they believed that after the

---

*Chris Hedges, "The Christian Fascists are Growing Stronger," Truthdig.com, June 6, 2010.
**Theonomy comes from two Greek words: *theos*, meaning "God," and *nomos*, meaning "law."
***In presenting a theonomic view of biblical law, the Chalcedon Foundation is often referred to as promoting theocracy and "dominionism." See www .chalcedon.edu/blog/blog.php.

coming of Jesus, the harsher bits of the Bible had been (at least to some extent) transformed by the "New Covenant" of Jesus' "Law of Love."

By contrast, the leaders of Reconstructionism believed that Old Testament teachings—on everything from capital punishment for gays to the virtues of child-beating—were still valid because they were the inerrant Word and Will of God and therefore should be enforced. Not only that, they said that biblical law should be *imposed* even on nonbelievers. This theology was the American version of the attempt in some Muslim countries to impose Sharia (Islamic law) on all citizens, Muslims and non-Muslims alike.

It's no coincidence that the rise of the Islamic Brotherhoods in Egypt and Syria and the rise of North American Reconstructionism took place in a twentieth-century time frame—as science, and modern "permissiveness" collided with a frightened conservatism rooted in religion. The writings of people such as Muslim Brotherhood founder Hassan al-Banna and those of Rushdoony are virtually interchangeable when it comes to their goals of restoring God to His "rightful place" as He presides over law and morals. According to al-Banna, Islam enjoins man to strive for a segregation of male and female students, a separate curriculum for girls, a prohibition on dancing, and a campaign against "ostentation in dress and loose behavior." Islamic governments must eventually be unified in a theocratic Caliphate. Or as the late Reconstructionist/Calvinist theologian David Chilton (sounding startlingly al-Banna-like) explained:

> The Great Commission to the Church does not end with simply witnessing to the nations. . . . The kingdoms of the world are to become the kingdoms of Christ. . . . This means that every aspect of life throughout the world is to be brought under the lordship

of Jesus Christ: families, individuals, business, science, agricul-
ture, the arts, law, education, economics, psychology, philosophy,
and every other sphere of human activity. Nothing may be left
out. Christ "must reign, until He has put all enemies under His
feet" (1st Cor. 15:25). . . . Our goal is a Christian world, made up
of explicitly Christian nations. How could a Christian desire anything else? . . . That is the only choice: pagan law or Christian law.
God specifically forbids "pluralism." God is not the least bit interested in sharing world dominion with Satan.*

It was my old friend, the short, stocky, bearded, gnomelike,
Armenian-American Rousas Rushdoony who in 1973 most thoroughly laid out the Far Right/Religious Right agenda in his book
The Institutes of Biblical Law. Rushdoony changed the definition
of salvation from the accepted Evangelical idea that it applies to
individuals to the claim that salvation is really about politics.
With this redefinition, Rushdoony contradicted the usual reading
of Jesus' words by most Christians to mean that Jesus had not
come to this earth to be a political leader: "My kingdom is not of
this world" (John 18:36).

According to Rushdoony, all nations on earth should be obedi-
ent to the ancient Jewish/Christian version of "God's Law," so that
the world will experience "God's blessings." Biblical salvation will
then turn back the consequences of The Fall, and we'll be on our
way to the New Eden. To achieve this "turning back," coercion
must be used by the faithful to stop evildoers, who are, by definition, *anyone* not obeying all of God's Laws as defined by the Reconstructionist interpretation of the Bible.

---

*David Chilton, *Paradise Restored: A Biblical Theology of Dominion*, 6th ed.
(Tyler, TX: Dominion Press, 1999), 271.

Most theologians argue that the New Testament Law of Love "corrects" or "completes" the Old Testament Law of Retribution. Not the Reconstructionists. Rushdoony's son-in-law Gary North has argued that in the Sermon on the Mount the commandments about love are only "recommendations for the ethical conduct of a *captive* people."* North says that Jesus' commands that we agree with adversaries quickly, go the second mile, turn the other cheek, and so forth are no more than instructions on how to survive captivity while being ruled by unbelieving sovereigns as the Jews were ruled by the Romans in Jesus' day. Once Christians are in charge, according to North, rather than turning the other cheek to our enemy, we "should either bust him in the chops or haul him before the magistrate, and possibly both." North adds, "It is only in a period of civil impotence that Christians are under the rule to 'resist not evil.'"**

How far would the Reconstructionists go? North, writes, "The question eventually must be raised: Is it a criminal offence to take the name of the Lord in vain? When people curse their parents, it unquestionably is a capital crime (Exodus 21:17). The son or daughter is under the lawful jurisdiction of the family. The integrity of the family must be maintained by the threat of death. Clearly, cursing God (blasphemy) is a comparable crime, and is therefore a capital crime (Leviticus 24:16)."***

Here's a good summary of the Reconstructionists' extremism from Frederick Clarkson (coauthor of *Challenging the Christian Right*):

---

*Gary North, *Tools of Dominion* (Tyler, TX: Institute for Christian Economics, 1990), 845.
**Greg Loren Durand, "Judicial Warfare: The Christian Reconstruction Movement and Its Blueprints for Dominion," Crownrights.com, www.yuricareport.com/Dominionism/HistoryOfReconstructionMovement.html.
***Gary North, *The Sinai Strategy: Economics and the Ten Commandments* (Tyler, TX: Institute for Christian Economics, 1986), 59–60.

Epitomizing the Reconstructionist idea of Biblical "warfare" is the
centrality of capital punishment under Biblical Law. Doctrinal
leaders (notably Rushdoony, North, and Bahnsen) call for the
death penalty for a wide range of crimes in addition to such con-
temporary capital crimes as rape, kidnapping, and murder. Death
is also the punishment for apostasy (abandonment of the faith),
heresy, blasphemy, witchcraft, astrology, adultery, "sodomy or homosexuality," incest, striking a parent, incorrigible juvenile delinquency, and, in the case of women, "unchastity before marriage."
According to North, women who have abortions should be publicly executed, "along with those who advised them to abort their
children." Rushdoony concludes: "God's government prevails, and
His alternatives are clear-cut: either men and nations obey His
laws, or God invokes the death penalty against them." . . . The Biblically approved methods of execution include burning (at the
stake for example), stoning, hanging, and "the sword." . . . People
who sympathize with Reconstructionism often flee the label because of the severe and unpopular nature of such views."*

Here is how I imagine a Reconstructionist version of the Sermon
on the Mount would read, inclusive of Reconstructionist "inside"
theological/political code words like "Law-Word":

Blessed are those who exercise dominion over the earth: for theirs
is the kingdom of heaven. Blessed are those who deport the immi-
grants: for they shall be comforted. Blessed are those who agree
that the significance of Jesus Christ as the 'faithful and true witness' is that He not only witnesses against those who are at war

---

*Frederick Clarkson, "Christian Reconstructionism: Theocratic Dominionism
Gains Influence," *The Public Eye*, March–June 1994, www.publiceye.org/
magazine/v08n1/chrisre1.html.

against God, but He also executes them: for they shall inherit the earth. Blessed are those who subdue all things and all nations to Christ and His Law-Word: for they shall be filled. Blessed are those who say that those who refuse to submit publicly to the eternal sanctions of God must be denied citizenship: for they shall obtain mercy. Blessed are the Calvinist Christians who are the only lawful heirs to the Kingdom: for they shall see God. Blessed are those who know that turning the other cheek is a temporary bribe paid to evil secular rulers: for they shall be called sons of God if they bust their enemies in the chops. Blessed are those who have taken an eye for an eye: for theirs is the Kingdom of Heaven. Blessed are ye when ye know that the battle for My sake is between the Christian Reconstruction Movement and everyone else. Rejoice, and be exceedingly glad: for great is your reward in heaven. For so we are to make Bible-obeying disciples of anybody who gets in our way, and kill those who resist.

I remember first meeting Rushdoony at his home in Vallecito, California, in the late 1970s. (That was where I also met Gary North for the first time.) I was accompanied by Jim Buchfuehrer, who had produced the antiabortion documentary series of films with me that featured my father and Dr. C. Everett Koop. (Koop was an ultra-Calvinist who would become Ronald Reagan's surgeon general.) The movie series and book project *Whatever Happened to the Human Race?* were Koop's and my brainchild. He had seen Dad's and my first film series—*How Should We Then Live?*—and Koop wanted to team up to expand on the last episodes, in which Dad had denounced the "imperial court" for "stripping the unborn" of their right to life. I talked my father into doing the project.

The impact of the two film series, as well as their companion books, was to give the Evangelical community a frame of reference through which to understand the "secularization of American

culture" and to point to the "human life issue" as the watershed
between a "Christian society" and a utilitarian, relativistic "post-
Christian" future. By the time the films had been viewed by millions
of American Evangelicals, Dad had become the leader of those Evangelicals who took a "stand" on the "life issues." And the films made
the Reconstructionists believe that perhaps in Francis Schaeffer and
his up-and-coming son they might have found new allies. So I began
to get messages that Rushdoony urgently wanted to meet me.

I was struck by the similarity between the adulation Rushdoony received in his compound and the adulation my father enjoyed at L'Abri, although Rushdoony's outfit was much smaller.
As in L'Abri, the man at the center of all the activity was treated
with deference bordering on idolatry. Since Rushdoony was also
so similar in build and manner to my father, he struck me as a
sort of imposter, even wearing a beard very much like Dad's!

Rushdoony's manner was both condescending and fatherly, as
if he wanted to ingratiate himself to me and recruit me for his
team, all the while instructing me. We spent three days together
talking. Rushdoony spoke earnestly and with plenty of hand-on-
arm touching and "fatherly" good humor. On the second visit, a
few months later, Rush (as his friends called him and as he asked
me to call him) introduced me to his biggest financial benefactor,
Howard Ahmanson.* Now *that* got my attention! Most religious
leaders would rather share their wives than their major donors.

---

*Howard Ahmanson Jr. is heir to the Home Savings bank fortune. Howard be-
came Rushdoony's financier and served as a board member of Rushdoony's
Chalcedon Foundation. In the 1970s Ahmanson started the career of Marvin
Olasky, who became an important figure in Evangelical media. Howard, like me,
later renounced his association with the Reconstructionists, even going so far as
to quit the Republican Party in 2009 and reregister as a Democrat. He also
stopped by my home in 2010, along with his charming wife, Roberta, to tell me
that he liked my memoir *Crazy for God* (New York: Carroll and Graf, 2007).

Howard started writing my religious media production company (Schaeffer V Productions) handsome checks for amounts totaling several hundred thousand dollars. Howard and I became friends (we still are), and while using his money to churn out Religious Right films, books, and newspapers, I also got Ahmanson to help my friend attorney John Whitehead to found the Rutherford Institute.

I was the institute's first fund-raiser as well as a founding board member. The Rutherford Institute was just one more example of the impact of Rushdoony's ideas. Whitehead was inspired by Rushdoony's political theology of "reclaiming America for God" and also personally encouraged by him to start what Whitehead pitched as "our version of the ACLU."*

The Rutherford Institute spawned many imitators, from Pat Robertson's legal foundation to James Dobson's legal program. A whole crop of Evangelical leaders suddenly wanted to cash in on the save-America-through-the-courts game, with its fund-raising (and publicity-making) grandstanding possibilities. Typically, Rutherford got involved with defending what in our Rutherford Institute newsletters we claimed were religious civil liberties: For instance, when Reconstructionist homeschool families were investigated by education or child welfare agencies, the Rutherford Institute would intervene to defend them.

What first put the Rutherford Institute on the Evangelical map was its association with Rushdoony, Ahmanson, and me. In 1980–1981 I produced and directed a film project (authored by Whitehead), *The Second American Revolution*, that not only brought Whitehead and the Rutherford Institute a large Evangelical following, but also painted the Evangelicals as victims of a "secular-humanist" America bent on "stripping Christians of our civil rights."

---

*Whitehead has since changed some of his positions on political and theological issues. He's more moderate.

We also produced a best-selling book of the same title that White-head wrote. Ahmanson funded the film portion of the project with a check for $150,000, and Dad and I were Whitehead's key advisors throughout the project.

When we talked, Rushdoony spoke about "secular America" as if it were an enemy state, not our country. He talked about how "we" should all use cash, never credit cards, since cards would make it "easy for the government to track us." Rushdoony held forth passionately about the virtues of gold, how very soon the conflict between the Soviet Union and America would lead to war. Rushdoony also noted that Vallecito was "well located to survive the next war" given "the prevailing wind directions" and its water supply.

Since I was the son of someone Rushdoony regarded as a rival, I had to be handled delicately. For the heir apparent to the growing Schaeffer movement to join Rushdoony would have been quite a coup. During our half-dozen or so meetings, Rushdoony made every effort to reel me in and constantly proposed ways we could all cooperate and "join forces," as he put it. Rushdoony was polite when talking about Dad, but nevertheless made it very clear that my father just didn't "go far enough." Dad, Rushdoony said, was "not consistently Calvinist." Dad had failed to present the "full Re-formed solution." Rushdoony added that my father's "analysis of the problem of secular humanism is good," but that the only "real solution" to modernity is the "*full application* of the biblical law."

The bizarre scope of Reconstructionists' ambition—"insanity," as my father often called it—is clear in the table of contents of Rush-doony's 890-page *The Institutes of Biblical Law,** wherein he

---

The Institutes of Biblical Law. Table of Contents—The Third Commandment. Swearing and Revolution. The Oath and Society. The Oath and Authority. The Fourth Commandment. The Sabbath and Work. The Sabbath and Law Appen-

commented on the world, its history, and its future in the light of what the Bible "says." Rushdoony provided Reconstruction theory for law, politics, jurisprudence, and social morality, just about everything except a Reformed Calvinist recipe for chicken soup!

The message of Rushdoony's work is best summed up in one of his innumerable Chalcedon Foundation position papers, "The Increase of His Government and Peace."** He writes, "The ultimate and absolute government of all things shall belong to Christ." In his book *Thy Kingdom Come****—using words that are similar to those the leaders of al Qaida would use decades later in reference to "true Islam"—Rushdoony argues that democracy and Christianity are incompatible: "Democracy is the great love of the failures and cowards of life," he writes. "One [biblical] faith, one law and one standard of justice did not mean democracy. The heresy of democracy has since

---

dix: The Economics of Sabbath Keeping—by Gary North. The Fifth Commandment. The Authority of the Family. The Economics of the Family. Education and the Family. The Family and Delinquency. The Sixth Commandment. The Death Penalty. Hybridization and Law. Abortion. Restitution or Restoration. Military Laws and Production. Taxation. Quarantine Laws. Dietary Rules. Social Inheritance: Landmarks. The Seventh Commandment. Marriage. Family Law. Marriage and Monogamy. Incest. Sex and Crime. Adultery. Divorce. Homosexuality. The Transvestite. Bestiality. The Eighth Commandment. Dominion. Theft. Restitution and Forgiveness. Liability of the Bystander. Money and Measure. Usury. Landmarks and Land. The Virgin Birth and Property. Fraud. Eminent Domain. Labor Laws. Prison. The Rights of Strangers, Widows, and Orphans. The Ninth Commandment. Corroboration. Perjury. False Witness. Slander Within Marriage. Slander as Theft. Judges. The Responsibility of Judges and Rulers. The Court. The Procedure of the Court. The Judgment of the Court. The Tenth Commandment. Covetousness. Special Privilege. The System. Notes on Law in Western Society . . . etc.

**Rousas John Rushdoony, "The Increase of His Government and Peace" (Vallecito, CA: Chalcedon Foundation, December 1967).

***Rousas John Rushdoony, *Thy Kingdom Come: Studies in Daniel and Revelation* (Fairfax, VA: Thoburn Press, 1970).

then worked havoc in church and state. . . . Christianity and democracy are inevitably enemies."*

The impact of Reconstructionism (often under other names) has grown even though Rushdoony has largely been forgotten even in Evangelical circles, let alone the wider world. He made the Evangelical world more susceptible to being politicized—and manipulated by some very smart people. Religious leaders like Jerry Falwell who once had nothing to do with politics per se were influenced by the Reconstructionists. That in turn moved the whole Evangelical movement to the right and then into the political arena, where it became "normal" for Evangelical leaders to jump head first into politics with little-to-no regard for the separation of church and state.

Non-Evangelicals with political agendas have cashed in on the Evangelicals' willingness to lend their numbers and influence to one moral crusade after another, or rather I should say, *to one political crusade after another masquerading as moral crusades.* For instance, conservative Roman Catholic Princeton University Professor of Jurisprudence Robert George was an antiabortion, anti-Obama, anti-gay-rights, and anti-stem-cell-research "profamily" activist, and he found ways to effectively carry on the Reconstructionist agenda while truthfully denying any formal connection to people like Rushdoony. Take George's brainchild: the "Manhattan Declaration: A Call of Christian Conscience." This was published in 2009 as an anti-Obama manifesto, and many Evangelical leaders signed on. George may not have been following Rushdoony or have ever read his work, *but the Evangelicals who signed on to George's agenda would never have done so if not for the influence of Reconstructionism on American Evangelicals decades before.*

---

*Ibid., 67.

The "Manhattan Declaration" reads:

We will not comply with any edict that purports to compel our institutions to participate in abortions, embryo-destructive research, assisted suicide and euthanasia, or any other anti-life act . . . nor will we bend to any rule purporting to force us to bless immoral sexual partnerships, treat them as marriages or the equivalent, or refrain from proclaiming the truth, as we know it, about morality and immorality and marriage and the family. We will fully and ungrudgingly render to Caesar what is Caesar's. But under no circumstances will we render to Caesar what is God's.*

In case you've never heard of George, he's been a one-man "brain trust" for the Religious Right, Glenn Beck, and the Far Right of the Republican Party as well as for the ultraconservative wing of the Roman Catholic Church. Here's how the *New York Times* introduced him to its readers:

[Robert George] has parlayed a 13th-century Catholic philosophy [the natural law theory] into real political influence. Glenn Beck, the Fox News talker and a big George fan, likes to introduce him as "one of the biggest brains in America," or, on one broadcast, "Superman of the Earth." Karl Rove told me he considers George a rising star on the right and a leading voice in persuading President George W. Bush to restrict embryonic stem-cell research. . . . Newt Gingrich called him "an important and growing influence" on the conservative movement, especially on matters like abortion and marriage. "If there really is a vast right-wing conspiracy,"

---

*Robert George, "Manhattan Declaration: A Call of Christian Conscience," November 20, 2009, www.manhattandeclaration.org/the-declaration/read.aspx.

the conservative Catholic journal *Crisis* concluded a few years ago, "its leaders probably meet in George's kitchen."*

I confronted George on a panel discussion entitled "Campaign '08: Race, Gender, and Religion" at Princeton University. We butted heads over what he'd been mischaracterizing as presidential candidate Obama's "proabortion" position. At the time we met on that (six-person) panel, George was one of McCain's key advisors and I (a former Republican) was blasting George's man for having sold out to the Religious Right, which McCain had once called "agents of intolerance." In introducing myself to the Princeton audience, I mentioned that McCain had written a glowing endorsement for one of my several books on military-civilian relations.** I also admitted that I'd actively worked for McCain in the 2000 presidential primaries against W. Bush by appearing—at McCain advisor Mark Salter's oft-repeated urgent request—on several religious and other conservative talk shows (for instance, on Ollie North's top-rated talk show) on McCain's behalf. (In those days McCain was being attacked by the likes of Religious Right leader James Dobson for not being "pro-life" enough.)

Before our confrontation George had written that "many more unborn human beings would likely be killed under Obama than under McCain."*** While challenging him, I argued that electing either McCain *or* Obama would change nothing regarding the availability

---

*David Kirkpatrick, "The Conservative-Christian Big Thinker," *New York Times*, December 16, 2009.

**Frank Schaeffer and Kathy Roth Douquet, *AWOL: The Unexcused Absence of America's Upper Classes from Military Service and How It Hurts Our Country* (New York: HarperCollins 2006).

***Robert P. George, "Obama's Abortion Extremism," *Catholic Online Opinion*, October 16, 2008, Witherspoon Institute, www.catholic.org/politics/story.php?id=30081.

of abortion. I said that I thought that there would be fewer abortions if women had access to the better health care and the other social services that Obama was proposing during his campaign.

George's "Manhattan Declaration" was signed by more than 150 American "mainstream" (mostly Evangelical) conservative religious leaders. They joined to "affirm support for traditional marriage" and to advocate civil disobedience against laws contradicting the signers' religious beliefs about marriage and/or the "life issues." The drafting committee included Evangelical Far Right leader Charles Colson.

It was the Reconstructionists who, along with several less extreme activists like my father, created the climate in which the likes of George, Colson, and Beck have been taken seriously by many Evangelicals. Without the work of the Reconstructionists, the next generation of religious activists (trying to use the courts, politics, and/or civil disobedience to impose their narrow theology on the majority of Americans) would have been relegated to some lonely street corner where they could gather to howl at the moon. Instead, the twenty-first century's theocrats (though they'd never so identify themselves) enjoyed the backing of Fox News, were tolerated at places like Princeton University, and could be found running most Evangelical organizations.

When I was with Rushdoony and the other Reconstructionist leaders, what struck me was their total lack of humanity in the context of their own theologically self-described "fallen nature." For those so certain that the faculty of Reason in mankind is fallen into "total depravity," they seemed pretty sure of their own ideas. (Maybe they explain this given that according to Calvinist theology, they are now "regenerate.") They certainly didn't behave as if they believed that they, too, were "fallen."

Where my parents, through L'Abri, ministered to many people who disagreed with them, to people who lived "sinful" lives, and to people who were officially apostate, Rushdoony and company sneered at and/or denounced anyone not in total agreement with them. Where Mom and Dad tried to rehabilitate The-God-Of-The-Bible, Rushdoony relished The-God-Of-The-Bible's mean side and, as it were, egged The-God-Of-The-Bible on to do His worst. Where Mom said that there were lots of things she didn't understand in the here and now and that we'd have to wait until "we get to Heaven to know, Dear," Rushdoony and company had an answer to every question.

What was missing in the Rushdoony netherworld were the *actual people* they talked so cheerily about either converting or, if need be, killing when the stoning got under way after America was in their hands. By contrast in L'Abri, the "They" on the "Other Side" were our friends and were living in our home.

When I was a child, before the culture wars started, "Secularists" and "Secular Humanists" weren't faceless threats to be killed or converted or written off in countless "position papers." They had names like Alice. And Mom and Dad cared about their students' souls, not about how their students would vote in the next election.

My parents, like most Evangelicals of that era, cared most about people's "relationship to Christ," not their relationship to the Republican Party. And had someone, like a Robert George, approached them with a document calling for a "stand" against an American president, they would have been shocked and/or laughed in his face. But that was then.

CHAPTER 6

A Very Small, Tragically Immodest Speedo Bathing Suit (and *Roe v. Wade*)

When I compared what I thought of as Normal People to my family, I envied them. They smoked, drank, laughed, never witnessed to anyone, and sometimes even danced to the music from the snack-bar jukebox on the beach. Mostly they didn't seem haunted by the idea that they were foot soldiers in a war between God and Satan. In The Battle Of The Heavenlies, much was expected of Us Real Christians when it came to doing our bit. This ongoing contest was won or lost one person at a time. The outcome of every battle depended on whether or not the Souls of the people we converted (or didn't convert) went to Heaven or Hell. It also decided their fate after the Resurrection: to burn forever in the "lake of fire" or to enjoy their indestructible bodies for eternity, doing who knew what.

PHOTO: *Mom and me in 1957*

117

"Mom?" the ten-year-old version of me asked one night after Mom had read me the creation story (again) and Eve had (again) been tempted by Satan, sinned, and taken us all down with her (again).

"Yes, Dear?"

"Why did God create Satan?"

"God did *not* 'create Satan,' my Dear!" said Mom, and she shot me a hurt glance as if to say that the phrasing of my question had been needlessly unkind to both God and to her. "He created lovely angels, and one of them was Lucifer, the highest-ranking angel. Lucifer didn't want to serve God. But Satan can't change God's Purposes! Meanwhile, *we* have to bring people to Christ to help God win. Do you understand?"

"But, Mom, what I don't understand is *why Jesus* doesn't just bring everyone to Jesus?"

"Then they'd have no choice, and He doesn't force anyone."

"But Dad says we're elected."

"Yes, and that's because God knows what will happen, Dear, but we still choose."

"How?"

"Because as it says in the Bible, 'All things are possible with God.'"

"It seems like a lot of bother," I said.

"It's God's Plan, Dear," said Mom in a tone that clearly indicated that, while she welcomed all questions about the Lord, I should nevertheless not question to a point that seemed to open the door to the sort of doubts that can lead us far from the Lord. Mom's tone softened as she added, "Darling, we're finite, so we just *can't* finally explain these things."

"But, Mom, *why* do we have to tell people about Jesus when God already knew who will be saved before He made them, and why did He make anyone to be Lost anyway?"

"Because, Dear, that way we get to participate in His Plan and also show that we love Him."

"But it seems so dumb!"

"No, Darling," said Mom, shooting me an alarmed look and beginning to speak rather quickly. "There's a *difference* between asking legitimate questions and questioning God in a way that makes it seem as if we're rebelling against Him. I'd be careful if I were you about using the word 'dumb' in this context, and for another thing, that's *such* an *American* word and not terribly sophisticated, and to use *that word* is *not* the sort of use of vocabulary that *I* know that you know, Dear, which is the reason I only read *good books* to you, so *please* say, 'I don't fully understand,' or 'That concept seems contradictory' but avoid the sort of words that make it sound as if you're being raised by ordinary American Christians who derive their tragically limited vocabulary from what they hear Billy Graham say, read on cereal boxes, and see on television!"

I grew up feeling that Mom, Dad, my sisters, and I were a separate species from the Normal humans I would see going about their business as if there were no Battle Of The Heavenlies. We were Set Apart From The World. We had no TV and no American cereal boxes either. And we'd done it to ourselves—on purpose! God *wanted* us to walk among Normal People as His Chosen Outcasts.

By the time I was eight or nine, the only conversations I felt comfortable having with strangers were those that happened *out* of my parents' and sisters' earshot. When they weren't around, I could temporarily pretend to join the human race. Lying was necessary because otherwise I'd attract The Look and The Uncomfortable Silence that always followed any truthful answer to the question "So what does your father do?" If my sister Susan was there, or worst of all Mom, I'd have to mumble something truthful about being missionaries and Dad being a pastor, and then I'd pray Mom wouldn't launch into the explanation of how God had called our family "to live by faith alone," otherwise known as "The L'Abri Story."

"But what do you live *on*?" a perplexed British vacationer on the beach near Portofino might ask the cringing eleven-year-old version of me after hearing Mom talk about "living by faith."

"People help out," I'd mutter, while scanning all possible escape routes.

If Mom were within earshot, in other words anywhere within a mile or so, she'd offer a glowing and animated explanation: "The Lord answers our prayers as a demonstration of His existence to an unbelieving world. We live by *faith* alone!"

"So strangers send you money?"

"Yes, as the Lord moves their hearts!" Mom would say.

The listener, who had been expecting something like "We're living in Switzerland while Dad's on business" would give me The Look and sidle off. If the listener didn't sidle off while the going was good, Mom might pull out a witnessing aid or a tract and share the Gospel right then and there.

This sharing of Jesus with strangers would be done *to* some inoffensive agnostic, Anglican, Catholic, or Jew—in other words, to someone of a different (or no) religious persuasion. The target might have been on the way to the snack bar for a slice of pizza and an espresso and instead would end up pressed into a one-on-one Evangelistic rally as her reward for politely remarking on the fine weather.

Sometimes Mom brought her Gospel Walnut and/or "The Heart of Salvation" booklet along to the beach, and she'd use those on The Lost. The witnessing aid was an actual walnut hollowed out and packed with a long strand of ribbon: black for your heart filled with sin, red for Jesus' blood, white for your heart once it was washed of sin, and gold for Heaven, where you'd be headed *pro-*

vided you prayed the Sinner's Prayer right then and there and asked Jesus to come into your heart *and* to be your Personal Savior, while Mom acted as a midwife for your second birth *before* the pizza oven exploded and killed you (or you got cancer—whatever) and it was "too late."

"Mom, can you be saved *after* you die?" the five-, six-, seven-, and eight-year-old versions of me repeatedly asked, rather hoping that you could so that there would be less pressure to save everyone *right now*, not to mention that *I* would get more time, too.

"No, Dear, the Bible is *very clear*. Hebrews 9:27 says we're 'destined to die once, and after that to face judgment.' Another passage that tells us there's no chance after death in Luke 16. The parable is about that rich man who died and went to Hell. He's told a chasm separates Heaven and Hell. Difficult as it is to fully understand, we know there's an Eternal Separation as the Punishment for people who won't accept Jesus Christ while they have the chance right now."

"What about the ones that never hear the Gospel?"

"They're all Lost, so that's why we have to *always* witness!"

Because there were *no more chances* after death, we Schaeffers were responsible for Every Lost Person we ever encountered—including all the Italians we met, except for Dino and Lorna in Milan because they'd come to L'Abri and already been saved. Dad said, "They're probably the only Real Christians in Italy, but they don't count because Lorna is English."

Sometimes Mom would leave the Gospel Walnut in her room and bring along "The Heart of Salvation" instead, a booklet about ten inches by ten inches cut out in a heart shape and made of five pages: black, red, white, gold, and green. Mom had taught my sisters and me a cheerful little ditty to sing as she turned the pages: "My heart was BLACK with sin, until the Savior came in! His precious

RED blood, I know, has washed it WHITE as snow! In His Word I am told, I'll walk the streets of GOLD! A wonderful, wonderful day, He washed my sins away!"

The props for witnessing that Mom carried were in her gospel-sharing repertoire only until the early 1960s. My parents had deployed witnessing aids in their ministries back in the States, but I caught only the tail end of Mom and Dad's fundamentalist incarnation. Once a bit of European sophistication rubbed off on my parents, their witnessing methods changed. They became more subtle. The Gospel Walnut was retired and replaced with conversations about philosophy, art, and politics. But these "conversations" were then steered and inevitably ended with a consideration of the Meaning of Life. And THAT, of course, led to a "discussion" about that "feeling of guilt we all have" and you can guess Who the only Answer to *that* feeling was.

Anyway, once our "The Heart of Salvation" song ended, we'd add, "Green is the color that shows how a child who loves Jesus will grow." I don't know why the explanation of the green page had to be delivered as a brief soliloquy after the song. But the recipient of our serenade never asked about that, mostly because by then his eyes had glazed over, and he (or she) was backing away and/or rooted to the spot in a horrified Normal-Pagan-and/or-Theologically-Confused-Liberal-Vacationing-Anglican-caught-in-the-headlights-of-an-oncoming-Born-Again-Express-Train sort of way.

If the recipient of the Schaeffer family's attentions happened to be a forty-year-old Italian businessman, standing barefoot on the cracked sandy concrete floor of the snack bar terrace while clad only in a Very Small, "tragically immodest" Speedo bathing suit, chest hair black and oily against his leathery tan chest, redolent and glistening with the tangy extra-virgin olive oil he used as suntan lotion, a cigarette in one hand and a glass of Campari in the other, the bulge of his genitals outlined in startling detail as he casually adjusted them by scratching, then shifting his generous package *while* reaching *within* his Speedo *while* we sang, the scene would become surreal. Here was the epitome of The World, a caricature of Fallen Humanity being confronted not just by The Gospel, but also by four (or post-Priscilla-leaving-home three) Very Virtuous Women and one little boy. The women were radiating disapproval of the man's Speedo and his clearly visible genitals—balls to the left, penis folded to the right—while *also* exuding a severe love for his Soul. The little boy was thinking of bolting for the water and swimming to the horizon.

As Mom would turn the pages while we sang, she'd point to her heart and then to the man's heart, tapping him firmly on his chest, thereby making his Pagan Saint Medallions and assorted gold charms, including his *cornuto* (an inch-long horn-shaped amulet carved from red coral to protect against the evil eye), to bounce. After we sang, the Lost Italian (who could not under-stand English) would nevertheless clap while smiling at us chil-dren, especially at my "developing" sisters. Perhaps all American families burst into songs as a way to greet strangers. "*Congratu-lazioni!*" he'd exclaim somewhat nervously, then try to turn away.

The Pagan Symbols dangling around his Lost Oily Neck were all the proof we needed—his alcoholic drink, cigarette, and penis wrapped around his thigh aside—that our target was Very, *Very* Lost. Had he been even moderately born again, he'd long since have tossed out his "Catholic trinkets." When Israel committed spiritual adultery, God called His people "whorish women" and accused them of fornication (Ezekiel 16:26–32 and Jeremiah 3:1–25). And we *knew* that the Roman Catholic Church was *even worse* than Is-rael when it chased after False Gods and Strange Women!

If on the off, off chance the Lost Italian showed interest and—after changing into born-again modest boxer-type swimming trunks—wanted a longer answer as to why he should take off his Pagan Saint Medals, Mom would have said, "What does the Bible say about Your Catholic Idols, you ask? That little horn miniature carrot thing you wear was once sacred to worshippers of the Moon Goddess! In your Catholic heresy, these *awful things* relate to the Virgin Mary standing on a lunar crescent! So turn with me to Exodus 20:4–5. Here let me show you! As you grow in the Lord, you'll get more familiar with your Bible! Here it is! 'Thou shalt not MAKE unto thee ANY graven image, or any likeness of anything that is in heaven above, or that is in the earth beneath, or that is in the water under the earth. Thou shalt not BOW DOWN thyself to them nor SERVE them.' Don't you Catholics MAKE graven images? Don't you then serve the moon goddess?"

"*Io suppongo di sì.*" (I suppose so.)

"Don't Catholics KNEEL down to statues of Mary?"

"*Io penso di sì.*" (I think so, yes.)

"Don't Catholics SERVE Mary?"

"*Ovviamente.*" (Obviously.)

"Don't Catholics BOW DOWN and kiss the foot of the pagan god Jupiter, which was renamed St. Peter?"

"*É vero.*" (Yes, that's true.)

"Then turn with me to Leviticus 26:1. Susan, please show this poor man where it is. See? 'You shall make you NO IDOLS nor GRAVEN IMAGE,' and THAT INCLUDES CORAL CARROTS, OR WHATEVER IT IS YOU CALL THAT SILLY THING! 'Neither rear you up a STANDING IMAGE. Neither shall ye set up any IMAGE OF STONE in your land to bow down unto it.' Don't Catholics rear up STANDING IMAGES?"

"*Io non lo so.*" (I don't know.)

"What do you mean 'I don't know'? Don't Catholics set up IMAGES OF STONE?! Haven't you ever been to St. Peter's Basilica? Turn with me to Deuteronomy 4:16. No, no, my poor Dear man, it's in the *Old* Testament! Here, Debby, you show him! He's obviously never even *seen* a Bible! 'Lest ye corrupt yourselves, and MAKE you a GRAVEN IMAGE, the similitude of ANY FIGURE, the likeness of MALE or FEMALE.' Don't you Catholics make graven images of MALE and FEMALE?"

"*Non importa.*"

"Debby, what did he say?"

"I think he said it doesn't matter."

"Oh, Dear, haven't you heard *anything* I've been telling you? Turn with me to Deuteronomy 16:22. Here I'll show you. 'Neither shalt thou SET thee up ANY IMAGE: which the Lord thy God HATES.' Don't Catholics SET UP ANY IMAGES? Yes! Doesn't God HATE those IMAGES?"

"*Io non lo so.*"

"Don't you know what God hates?"

To which our Italian might have answered "*Si!*" and torn off his wicked trinkets and been saved or kept his trinkets and muttered "*Vaffanculo!*" and remained as Lost as ever.

But this never happened. In all the years of witnessing, while on vacation we never saved one *cornuto*-wearing Italian, though several Italians, including the aforementioned Dino (and Lorna if you count English wives married to Italians), did come to L'Abri and returned to Dark, Lost Italy and started a home church in Milan. "But, sadly," as Mom once said, "even Dino still wears a medallion of some 'saint,' so I'm not entirely sure about him."

Dad preached at L'Abri's Milan branch once a month. He always purchased an excellent Motta Panettone (the cake typical of Milan usually prepared for Christmas) while passing through the Milan station. Panettone is a fine dry airy concoction that's so light and fluffy it melts in your mouth. Eating the treasured wedge Dad offered me, like some sort of Dad-coming-home sacrament, gave me a lifelong sensory association with the words "reaching the Italians for Christ" and the taste of candied orange. Any time I hear those words, I can *taste* candied fruit and even get a whiff of the cigarette smell Dad always carried home on his clothes after his long train ride. And even now any time I eat Panettone, I can't help but think about the Lost Italians.

Anyway, unaware that his medallions had given him away and blithely oblivious to his impending doom on Judgment Day and/ or if the pizza oven exploded right then and there, our Very Lost Italian just smiled, then wandered off with a transitive-verb-type shrug (i.e., to raise the shoulders, especially as a gesture of doubt, disdain, or indifference).

Once his back was turned to us, Mom shuddered, thereby directing my attention to his bottom and how the Lost Man's Speedo was riding up *and* down. This caused a sharp disapproving intake of breath by my mother since we could all see the Top Of His Crack *and* the twin-crescent-moon-like Lower Parts of his Bottom's Cheeks protruding *beneath* the all-too-brief briefs, with the suntan-line-demarcated Very White Cheek Flesh winking slyly at us as he walked away.

During these demonstrations Dad stayed away. In our pre-sophistication days, Mom often chided him for his cold heart when it came to Reaching Out To The Lost in public places. But back then Dad did carry tracts with him, which he'd scatter anonymously, sort of like rabbit droppings in a garden, evidence of the rabbit but with no actual rabbit there to confront the consequences for the missing lettuce (or in Dad's case, the nonbiodegradable Jesus litter).

Throughout my early childhood, we Schaeffers were busy littering train seats, café tables, and assorted telephone booths all over Switzerland, Italy, and the rest of Europe with four- and five-page luridly illustrated little booklets "in the local language in case someone is led to read it," as Dad said. They had titles in French and Italian, such as "What Must I Do to Be Saved?" or "Is There a Heaven and Hell?" and "Where Will I Spend Eternity?" Sometimes as our train roared through Italian or Swiss towns, Dad would fling handfuls of tracts from the train window at astonished passersby.

My lack of zeal for evangelizing worried me. My reluctance to witness always conjured up Jesus' dire warning: "But whoever denies me before men, I also will deny before my Father who is in heaven" (Matthew 10:33). To even be *inwardly embarrassed* was a denial. I knew God saw the nine-year-old version of me hiding behind the snack bar, wedged between the jukebox and the pile of folded deck chairs when Mom declared open season on The Lost. Not only had I *not* done enough to save some Lost Soul; I'd also let Jesus down in the Battle of the Heavenlies! "See!" Satan would say to God while laughing nastily and pointing down at me where I was trying to shrink into myself or (chameleonlike) meld with the pavement. "Your servant Frank Schaeffer is only *pretending* to sing along with his mother! He's moving his lips, but do you hear his voice? No! And why not? Because he doesn't *really* love you!" Another nail driven into my Lord's hands and feet by my Sins: in this case, my lack of enthusiasm combined with a timid lip-sync demonstration in the vain hope that the pretty eleven-year-old English girl I'd just met the day before on the beach—and who Had Actually Smiled At Me Even After She'd Met Mom—would *not* hear my voice, identify it, turn, and see me standing with my family singing.

Besides evangelizing, we Schaeffers did our small part to help God win the Battle Of The Heavenlies by wearing *modest* bathing suits. Dad and I wore long boxer-shorts-style suits—not skin-tight, genital-outlining Speedos. Our women wore 1950s-type skirted suits, which gave the swimsuit the look of a child's play-suit with a nice modesty skirt (or ruffle) to block one's view of the important-to-always-hide (vicinity of) that Most Private Place.

In contrast to Us Real Christians, The Lost wore ever-smaller bathing suits each year. And our modest-bathing-suit-wearing Mission-To-The-Lost failed. In fact, by the late 1960s some of The Lost started going topless. And their immodest contagion even began to infect America. That's what hippies and American feminist women were: wannabe French and Italian Topless Pagans trying to turn the whole of heretofore chaste America into a scratch-your-balls-in-public Paraggi beach!

Those wannabe Europeans in America started to get their way—with the legalization of abortion, the ultimate affront to Christian conservative values. After the *Roe v. Wade* ruling, Christian America was convinced that the proselytizing shoe was on the other foot. Now it was the secular world that was forcing Us Real Christians to listen to *their* version of "The Heart of Salvation" and don tiny bathing suits as *they* evangelized Us God-fearing Americans with the Gospel Of Guiltless Fucking!

Before 1973, abortion was already being legalized state by state without starting a civil war. No one got shot in 1959 when the American Law Institute (ALI) proposed a model penal code for state abortion laws. The code proposed legalizing abortion for reasons including the mental or physical health of the mother, pregnancy due to rape and incest, and fetal deformity. On April 25, 1967, the governor of Colorado, John Love, signed the first liberalized ALI-model abortion law in the United States, allowing abortion in cases of mental or physical disability of either the child or mother or in cases of rape or incest. No buildings were firebombed, nor did the Republican Party decide to define itself as "pro-life" and fight every election, local, state, and national, by declaring its antiabortion credentials. There were even Southern Baptist leaders on the record as being in favor of abortion rights. For instance, Dr. W. A. Criswell (a two-term president of the

Southern Baptist Convention) and my father (in later years) argued over abortion. Criswell was on record saying he didn't think
life began until a baby took his or her first breath.

Laws were passed in California, Oregon, and North Carolina
legalizing abortion, and no one chained himself to any clinic gates.
In 1970 New York allowed abortion on demand up to the twenty-
fourth week of pregnancy. Governor Nelson A. Rockefeller signed
a bill repealing the state's 1830 law banning abortion after "quick-
ening" (the ancient term indicates the initial motion of the fetus as
felt by the mother). Rockefeller's life was not threatened by people
nailing up "wanted" posters listing his home address and where
his children went to school. Similar laws were passed in Alaska,
Hawaii, and Washington State without the Democratic Party
changing its platform to become thereafter "The Abortion Party"
(as Republicans would soon label it).

By the end of 1972, a total of thirteen states had an ALI-type
law, and none had sparked a culture war. Four states allowed
abortion on demand, and there were no mass demonstrations,
let alone assassinations of doctors. Even ultraconservative Mississippi permitted abortion for rape and incest, while Alabama allowed abortion for the mother's physical health. Ronald Reagan
(albeit somewhat absentmindedly) was pro-choice. No clinics in
New York State, Alaska, or California (where abortion was legal)
were being bombed.

On January 22, 1973, the U.S. Supreme Court issued its ruling in
Roe v. *Wade*. The incremental state-by-state approach to finding a
more humane (not to mention realistic) way to deal with unwanted pregnancy than the nefarious "back-alley" abortion ended
with a smash. In *Roe*, the right to privacy was discovered to be
"broad enough to encompass" a right to abortion. *Roe* adopted a
trimester scheme of pregnancy. In the first trimester, a state could

enact no regulation to protect a fetus. In the second trimester, a state could enact some regulation, but only for the purpose of protecting maternal health. In the third trimester, even after viability,* a state could (but did not have to) "proscribe" abortion, provided it made exceptions to preserve the life and health of a woman seeking an abortion.

Then the *Doe v. Bolton* ruling (also in 1973) defined health to mean "all factors" that affect a woman, including "emotional, psychological, familial, and the woman's age." In other words—in practical terms—if you could find a doctor willing to do the deed, abortion was made legal at a stroke in all fifty states, up to the moment before a fully grown baby was born.

Roe as "refined" by *Bolton* created the culture wars. This was a "life-and-death" matter sparking raw emotions to match: dead babies pitted against women killed by coat hangers. Unlike debates over prayer in public schools, the right to bear arms, racial issues, and gay rights, *Roe* offered no middle ground, let alone the psychological space for an incremental adjustment to a new sensitivity to women's rights. Unlike capital punishment, this issue wasn't about a few hundred murderers on death row but about everyone's daughters, wives, mothers, sisters, and girlfriends, not to mention about the fate of every baby conceived from then on.

As redefined by *Bolton, Roe* was extreme when compared not only to the heretofore more nuanced and gradual evolution of

---

*Fetal viability generally refers to the ability of a fetus to survive outside the womb, but the term is subject to interpretation. The *Roe v. Wade* ruling says, "With respect to the State's important and legitimate interest in potential life, the 'compelling' point is at viability. This is so because the foetus then presumably has the capability of meaningful life outside the mother's womb." See "Abortion Time Limits: Fetal Viability," *British Medical Association Journal,* June 17, 2005, www.bma.org.uk/ethics/reproduction_genetics/AbortionTime Limits.jsp?page=12.

abortion laws in America but also as compared to the laws defining access to abortion in other Western countries. And *Roe* was about Sex!

Matters sexual generate a special sort of heat in Sex-obsessed/ Sex-fearing America. Thus, the 1960s ruckus over the pill and "what it will lead to" was just a foretaste of what the battle over abortion became—and has remained.

Roe as restated by *Bolton* fed the passion that has burned within each successive generation of antigovernment protesters since the early 1970s. This has included the rise of the so-called Tea Party movement and the Far Right's vitriol-laced reaction to President Obama's twenty-first-century moderate legislative health care reform, including predictions of "Death Panels," and "government takeover." *Roe* even indirectly energized those members of the Far Right who didn't care about abortion per se or who were pro-choice libertarians. *Roe* had such far-reaching effects because *reactions* to *Roe* and *Bolton* set the scorched-earth, winner-take-all *tone* and *volume* of the political fights since 1973. And given the permissiveness of Roe and Bolton when taken together, they opened the door to a constant stream of news stories about late-term abortions like the following one that has kept antiabortion Americans enraged and the general population (even many pro-choice people) unsettled and queasy.

As the *New York Times* reported in January of 2011 (in the context of an article noting that 40 percent of all pregnancies in New York City end in abortion):

> The vast majority of abortions in New York—88 percent—take place in the first 12 weeks. All but 2 percent take place in the first 20. After that, women's options narrow. It's far too late for [abortion-causing] pills, and too late for most OB-GYNS. So, many women

are referred to specialists like Dr. Robert Berg, who occupy the outer edge of New York's abortion landscape, terminating pregnancies up to the legal limit of 24 weeks after conception. The procedure costs about $15,000, some of which is typically covered by insurance, and starts in his office, where he dilates the patient's cervix to approximate the effects of labor. He describes the process as "quite unpleasant." A day or two later, in an operating room at NYU Langone Medical Center, Dr. Berg removes the fetus, either intact, using his hands, or "destructively," using medical instruments. . . . Dr. Berg said, some patients seeking late-term abortions are "hostile to me, they're hostile to my office staff."

"I'm just a punching bag," he added. "I don't do well with that. Sometimes they won't even look at me the day of the procedure; they won't speak to me. That I despise. I really hate that. They were referred to me because I do it safely and expeditiously," the doctor continued. "To be treated like garbage—and my staff—is really very upsetting."

Abortion is complicated, even in New York.*

The words "abortion is complicated" must be the understatement of all time. The writer might also have added that people's views on abortion are often more personal than political, let alone strictly rational. In that light, and before offering my opinion on the fight at the heart of our culture wars, I think a disclosure is needed.

By the age of seventeen I'd either slept with or tried to sleep with or wanted to sleep with every girl with a heartbeat I'd met since I was about twelve. I was a virtual caricature of the irresponsible young male, the type who becomes (as much as anything

---

*Ariel Kaminer, "Abortion: Easy Access, Complex Everything Else," *New York Times*, January 21, 2011, www.nytimes.com/2011/01/23/nyregion/23critic .html?ref=nyregion.

else) the reason for many women's need for access to abortion. When I was fifteen, one girlfriend (not Genie) told me I'd gotten her pregnant and demanded that I marry her. (This was in the context of L'Abri, where if you "got someone pregnant," marriage was the recommended choice to "fix" the "problem." In Evangelical circles young marriage was not unusual). She said, "I already had two abortions with other boyfriends and won't do that again." (She was a nineteen-year-old L'Abri student from America.) I said, "Have another abortion; I'm not marrying you." She turned out not to be pregnant. But in the "God-sees-the-heart" department, I'd proved that I was just as callous as anyone else.

When Genie got pregnant two years later, we decided to "keep" Jessica (what an oddly condescending term to use about my daughter). Abortion was not a very real possibility to us given Genie's and my backgrounds. We were in Switzerland, where in 1969 abortion was illegal. That didn't mean it wasn't available. My previous girlfriend had her two illegal abortions in South Carolina in a "back-alley" arrangement, actually from a respectable local doctor, and everyone knew that in Switzerland (even at that time) plenty of private health clinics opened their doors to women "in need."

When Genie found she was pregnant and told her parents that she wanted to get married, they told her she could come home and didn't need to marry. They were Roman Catholics, they were exceptionally kind, and they would have supported her choice to either keep the baby or have it adopted. They also would have made their disapproval of abortion clear.

Yes, I did love Genie, and she loved me, or at least we each had experienced an intense and passionate teen version of love. And we were living in a community that actually behaved as Jesus instructed His followers to behave when it came to not judging but rather offering unlimited support. We weren't well off, though; in fact we had nothing but a room full of my paintings and a free place to live. But pre-*Roe*, perhaps like most people, my parents' attitude to abortion was one of silent ambivalence. They didn't approve of abortions (back then few people did, including Planned Parenthood, which in its official publications as late as 1968 called abortion murder). But the "issue" had no heat. It certainly wasn't political as it was to become and was probably one of those things about which both Mom and Dad would have said, "I wouldn't do this myself, but if you do, I'd understand even if I advised against it." I know that they had comforted women who had had abortions (like that previous girlfriend of mine) just as they also cared for many single mothers who'd kept their children.

Actually, Genie and I never discussed abortion, even when we discovered she was pregnant. All we debated was if we were going to stay together or if Genie would do what her parents wanted and go home to begin college. I guess we assumed that the future of her pregnancy would be decided after Genie's decision whether to stay with me or not. She'd already partly "voted" for me by having a friend of hers steal her passport out of her mother's underwear drawer and express-mail it to New York, where Genie had traveled to join me at the first show of my paintings at the Frisch Gallery. You see, she'd flown home after being in Europe for six months; she was supposed to have been there for three weeks, then stumbled on L'Abri (and me) and stayed.

Genie had returned to her parents not knowing she was pregnant. And then, after only ten days at home, Genie joined me in New York against her parents' wishes. Then we headed back to Europe via boat (also against their wishes) and only on the boat did Genie begin to suspect that she might be pregnant. We really didn't know if we would have the support of my family, let alone the rest of the L'Abri staff. At the time I thought Dad might just get so angry he'd throw us out. In fact, Dad, Mom, and most of the L'Abri people treated us with dignity and compassion.

For an unmarried Schaeffer child, having Sex was something to be hidden. Sure, my parents knew I'd been chasing any female who moved and I was now sleeping with Genie, but knowing and *acknowledging* something are two different things. Mom talked about everything related to procreation but fell strangely silent when it came to her son's actual sex life. The Talks Mom gave me did no good. Informed or not, I was never going to go up to Mom and say, "I need a condom because I'm fornicating." There was a pharmacy up the road run by people Mom and Dad knew. I was too embarrassed to ask for condoms. And the pill was still something relatively new, and Genie was like me in that she wasn't about to ask my (or her) parents for an introduction to some doctor to get a prescription. Contraceptives weren't readily available. You had to ask a grown-up. Besides, Genie and I were like many teens: believers in our exception from consequences.

Did I choose fatherhood? No, I lived in the moment.

Was I a good father? No, I was an insecure kid with a temper.

I slapped my daughter. I also loved Jessica, but there were plenty of days I resented being "saddled" with a child. I'm a better grandfather than I ever was a dad. I don't think Jessica would have been better off dead, but I was often mean.

The 1970s Evangelical antiabortion movement that Dad, Koop, and I helped create seduced the Republican Party. By the early 1980s the Republicans were laboring under the weight of a single-issue religious test for heresy: abortion. I was there—and/or Dad was—participating in various meetings with Congressman Jack Kemp, Presidents Ford, Reagan, and Bush, Sr., when the unholy marriage between the Republican Party and the Evangelical Reconstructionist-infected "pro-life" community was gradually consummated. Dad and I—as did many other Evangelical leaders like Jerry Falwell—met one on one or in groups with key members of the Republican leadership quite regularly to develop a "pro-life strategy" for rolling back *Roe v. Wade.* (Senator Jesse Helms named Dad as his favorite author when asked by the *American Spectator* magazine to name his favorite books.)

And that strategy was simple: Republican leaders would affirm their antiabortion commitment to Evangelicals, and in turn we'd vote for them—by the tens of millions. Once Republicans controlled both houses of Congress and the presidency, "we" would reverse *Roe*, through a constitutional amendment and/or through the appointment of antiabortion judges to the Supreme Court or, if need be, through civil disobedience and even violence, though this was only hinted at—at first.

When Evangelical and Republican leaders sat together, we discussed "the issue," but we would soon move on to the practical particulars, such as "Will blue-collar Catholic voters join us now?" (They did.) Soon Evangelical leaders were helping political leaders to send their message to the "pro-life community" that they—the Republican leaders—were on board.

For instance, I organized the 1984 publication of President Ronald Reagan's antiabortion book with Evangelical Bible publisher Thomas Nelson. Reagan's book had first appeared as an essay in the *Human Life Review* (Spring 1983). I was friends with *Human Life Review* founder and editor: the brilliant Roman Catholic antiabortion crusader Jim McFadden. He and I cooked up the presidential project over the phone.

The president's book expressed his antiabortion "views" as ghostwritten by McFadden in order to cement the Reagan "deal" with the antiabortion movement. We called the book *Abortion and the Conscience of the Nation.* I suggested to Reagan's people that two Schaeffer family friends—C. Everett Koop and Malcolm Muggeridge (a famous British writer/social critic and convert from Far Left politics to rabid Far Right Roman Catholicism with whom my father once led a huge pro-life demonstration in Hyde Park, London)—provide us with afterwords to "bulk out" an otherwise too brief book, which they did within a week or two after I called them.

Once they were "on board," Republican leaders like Senator Jesse Helms and Congressmen Jack Kemp and Henry Hyde (to name but three whom I met with often, in Jack's case in his home, where I stayed as a guest) worked closely with my father and me, and we (along with a lot of other religious leaders) began to deliver large blocs of voters. We even managed "our" voters for the Republican Party by incessantly reminding our followers of "the issue" through newsletters, TV, and radio broadcasts. For instance, I worked closely with James Dobson in the early days of his "Focus on the Family" radio program, and I was on his show several times. He offered my "pro-life" book *A Time for Anger* as a fund-raising fulfillment and distributed over 150,000 copies. The book eventually sold over half a million copies.

No one seemed to notice (or mind) that the Republicans weren't really *doing* anything about abortion other than talking about it to voters. And by the mid- to late 1980s the cause shifted: We Evangelicals paid lip-service to "stopping abortion," but the real issue was keeping Republicans in power and keeping Evangelical leaders in the ego-stroking loop of having access to power.

Fast-forward thirty years to the early twenty-first century: The messengers, leaders, and day-to-day "issues" changed, but the *volume* and *tone* of the antigovernment "debate" and the anger in reaction to the Obama presidency originated with the antiabortion movement. To understand where that anger came from and who first gave voice to it, consider a few prescient passages from my father's immensely influential book (influential within the Evangelical ghetto, that is) *A Christian Manifesto*, which was published in 1981.

As you read these excerpts, bear in mind what would take place in the health care "debates" over what came to be disparaged as "Obamacare" thirty years or so after my father's book was read by hundreds of thousands of Evangelicals. Anti-health-care-reform rhetoric—"Death Panels!" "Government Takeover!" "Obama is Hitler!"—that the Far Right spewed in the policy debates of 2009 and beyond seemed to be ripped from the pages of Dad's and my writings. Note the ominous rhetorical shadow Dad's book cast over a benighted and divided American future, a future that produced the climate of hate that eventually spawned the murder of abortion providers such as Dr. George Tiller in Wichita in 2009.

The "background noise" of harsh words also foreshadowed the 2011 shooting of Congresswoman Gabrielle Giffords in Tucson. I don't for a moment believe that this tragedy was related to the abortion issue, let alone to Dad or to me. But irrespective of whose "fault" the killings and attempted killings were on that day, one thing *is* certain: *The furious political climate at that time meant that no one was surprised when a deranged young man opened fire on a political leader.*

In a country awash in weapons and wallowing in the rhetoric of rebellion against an "evil" government, sporadic outbursts of murder tinged with political overtones seem as inevitable as they seem horribly "normal." It doesn't seem like much of a stretch to foresee a day when a "secessionist" group and/or members of some "militia"—let alone one lone individual—will use their U.S. passports, white skins, and solid-citizen standing as a cover for importing a weapon of mass destruction to "liberate" the rest of us from our federal government's "tyranny" and/or to "punish" some city like New York, known as the U.S. "abortion capital" or San Francisco as the place that "those gays have taken over." And the possibility of an assassination in the same vein is a never-ending threat. What we fear most from Islamist terrorists could also be unleashed on us by our very own Christian and/or Libertarian activists.

Here's a bit from *Manifesto* on how the government was "taking away" our country and turning it over to Liberals, codenamed by Dad as "this total humanistic way of thinking":

> The law, and especially the courts, is the vehicle to force this total humanistic way of thinking upon the entire population.*

And this:

> Simply put, the Declaration of Independence states that the people, if they find that their basic rights are being systematically attacked by the state, have a duty to try and change that government, and if they cannot do so, to abolish it.**

Then this:

> There does come a time when force, even physical force, is appropriate. . . . A true Christian in Hitler's Germany and in the occupied countries should have defied the false and counterfeit state. This brings us to a current issue that is crucial for the future of the church in the United States, the issue of abortion. . . . It is time we consciously realize that when any office commands

---

*Francis Schaeffer, *A Christian Manifesto* (Westchester, IL: Crossway Books, 1981), 49.
**Ibid., 128.

what is contrary to God's law it abrogates its authority. And our loyalty to the God who gave this law then requires that we make the appropriate response in that situation.*

In other words, Dad's followers were told that (1) force is a legitimate weapon to use against an evil government; (2) America was like Hitler's Germany—because of legal abortion and of the forcing of "Humanism" on the population—and thus intrinsically evil; and (3) whatever would have been the "appropriate response" to stop Hitler was now *appropriate to do here in America* to stop our government, which Dad had just branded a "counterfeit state."

Dad's books sailed under the radar of the major media, which weren't paying much attention to religious books despite the powerful influence they were having on the direction of American politics. *Manifesto* sold more than 1 million copies in Evangelical bookstores. It also set the stage for countless acts of civil disobedience and antiabortion vandalism. The book became the "Bible" for such activist antiabortion groups as Operation Rescue and for Far Right leaders like Dr. James Dobson (of the Focus on the Family ministry), who would (from then on) often quote from Dad's (and my) books on air. And *Manifesto* was far from unique. It was just the first drop of what would become a river of Religious Right (and secular right-wing) books, radio shows, and TV programs viciously blaming "Liberals" and the U.S. government for all that was wrong in America.

Thirty years or so after Dad was comparing America to Hitler's Germany, Reverend Jeremiah Wright (then Senator Obama's pastor) thundered about sin, racism, and injustice. During the 2008

---

*Ibid., 117–118.

election, Wright was accused of treason by the conservative media for his "anti-American" views because in a fiery sermon he'd said "God damn America." Senator and (then) presidential candidate Obama suffered smear by association. But when my father and I had denounced America and even called for the overthrow of the U.S. government because it was "pro-abortion," and thus "humanistic" and "counterfeit," not to mention like Hitler's Germany, we were invited to lunch at the White House.

No one called us un-American. (We were white.)

Actually, we were profoundly *anti*-American. Dad and I contributed to a government-is-the-enemy climate in which eventually Timothy McVeigh found it thinkable to bomb the Murrah Federal Building in Oklahoma City. We had no personal connection to McVeigh, and he'd probably never heard of us, but some of our followers did kill abortion providers.

Dad and I both visited several of our antiabortion "troops," as Dad called them, in various jails serving sentences for blocking access to clinics. And Paul Hill, a Reconstructionist Presbyterian minister had read Dad's antiabortion books before Hill murdered Dr. John Britton and James Barrett (an abortion provider and his security escort) in 1994. James Kopp, who shot Dr. Barnett Slepian in 1998, had once written to Dad thanking him for his leadership. And Dad and I were close to the radical elements that started Operation Rescue, and they in turn were the breeding ground for individuals who began to break the law.

As I said, the same sort of "discourse" we'd used to denounce abortion when calling it "murder" and to predict that euthanasia and infanticide were going to be the "next step" resurfaced with a vengeance during the Obama presidency. The idea that the government was illegitimate also exploded, this time with a personal (often race-tinged) twist directed at President Obama: "He wasn't born here!" "He's not a real American!" "He was born in Kenya!" "He doesn't believe America is exceptional!" and so forth.

Some anti-Obama agitators even seemed to be trawling for assassins. For instance, one group started selling a Psalms 109:8 anti-Obama bumper sticker that read, "Let his days be few; and let another take his office." The underlying message was clear (at least to anyone raised in a Bible-believing home). The next verse in that Psalm reads, "Let his children be fatherless, and his wife a widow."

Dad and I were rewarded by the Republican leadership— admittedly before some of Dad's fans were killing doctors but *after* we were spreading antigovernment and anti-American venom— for our "stand." By the end of the 1970s the Republicans depended on agitators (or "prophetic voices") like us to energize their rank and file.

They still do. A multi-billion-dollar industry grew from the antiabortion movement's roots. Its sole business became the "winding up" of white middle- and lower-middle-class undereducated (often overtly anti-higher-education) religious fundamentalists and their fellow "patriotic" secular libertarian Far Right travelers. By the early twenty-first century these "just folks" were the core of the base of the Republican Party. (William F. Buckley, call your office!) As Rupert Murdoch, Fox News, Sarah Palin, Rush Limbaugh, Glenn Beck, Robert George, and others discovered, selling perpetual anger (not to mention self-pity and a sense of outraged victimhood) to the proudly misinformed leads to fortune.

Since my father's death in 1984 and in spite of his work having contributed to several murders of doctors, not to mention to a troubled period of American history in which threats against our leaders became more and more common, he's suffered no loss of admirers in top Evangelical circles. For instance, during the 2008 primary campaign, when Arkansas governor and presidential candidate (and Southern Baptist minister) Mike Huckabee was asked by Katie Couric to name the one book he'd take with him to a desert island, besides the Bible, he named Dad's book *Whatever Happened to the Human Race?* a book in which Dad had compared post–*Roe v. Wade* America to Hitler's Germany and Stalin's Russia. And here's how another "respectable" Evangelical leader endorsed my father's books. "[*How Should We Then Live?*] is a modern-day classic, one of Schaeffer's books that awakened me to how biblical truth affects all of life," writes Charles Colson.*

To the post-*Roe* Right, hating the American government became the new patriotism. And, yes, other issues were involved besides *Roe* in goading Evangelicals and other members of the Right into a defensive crouch, but those issues—racial integration, a ban on prayer in public schools, gay rights, immigration and so on— paled in comparison to the slam-dunk blanket legalization of abortion when it came to stoking the flames of alienation.

Abortion is still the perfect winner-take-all means for inflaming the "base" of both sides, which have a Pavlovian response to even hearing the code words "choice," "life," "family values," and "abortion." I know. I raised over $5 million to make those two antiabortion documentary film series with Dad, including the one with Dr. Koop, and to fund our nationwide series of seminars. Over 100,000 people attended the more than forty seminars we ran, and the movies were later seen by millions of people in tens of thousands of churches, not to mention the best-selling books that went with the movies.

---

*www.amazon.com/How-Should-We-Then-Live/dp/1581345364/ref=sr _1_1?s=books&ie=UTF8&qid=1285237692&sr=1-1.

And here's the part my pro-choice friends won't like me mentioning and that I rarely see discussed in the Left's version of the Right's echo chambers: Pro-choice advocates were as much to blame for the start of the culture wars as the people on the antiabortion side who reacted to *Roe*.

It takes two to start an all-consuming culture war. Pro-choice advocates made some mind-bogglingly dumb (and extreme) choices in the tactics they used to pursue abortion rights. Both sides missed the point: The abortion "issue" intersects with *actual lives* and *emotions*. The antiabortion side talked about abortion as if women with lives, hopes, and dreams weren't at the heart of the question. And the pro-choice advocates seemed to forget something, too: that the "fetal tissue" they dismissed as irrelevant looked very much like the rest of us when seen in an ultrasound image, or, as my mother lamented about her lost baby, "He had all his little fingers and toes."

CHAPTER 7

The Girl
Who Let Me

Time travel was possible in the Swiss Alps. By mid-April the crocuses had faded, but if I wanted to revisit early spring, all I needed to do was to walk up the path above the village. Changing altitude meant I could find yellow, purple, and white crocuses. I could pick which week or month I wanted to visit and turn the clock forward or back. In the lower valleys crocus and anemones flowered early with the snowmelt. Then they disappeared, with only their leaves remaining. But as the season advanced, I could pick a large bunch of field flowers for Mom in May above our house and then pick the same kinds of flowers for her again a month later a half a mile higher up the mountain long after our village's hay fields were cut.

But when it came to Girls, no matter what season, they had either bloomed and were taken or they were stuck in a perpetual winter and uninterested in pollinating. And at L'Abri they were twenty and I was thirteen. I knew that Girls didn't need what I needed—*to pollinate!*—and that there was no way to hurry, let

PHOTO: *Mom pounding on her old manual typewriter in 1962*

145

alone manipulate, their seasons, no way to bridge the gap between their ages and mine, their mysterious chaste winter and my ardent spring. Unlike field flowers, Girls didn't fit any perennial patterns that would help predict when they were *supposed* to bloom. I knew nothing of their pollination prospects other than Mom's mantra about "before" and "after" that all-important Wedding Night.

I'd look at Girls but knew that they weren't looking back at me—That Way. Desire seemed to be a one-way street. Women seemed maddeningly whole, whereas I was anxiously incomplete. I regarded what I wanted to do *to* Girls as my very own special Sinful Need. I figured that I'd have to somehow trick some Girl into letting me fulfill My Need before she figured out what was going on.

Of course, this was *if* I were to pollinate *before* my Wedding Night. After that, according to Mom, a miracle would happen and the heretofore uninterested female whom God had picked out for me would *willingly* take off *all* her clothes *any time I asked her to,* and best of all, then it would be OKAY with Mom and also with God!

"Men," Mom said, "are notorious." Girls who didn't wait "fell pregnant." Girls were victims of boys. Mom presented premarital sex as something boys did *to* Girls not *with* Girls. The import of Mom's instructions was to beg me to curb my Desires long enough so that I wouldn't join the ranks of "those sorts of men"—the predators—who made some poor girl "stumble."

So when any Girl had let me do anything to her, on some rare occasion and as if by chance, I was surprised. I assumed that she was just being absentminded. Patti (the daughter of a family of visiting missionaries) let me hold her hand when I was six and she was seven. I kissed Jennifer (the daughter of a L'Abri worker) when we were nine, but that was just a good-bye kiss on her unexpectedly proffered cheek after her birthday party. Her sister Amy was sixteen *and had breasts* and wore *tight* red-and-green plaid capri pants and *form-fitting* sweaters. I *wanted* Amy, *not* Jennifer!

Despite my mother's best efforts to explain the depths of Female Mystery to me, I was in love with at least one of Our Girls out of every batch who lived in our chalet. I would hang around The Girl Of The Moment full of longing and misinformation as to what Girls want, let alone *when* they might want it. Gauzy descriptions of What Happens On Your Wedding Night and/or King David's Sin and how to get an *actual* twenty-year-old named Jane—who was visiting us from Wisconsin and who had short sassy blond hair that positively sparkled in the sunlight *while* framing a perfect face *and* dazzling blue eyes—to kiss the twelve-year-old version of me was another matter altogether.

The Girl Who Let Me was French and the same age as me when we met in the summer of 1964. We were both thirteen. She was the village pastor's niece visiting from France. It was early July, so the hay field above the back road was full of field flowers—Queen Anne's lace, ox-eye daisies, and buttercups—tangled up with the tall grass into lovely swaying thickets of vivid color. Swiss Alpine meadows are made mostly of flowering plants. The day was warm and the dense two-to-three-foot-tall hay field–flower meadow provided sweet-smelling privacy, a screen to shield us when we lay down while being serenaded by crickets.

I'd happened to walk past the village parsonage that morning. It was a large three-story house about a quarter of a mile from ours. The Girl Who Let Me was standing by the gate. That's where we met. Like all the state-owned buildings in the canton of Vaud, the village parsonage had solid shutters painted with wide green-and-white stripes, and it was made of imposing masonry.

I'm guessing that The Girl Who Let Me had been looking at the mountains, waiting for a boy, any boy, to come along. I wish I could remember her name. I said hello, and she said hello, and I said I lived up the road—not mentioning that I was one of the weird missionaries, though later she told me she knew who I was because her uncle disapproved of us Schaeffers and said so. Anyway, that first day she didn't ask awkward questions. I asked her where she was from, and she answered Paris, and then, with a sudden flash of inspiration, I asked her if she'd like to go for a walk because the crocuses were still blooming only a fifteen-minute hike up the steep path.

She said yes!

Just as we got deep into the pine and beech forest after walking about a half a mile up the trail (which cut almost vertically into the woods from our back road up to the peaks above us), The Girl Who Let Me put her hand in mine. *She actually initiated the contact by slipping her fine-boned delicate cool little fingers into my palm.* I didn't dare to look at her in case that would make her realize what she'd done since I assumed this hand-holding was some sort of mistake. Maybe she was so used to pairing up two by two for school walks—as the Swiss and the French made their youngsters do when forming them up in rows—that we weren't really holding hands the way I hoped we were (like a married couple On Their Way To The Wedding Night) but just doing something she thought all children had to do on walks.

One of the great things about The Girl Who Let Me—besides the fact she *kept* holding my hand the way I hoped some Girl would someday and that "someday" was *miraculously today*—was that she turned to me and said, "*Tu es très mignon*" (You're very cute). Oh, for the chance to walk up my mountainside into that spring day again. I'd like to really talk to her this time. I'd like to ask her who taught her how to keep gently guiding my hand away from her lap and how many babies she has had during the years since we met and whom she married and if her life has been happy and if she remembers me. Mainly I'd like to thank The Girl Who Let Me.

Does she, like me, bathe her grandchild toddlers these days while singing "Ba Ba, Black Sheep" at the top of her lungs and then howling with them "like wolves"? Does she draw pictures for her grandchildren of "bad kitties" knocking over plates and glasses while the cats are jumping over a table chasing mice? Is Beatrix Potter's *A Tale of Two Bad Mice* also a favorite in her household? Has it surprised The Girl Who Let Me that the best thing that ever happened to her is her grandchildren's love? Does she feel disconnected from that thirteen-year-old French girl who let that American boy hold her hand? Could she please send me a picture of herself as she was then and one of herself now with her family around her because I can't remember her face, only that her hair was light brown and a bit frizzy, and that she was so very slender, and that her Nipple was a pale translucent mauve that matched the lavender crocuses on the mossy bank just above where we were lying.

We kissed in the woods. She let me touch her breast after I managed to push her bra up, or rather push a cup up—after she opened her blouse (matter 'a fact as you please). It wasn't a big lacy contraption like the ones on our chalet's laundry line. It was simple, small, and made of a flower print decorated with tiny pink rosebuds. The problem was that I couldn't kiss her *and* stare at The Nipple, so I intermittently did one activity while pretending not to do the other since I was more interested in *seeing*—AT LAST—than in kissing. And that's why I can't remember her face. Seeing The Nipple was like looking into the sun; it obliterated my ability to perceive almost anything else.

The Girl Who Let Me used her tongue's tip and flicked it back and forth over my tongue tip so quickly that it felt like the electric toothbrush Dad had recently purchased and let me try out. I was startled. I'd never been told that tongues would be involved! I knew all about how "Your precious seed will swim up into your wife's womb and meet the precious egg," but Mom said nothing about tongues.

I kissed The Girl Who Let Me with my mouth closed. Then, during the *second kiss* I suddenly felt this little wet sliver of *something* push through my lips, past the gate of my teeth, and then *meet my tongue* and flick back and forth at a rate of about fifty revolutions per second. I was fascinated and delighted. She was *doing* something *to* me *on purpose.*

She initiated all phases of our physical contact, while I carefully lay *across* and *away* from her at a right angle, not on her. I was keeping my crotch pressed firmly to the ground. I didn't want this wonderfully accommodating and supremely kind Girl to feel my dreadful erection pressing against her, something I was embarrassed by and knew that she—and of course all Girls—would hate! I was sure she'd jump up and run for home if she discovered my shame.

Even after I learned that Girls don't mind feeling an erection pressed against them, for several years after kissing The Girl Who Let Me I thought that the light speed-tongue-flicking method was the proper way to use tongues when kissing. It took several more encounters for me to understand that maybe The Girl Who Let Me was as inexperienced as I was that blissful morning and that maybe she'd heard about tongues from a friend and misunderstood the technical details. Still, I had good reason to trust her expertise: The Girl Who Let Me was *French.* Mom always said that the French were "tragically promiscuous."

Later, when I kissed other Girls, I assumed that they didn't know the right way to kiss. Their tongues moved *so slowly*. I resisted all newfangled tongues thrust all the way into my mouth like slow writhing snakes. I loyally stuck to what I'd been taught by The Girl Who Let Me. After all, she'd been so kind—not once but every day for two golden nipple-exposing, tongue-flicking, hand-holding weeks.

What did The Girl Who Let Me want that afternoon? By patiently guiding my straying hands away from her lap (again and again), she made it clear that kissing—and a glance at The Nipple—was all I was going to get. And, of course, with an erection to hide, there was no climbing on top.

It was one thing to stick my Little Thing into my ice sculpture. Who cared if Seth saw my erection? We experimented all the time. How far could we pee over a cliff? What did it feel like to shove a twig up It? (Big mistake.) Could we write our names with pee in the snow? But Seth seeing my Little Thing was one thing. A Girl seeing It, let alone feeling It pressing against her, presented a whole different magnitude of mortification.

The Girl Who Let Me and I had a spiritual connection, too, that gave our inexpert tongue flicking a friendly foundation. As I said, her uncle was the village Protestant state church pastor. Even though he was a "liberal Barthian," as Dad had called him, nevertheless The Girl Who Let Me and I were both connected to the pastoring trade. Also, she wasn't a villager but an outsider like me. So when one bright morning I walked down the path to the vicarage gate, and she wasn't there, my heartsick pang cut deep.

She'd said nothing about leaving! I walked back to the vicarage every day for the rest of the summer. The Girl Who Let Me never was at the gate again. I finally asked Alice where The Girl Who Let Me was. Alice (who always knew everything about my doings) said that "*ta petite amie*" had returned to France.

By early fall I drummed up my courage to go right up to the front door of the vicarage and ask the pastor where his niece was and if I could have her address. He told me that she'd been sent back to France early *because of me* and never to come to his house again. I spoke French to him, but he answered in English, as if to emphasize that I was most certainly an unwelcome outsider. I was a "bad influence," he said. And he also said that his niece had traveled to Huémoz to breathe "good mountain air," not to be "molested by American boys." And, he added a parting shot in haughty Swissified English, "what a large pity it is that ze authorities were so foolish as to have giving your family residency permit C for unfolding of your sect amongst us!" (The Swiss were not generous with giving residency permits to foreigners. The most coveted permit was the full residency, unlimited "Permit C." My parents had these permits, but other workers at L'Abri rarely got them, and this was a subject of constant prayer, "that the hearts of the commune of Ollon officials might be moved").

I'm sure The Girl Who Let Me didn't tell her uncle about us, let alone what she let me do. She had always greeted every mention of her uncle with a sigh. So how did he know I'd "molested" his niece? Maybe the hay wasn't high enough by the edge of the forest path, and he'd been scanning the mountainside above the vicarage using binoculars. I could only be thankful that my parents and this local Swiss pastor weren't on speaking terms.

Four years after The Girl Who Let Me and I were kissing on that mountainside, I got Genie pregnant and she turned out to be my wife. If the Girl Who Let Me ever reads this, then I'd like to say to her—rather to you, *Ma Chérie*—that all this stuff about waiting for the "right time and right age" and "right person" is nonsense. How long do we think we have? Many of my friends say they envy me my grandchildren. That's odd. Measured by their idea of success and how to achieve it, Genie and I and our children have taken the "wrong path" by having children "too young." And the strange thing is that my aging and envious friends' childless children are doing *just what their parents pushed, begged, even forced them to do*: "succeed," with a vengeance, while putting having children on hold.

Serendipitous, messy, and joy-filled bodily-fluid-lubricated natural life, babies, and grandbabies (in other words, Love) matter most to me. I hope, *Ma Chérie*, that you found your own version of what Genie and I (and you and me almost) stumbled into by dumb luck and horny abandon—a life full of children, grandchildren, and friendship.

When I run into the sorts of striving people who are *shocked* if you have a child before age thirty-five or so, if at all, as they chase a second master's degree and who act as if Nature and Love are a mere footnote to Career, Mom's example of putting Life first kicks in. Mom's idea that Family is a blessing has proved true. I am glad I had babies at the "wrong" age. Whatever path led to two-year-old Lucy and me working on my old broken Pinocchio, as we glued him back together, let alone her joy as she hugged me and exclaimed, "Thank you *so much*, Ba, for fixing him!" is an experience I'd choose a thousand times over anything my career has ever offered me. And six-month-old Jack grabbing my nose and shrieking with delight while radiating effervescent joy is not *a* blessing but *the* blessing of my life.

When at age seventeen, you get your girlfriend pregnant, and later your own children start families fairly young, you wind up with grandchildren the same ages as some of your friends' children. So when Genie and I walk around with Amanda (age eighteen) and Ben (age fifteen), people assume they're our kids. "You're too young to be grandparents of a eighteen-year-old!" they exclaim with a smile, as if offering Genie and me a compliment. What's really happening is that we've upset their idea of what it means to be good, upstanding, twenty-first-century, kids-canwait, upper-middle-class whites.

Most upper-middle-class white North Americans think that it's normal for black, brown, and Latino people to have grandchildren "too early." But upper-middle-class whites aren't supposed to have kids early, let alone have teenage grandchildren before they're in their sixties. Sure, we live in a nice house overlooking the Merrimack River, and between us, Genie and I have ancestors who sailed on the *Mayflower* and one (Genie's mother's great-great . . . grandfather) who signed the Constitution of the United States. So we *seem* okay as far as that goes, at least to the sort of people who *really care* about trying to get their children into Harvard. But I think that some of our snobbier friends suspect that Genie and I may also lead Wolfman-at-full-moon-type double lives. Maybe at night we turn into junk-food-loving porkers, sneak off to a trailer park with our brood of kids and grandkids, and lounge in a Winnebago surrounded by broken-down cars up on blocks, watch wrestling on TV, buy liquor with ill-gotten food stamps, scarf corn chips and bean dip, gain weight and put on dreadful sweat pants, sprout mullet haircuts, then trudge the isles of Wal-Mart until dawn breathing the plastic smell and loving it while, with each step, the cheeks of our suddenly gigantic bottoms rise, quiver, fall, and rise again like massive sacks of Jell-O strapped to the hindquarters of water buffalo.

My parents put me on the Grandchild Path by their life example of putting people and relationships ahead of material possessions and even ahead of their theological beliefs. When it came to living, Mom was balanced and moderate. She believed in planning children whether she officially said God was sovereign or not. On the other hand, she didn't believe in planning too much, let alone think that material stuff, prestige, and Career could ever make anyone happy if he or she gave up (or postponed) Love, Family, and Children for a materialistic mirage.

But not all Evangelicals were as sensible as my parents were when it comes to family matters. Consider that in 2009 over 6,000 women met in Chicago for the "True Woman Conference," to call women to "Complementarianism"—in other words, to join the Reconstructionist Patriarchy Movement called by another less-forbidding name. The organizers used their conference to launch the "True Woman Manifesto." A clause in the preamble reads, "When we respond humbly to male leadership in our homes and churches, we demonstrate a noble submission to [male] authority that reflects Christ's submission to God His Father."

"We are believing God for a movement of reformation and re-vival in the hearts and homes of Christian women all around this world," the group's leader, Evangelical best-selling author/guru and "motivational speaker" Nancy Leigh DeMoss, said in her opening remarks. The other speakers at the conference included some of the foremost leaders of the twenty-first-century "mainstream" Evan-gelical world.* I'm guessing that none of those leaders would have publicly embraced Reconstructionism. Nevertheless, by lending their presence to that meeting, they were implicitly endorsing the Reconstructionist view of women and the "divine male headship of women ordained by the Bible" to which my mother paid lip-service

---

*Speakers included Pastor John Piper; Christian radio personality Nancy Leigh DeMoss; Southern Baptist Theological Seminary professor and antifeminist au-thor Mary Kassian; J. Ligon Duncan III, chairman of the board for the Council for Biblical Manhood and Womanhood; and Susan Hunt, an author and consul-tant to the Presbyterian Church in America's Women in the Church Ministry. The conference was organized by DeMoss's St. Louis–based ministry, Revive Our Hearts, a "women's ministry" that teaches that female "submission" to men will bring America back to God.

(when pressed) but contradicted by the way she lived her whole fiercely independent life.

Women are "called to encourage godly masculinity" by *submitting* to men, says the "True Woman Manifesto" those leaders assembled to sign. Women must "submit to their husbands and [male-only] pastors." According to this view of what I'll call Godly Groveling Women, women must "honor the God-ordained male headship" of their husbands by allowing their Men to rule them. Thus, selfish rights (as in the Bill of Rights) are "antithetical to Jesus Christ." So The Godly Groveling True Woman believes that she must (as it were) rent her womb to God (and thus to a Reconstructionist revolution in whatever name) in order to embrace "fruitful femininity."

In other words, roll over, Mom. Your Most Private Place is not yours, and it's not private. Your womb is God's, and He needs lots more Spiritual Warriors. And while we're at it, no more Talks. You're a second-class citizen, Edith, who must follow your husband's lead, for the Patriarchy Movement tells you so!

For those who missed the conference, the way to a "Complete Submission Makeover" was made easy. According to the True Woman Web site, "Don't miss out—take the 30-Day True Woman Make-Over to discover and experience God's design and calling for your life! Join Nancy Leigh DeMoss on a journey through Proverbs 31, 1 Timothy 2:9–10, and Titus 2:1–5. For thirty days, we'll send this email directly to your inbox, complete with biblical teaching; helpful links, printable downloads, and recommended resources."*

What Nancy Leigh DeMoss was doing with her "Complete Submission Makeover" was to extend the reach of a fringe funda-

---

*See www.truewoman.com.

mentalist movement—the "Quiverfull Movement"—into the Evangelical mainstream. (The name of the Quiverfull Movement alludes to Psalm 127:3: "Lo, children are an heritage of the LORD and the fruit of the womb is his reward. As arrows are in the hand of a mighty man; so are children of the youth. Happy is the man that hath his quiver full of them: they shall not be ashamed.")

Some Quiverfull leaders have argued against allowing daughters to attend college, as worldly outsiders might destroy their faith. Daughters, they say, should stay at home after they graduate from homeschooling. Daughters should practice being a "helpmeet" to their fathers, training to someday "serve" those godly husbands God will send their way. Some Quiverfull women are not allowed to drive. Others make lists of their daily tasks to submit to their husbands. Quiverfull wives *are* carrying on at least one of Mom's rules, however: They believe that it is their duty to be sexually available to their husbands at all times. If a husband strays because of a wife's refusal, it's her fault.

Mary Pride, the modern-day Patriarchy/Quiverfull Movement's female founder, was often quoted at the True Woman Conference. Pride paved the way for the modern-era "submission movement" decades ago. She did so with my help.

Pride was one of my mother's followers and began to write me fan letters in the 1970s after I'd emerged as a successful rabble-rousing antiabortion leader. By then I was doing the rounds, speaking at the biggest and most politicized churches of the day, including Jerry Falwell's Liberty Baptist. I was even pursuing my own Evangelical media side project: the business of publishing and promoting Far Right books.

As a moonlighting literary agent, I represented my parents, as well as Koop, Whitehead, and several other Religious Right and (emerging) neoconservative authors. I'd begun my book agent line of work by negotiating contracts for my parents and getting them some record-setting advances (at least by the standards of those more modest times in the world of religious publishing). Then I was asked by Koop to represent his part of the coauthorship of Dad's and his *Whatever Happened to the Human Race?* Other people asked me to pitch books for them, too, and eventually I signed on about twenty authors.

In the early1980s, Pride sent me a manuscript for her first book, *The Way Home*, which was to become the "Bible" for the big-family/homeschool movement. Pride told her life story—how she moved away from her feminist and "anti-natal" beliefs and embraced Christianity. She explained how she found "true happiness" in the "biblically mandated role of wives and mothers as bearers of children." Pride wrote that "the church's sin which has caused us to become unsavory salt incapable of uplifting the society around us is [the] selfishness [of] refusing to consider children an unmitigated blessing."* In *The Way Home* Pride pitched huge families as the only way for women to be truly happy and the only way to change America and bring it back to its so-called Christian foundation.

Pride was interested in more than women just having babies; she wanted those babies indoctrinated. So Pride called for unleashing a new generation of godly homeschooled children onto the slumbering American mainstream in order to reform it.

I met resistance when selling Pride's first manuscript because her antifeminism struck even some Evangelical editors as extreme. I eventually got *The Way Home* published by convincing Crossway Books publisher and editor, Lane Dennis, to take on the book even though he doubted it would sell. Dennis had said, "No women want to read a 'women's book' that tells women to give up their rights."

---

*Mary Pride, *The Way Home* (Westchester, IL: Crossway Books, 1985), 28.

After arguing for a while, I snapped back that unless he took on my new author, I'd pull the whole Schaeffer oeuvre from his company— a heretofore minor tract publishing mom-and-pop outfit (also a printing company for hire) that had recently turned into an Evangelical publishing powerhouse based on the sales of the Schaeffer books. I also told Dennis that Pride's book would "become a movement." The Schaeffer books, as well as those by Pride and other of "my" authors, put Crossway on the map. My own books sold well, too, such as *A Time for Anger: The Myth of Neutrality.**

Pride's overnight success occurred for several reasons. She was a capable writer and was speaking to Jesus Victims who could be swayed by "the Bible says" arguments. Pride's success was also yet more evidence of the backlash against *Roe v. Wade* and the genuine heartfelt fury it generated in many women. Pride cashed in on the Reconstructionists' semiunderground network of homeschool groups founded by Rushdoony and took the homeschool message to a wider audience. The public schools in many areas of the country had degenerated into educational failures, so Pride also scored points about homeschooling with many parents who wanted the best for their children, irrespective of their religious or political views.

By the time I signed up Pride as an author-client, I was connecting my expanding "stable" of Far Right authors to Crossway Books, Thomas Nelson Publishers, Word Books, Zondervan, and

---

*I also published *Is Capitalism Christian?* (Westchester, IL: Crossway Books, 1985), a book of essays that I edited and for which Congressman Jack Kemp served as my advisor—feeding me material in keeping with his (then-popular) "supply-side" economic theories praising unregulated capitalism. *Bad News for Modern Man* (Westchester, IL: Crossway Books, 1984) was about "the liberal takeover of America." *A Modest Proposal* (Westchester, IL: Crossway Books, 1984), coauthored with Harold Fickett, took a stab at Swiftian satire about abortion.

Tyndale House and also to the neoconservative (Roman Catholic) Regnery Gateway Publishers. Henry Regnery and I used to talk on the phone and strategize about breaking the "stranglehold of the liberal media." Regnery copublished books with me and printed special *Christian Activist* and/or "Franky Schaeffer" editions of several Regnery books. Regnery even created a new imprint called "Discipleship Books." Across the top of each book, in large bold type, the words appeared: "A Franky Schaeffer/Christian Activist Book." Our projects included *Target America: The Influence of Communist Propaganda on U.S Media* by James L. Tyson, (1985); *Panic Among the Philistines* by Bryan F. Griffin (1985); and *The Coercive Utopians* by Rael Jean Isaac and Erich Isaac (1985). The books published under our joint imprint received glowing reviews in *Commentary*, the *American Spectator*, *Chronicles of Culture*, the *Wall Street Journal*, and other to-the-right publications.

The *Christian Activist* was my widely circulated antiabortion, antiliberal freebee newspaper. I was editor and founder. (The *Christian Activist* was published by Schaeffer V Productions.) The Evangelical version of the *Christian Activist* hit a circulation of about 250,000 in the early 1980s. After I left the Evangelical world, I re-created it as a short-lived Eastern Orthodox paper that reached a circulation of about 50,000. I stopped publishing that, too. I'd come to see that my "Christian" activism was antithetical to the spirit of the kind of religion I was inspired by: the Eastern Orthodox embrace of sacrament and community. (The Orthodox Church has a right wing, too, but the Orthodoxy I embraced, not to mention my local parish, was not of that ilk.) My politics was changing. By then I saw the neoconservatives as a threat to America and beyond. War without end—often in "defense of Israel"— seemed to be all the neoconservatives were really about as they fixated on a worship of military brute force put in service of some fuzzy imperial idea of so-called American exceptionalism . . .

Back in the day, Regnery told me that the editions of his books reprinted with my name on them as copublisher and then promoted in my newspaper sold more than the original editions. As he once said, "With the Schaeffer name on it, I can sell anything to the Evangelicals, and there are lots of them!" My Regnery copublishing ventures also included books by such neoconservatives as writer Richard Grenier. I got his procolonial *The Gandhi Nobody Knows* published as a counterstatement to the film *Gandhi*. Conservatives had reacted to the movie negatively because it was "soft" on Gandhi, it was "hard" on white men and colonialism, and, worst of all, it made Hinduism look okay in comparison to our "Judeo-Christian heritage."

As I mentioned, Erich Isaac and Rael Jean Isaac were also my clients, or rather I should say briefly my authors. The Isaacs were academics and ardent Zionists, and they were leaders in such groups as Americans for a Safe Israel. Through the Isaacs I was put in touch with other radically pro-Israel neoconservatives. This "bridge-building," in turn, introduced me to Norman Podhoretz, the editor of *Commentary* magazine, who was using the Republican Party and/or being used by it to advance his single issue—support for the state of Israel—just as I was doing the same for my single issue: abortion.

Commentary had emerged in the 1970s as the neoconservatives' flagship publication. I regularly reprinted some of its articles as books or as essays in my newspaper. And when my mother raised $50,000 from her pal Dallas multimillionaire Mary Crowley (founder of Home Interiors and Gifts) to launch Mom's new book, *Forever Music* (1986), Podhoretz lent his support.

Mom used Crowley's money to rent Alice Tully Hall at Lincoln Center and hire the Guarneri Quartet. Mom's "best friends"— about five hundred of them—showed up for the gala concert, as did Podhoretz and his wife, Midge Decter, and their entourage.

(I had invited them. Mom had no contact with the *Commentary* crowd.)

By then (the concert was held April 27, 1986) I was on my way out of the Evangelical world and was involved only because of my support for my mother's concert. It was close to her heart: a way to promote her book on her love of music. She'd spent months researching the Steinway piano company, inclusive of visits to its factories. Mom used the story of the Steinway Company as the hook to get people interested in her views on art and music.

I remember laughing at the bemused expressions on the faces of the members of the quartet while they sipped drinks at the postconcert reception as they tried to figure out how the hell the same space could be occupied by these two groups: the cream of the New York neoconservative Zionist intellectuals *and* a passel of mink-draped, diamond-crusted Southern Baptist Texans asking everyone if they had a "personal relationship with Jesus Christ."

Anyway, I was in a good position to "launch" not only Pride's book but also any project I wanted to get behind. It was in this capacity as a brash young wheeler-dealer, literary agent/author/filmmaker to the Religious Right, and Evangelical/pro-life link to the emerging neoconservative movement that I launched Mary Pride. And she, in turn, started a large movement that—like so much else that has come from the Reconstructionist-inspired Religious Right since the 1970s—flew under the radar of the mainstream media.

Major newspapers let down their readers rather badly. Maybe they just couldn't bring themselves to take what they regarded as rube religion seriously. The *New York Times* didn't even bother to review Reagan's antiabortion book, failing to mark the moment when a U.S. president officially signaled that the Republican Party had become the antiabortion party and would from then on be defined by one social issue above all others. I think that the editors of many major North American newspapers had decided that *Roe* and *Bolton* had settled the abortion issue. These were rulings that many editors lent the prestige of their editorial page to time and again. (Perhaps that was why the media also ignored Mary Pride.)

Pride went much further than anyone else had in pushing an antifeminist, wombs-for-revolution, post-*Roe* counterattack on modernity. She even broke ranks with her former idol, Edith Schaeffer!

Pride denounced Mom's embrace of family planning and good Sex. Mom just wasn't hard-line enough for take-no-prisoners Pride. So in her first book she reprimanded Mom for extolling foreplay, sexy underwear, and other such sex-friendly instructions to Christian wives. In fact, Pride didn't seem to like anything that might dilute the *only real reason* for copulating: making Godly children.

"Where on earth did you dig up This Unfortunate Woman?!" Mom asked me after reading Pride's critique of her recommendations about black nightgowns and foreplay. "Really, Darling, how *could* you?"

Many Reconstructionist-influenced pastors began using Pride's materials almost as soon as they were published because (*at last*) here was a *woman* telling other women to *submit* to *men*. And as luck would have it, Pride and her husband were computer experts back when few people were. So Quiverfull adherents were some of the first Internet users to exploit the potential of home computers. Homeschool groups began to network, and Pride became the leader of the Evangelical homeschool movement, which she, second only to Rushdoony, created in its anti-American incarnation.

When I say "anti-American," I mean anti-American *as America actually is*: multicultural, pluralistic, gay embracing, multiethnic, and based on a *secular* Constitution and the *secular* rule of law.

Pride and company would have claimed to be patriotic, but their loyalty was to a "Christian America." They seemed to have nothing but contempt for America as it actually was. They also ignored America's complex roots, as described wonderfully by the historian and cultural critic Jacques Barzun, who writes:

> Our [American] spirit is watered by three streams of thought, originally distinct, but here mingled: The eighteenth century enlightenment view of progress toward social reason, or what we Americans know as the Jeffersonian ideal; The Romanticist view of man's diversity, inventiveness and love of risk by which society is forever kept in flux, forever changing; The native tradition of Deafness to Doctrine which permits our Federal system to subsist at the same time as it provides free room for carrying out the behests of our other two beliefs.*

The Christian homeschool movement drove the Evangelical school movement to the ever-harsher world-rejecting Far Right. This happened because Evangelical homeschoolers were demanding ever-greater levels of "separation" from the Evil Secular World. It wasn't enough just to reject the public schools. How could the Christian parent be *sure* that even the Evangelical schools were sufficiently pure? And so the Christian schools radicalized in order to not appear to be compromising with The World in the eyes of increasingly frightened and angry Jesus Victim parents.

My account here of the rise of the homeschool movement is *not* aimed at homeschooling per se but at parents who want to indoctrinate rather than educate. There are many secular and also

---

*Jacques Barzun, *God's Country and Mine: A Declaration of Love, Spiced with a Few Harsh Words* (1954; repr. Santa Barbara, CA: Greenwood Press, 1973), 134.

religiously moderate homeschool parents doing the best they can for their children, many of whom go on to successful and happy lives and do tremendously well in college. In a climate where the public schools have been allowed to rot, with plenty of help from neglectful parents and teachers, good parents have the right to do whatever is necessary to help their children get an education, including schooling children at home and/or sending them to private secular or religious schools.

That said . . . what, Pride asked, was the point of having all those children and then turning them over to public schools to be made into secular humanists and Jesus-hating pagans?

The irony was that Pride preached a dogmatic, stay-at-home, follow-your-man philosophy for other women while turning her lucrative homeschooling empire into a one-woman industry.* So Pride may be added to the list of powerful women who just *love* those "traditional roles" for *other* women. And Pride's successor in the Patriarchy Movement, the wealthy author/guru Nancy Leigh DeMoss, was also one of those do-as-I-say-not-as-I-do best-selling

---

*Pride published many more books after I quit as her agent (at almost the same time as I dropped out of the whole Evangelical movement). Her books include *The Way Home* (Westchester, IL: Crossway Books, 1985); *The Big Book of Home Learning* (Westchester, IL: Crossway Books, 1986); *The Next Book of Home Learning* (Westchester, IL: Crossway Books, 1987); *The New Big Book of Home Learning* (Westchester, IL: Crossway Books, 1988); *All the Way Home* (Westchester, IL: Crossway Books, 1989); *The Child Abuse Industry* (Westchester, IL: Crossway Books, 1986); *Schoolproof* (Westchester, IL: Crossway Books, 1988); *Unholy Sacrifices of the New Age* and *Ancient Empires of the New Age* (Westchester, IL: Crossway Books, 1988, The "Old Wise Tales" series: *Too Many Chickens, The Greenie, The Better Butter Battle, Baby Doe* (Nashville, TN: Wolgemuth and Hyatt, 1990); *The Big Book of Home Learning*, 4 vols.: *Getting Started, Preschool & Elementary, Teen & Adult, Afterschooling* (Westchester, IL: Crossway Books, 1991); *Pride's Guide to Educational Software with husband Bill Pride* (Westchester, IL: Crossway, 1997); and *Mary Pride's Complete Guide to Getting Started in Homeschooling* (Wheaton, IL: Harvest House, 2004).

career women doing high-paid speaking gigs *while* encouraging
other women to stay home and *submit* to their men.

Nancy Leigh DeMoss happened to be the daughter of a former
friend of my mother's, Nancy DeMoss, who was instrumental in
my parents' rise to Evangelical superstardom. Nancy DeMoss was
also pivotal in the role of facilitator and financier when it came
to seamlessly merging Reconstructionist ideology with the "respectable" mainstream Evangelical community. I worked closely
with Nancy on several projects. She generously supported my various Schaeffer-related antiabortion movies, books, and seminar
tours. She also took our message much further on her own by underwriting a massive well-produced antiabortion TV and print
media ad campaign inspired by our work.

Soon after the death of her wealthy husband, Arthur DeMoss,
Nancy DeMoss had become my mother's friend and an ardent
Schaeffer follower. She also took over her late husband's foundation
as CEO. Besides underwriting several Schaeffer projects, Nancy
contributed millions to Republican and other Far Right causes (including $70,000 to start Newt Gingrich's political action commit-
tee, GOPAC). She also helped the Plymouth Rock Foundation, a
Reconstructionist-aligned group.

When Nancy's daughter (the aforementioned Nancy Leigh De-
Moss) took Pride's ideas to a bigger audience than Pride could
have imagined, she was just taking the next logical step begun by
her mother. Like my sisters and I, the DeMoss siblings found
themselves in their parents' orbit. The DeMoss children became
coworkers in the "cause," much as I filled that role in my family.
Nancy's other daughter, Deborah, worked for Senator Jesse Helms.
Nancy's son Mark worked for Jerry Falwell before founding the
DeMoss Group, a PR firm used by the likes of Billy Graham's son
Franklin. But unlike the Schaeffers, the DeMoss clan had tens of

millions of dollars with which to back its pet Far Right schemes, one of which would be the Quiverfull Movement.

The Quiverfull and Reconstructionist Movements have made for some weird bedfellows. I mean that in both senses of the word: It's *weird* that these folks connected, given their differing agendas and theologies, *and* these are weird people. What unites many extremist groups is only their shared sense of grievance and victimhood. For instance, there are fundamentalist Christians making connections with some ultra-Orthodox Jewish patriarchy enthusiasts, among whom some women take the contraceptive pill to avoid menstruation on their wedding night (keeping those Levitical laws up to date) so that they can have sex and remain "clean" and are then given fertility drugs by their rabbis to reverse the process and get the baby-making going. As one Jewish women's "health" site says of such interventions:

> Physical contact between husband and wife is prohibited while the wife is niddah (impure). Therefore, a Halacha observant bride (one who follows the Talmudic "way" or "path") will want to schedule her wedding for a date when she will not be niddah. She may turn to her health care provider for assistance in assuring that the timing is correct. This is not merely a request to avoid menstruation on her wedding night. All bleeding needs to have ceased at least one week before the wedding, allowing her enough time to count seven clean days and then immerse in the mikveh (ritual purification) before she gets married.*

---

*This explanation of Jewish Orthodox purity regulations for women appears on Nishmat, a Web site for health care professionals. See Jerusalem Center for Advanced Jewish Study for Women, "Hormonal Cycle Manipulation for Brides," www.jewishwomenshealth.org/article.php?article=14.

The big-family agenda of the Patriarchy Movement reaches far and wide, across bizarre lines. For instance, some formerly notoriously anti-Semitic Roman Catholic groups in Poland want to return to a strict "many-children" world and now write appreciatively about the Orthodox Jews' many-children families. These Orthodox Jews are the people who are populating the West Bank of Israel with damn-international-law-peace-defeating "facts on the ground" (i.e., many children), as fundamentalist religious Zionists do their bit to drive the world back to their favorite period of history: the Bronze Age. And there are a number of leading Roman Catholics who are also part of this strange, informal, anticontraceptive alliance.

To plumb the depths of the tortured "reasoning" behind the Roman Catholic version of the Quiverfull Movement, consider the writing of Roman Catholic philosopher Elizabeth Anscombe. She's a heroine to today's leading conservative Roman Catholics. She wrote passionately in defense of the papal prohibition of contraception:

> In considering an action, we need always to judge several things about ourselves. First: is the *sort* of act we contemplate doing something that it's all right to do? Second: are our further or surrounding intentions all right? Third: is the spirit in which we do it all right? Contraceptive intercourse fails on the first count; and to intend such an act is not to intend a marriage act at all, whether or no we're married. An act of ordinary intercourse in marriage at an infertile time, though, is a perfectly ordinary act of married intercourse, and it will be bad, if it is bad, only on the second or third counts. . . . If contraceptive intercourse is permissible, then what objection could there be after all to mutual masturbation, or copulation *in vase indebito*, sodomy, buggery (I should perhaps remark that I am using a *legal* term here—not indulging in bad language), when normal

copulation is impossible or inadvisable (or in any case, according to taste)? It can't be the mere pattern of bodily behavior in which the stimulation is procured that makes all the difference! But if such things are all right, it becomes perfectly impossible to see anything wrong with homosexual intercourse, for example. . . . If you are defending contraception, you will have rejected Christian tradition. . . . It's this that makes the division between straightforward fornication or adultery and the wickedness of the sins against nature and of contraceptive intercourse. Hence contraceptive intercourse within marriage is a graver offence against chastity than is straightforward fornication or adultery."*

Here is how Robert George lauded this insane "argument" in his gushing Anscombe obituary:

In 1968, when much of the rest of the Catholic intellectual world reacted with shock and anger to Pope Paul VI's reaffirmation of Catholic teaching regarding the immorality of contraception, the Geach-Anscombe family toasted the announcement with champagne. Her defense of the teaching in the essay "Contraception and Chastity" is an all-too-rare example of rigorous philosophical argumentation on matters of sexual ethics. Catholics who demand the liberalization of their Church's teachings have yet to come to terms with Anscombe's arguments.**

Another Far Right Roman Catholic ideologue (and also an academic) even wrote a book calling on Christians, Jews, and Muslims

---

*G. E. M. Anscombe, "Contraception and Chastity" (London: Catholic Truth Society, 1975).
**Robert George, "Elizabeth Anscombe, R.I.P.: One of the 20th Century's Most Remarkable Women," *National Review*, February 3–4, 2001.

to join together in a *jihad against the secular West*. In *Ecumenical Jihad: Ecumenism and the Culture War* a former friend of mine, Peter Kreeft (a professor of philosophy at Boston College), called for "ecumenical jihad."* I met with Kreeft several times in my home in the 1980s and early 1990s while he was developing his "jihadist" ideas. I even published some of his articles in my *Christian Activist* newspaper.

Kreeft's was not a plea for blowing people up, and his book was published pre-9/11. His book was based on the fact that many believers in Roman Catholicism, Evangelical Protestantism, and Islam (at least in their fundamentalist forms) rejected the sexual revolution of the 1960s. Homosexuality is out, sex education is evil, and so on. Kreeft called on all believers to unite to overthrow "secularism" in the same antisecular spirit that Robert George channeled a few years later when trying to undermine the Obama administration through his brainchild, the "Manhattan Declaration." Kreeft called for an "alliance" of fundamentalist Protestants, Catholics, Jews, and Muslims to prosecute a culture war against what he viewed as the Western cultural elite.

Ecumenical Jihad was dedicated to Richard John Neuhaus, the late Roman Catholic convert priest, and to Charles Colson (who later teamed up with George to author the "Manhattan Declaration"). Neuhaus and I often talked on the phone when he was about to launch his Far Right *First Things* journal. Neuhaus asked me to contribute articles, which I did. According to what Neuhaus told me, *First Things* was supposed to be the pro-life version of Norman Podhoretz's *Commentary*. "To fill a gap," as Neuhaus put it to me.

---

*Peter Kreeft, *Ecumenical Jihad: Ecumenism and the Culture War* (San Francisco: Ignatius Press, 1996).

Podhoretz, who at first was friendly with Neuhaus, told me he broke with him over Neuhaus's "anti-American views," as Podhoretz put it. This was just after Neuhaus had started describing the U.S. government as an illegitimate "regime." As the *Washington Post* noted:

In an essay he wrote for *First Things*, [Neuhaus] likened the legal right to abortion to state-sponsored murder under the Nazi regime. "Law, as it is presently made by the judiciary, has declared its independence from morality," he wrote. "America is not and, please God, will never become Nazi Germany, but it is only blind hubris that denies it can happen here and, in peculiarly American ways, may be happening here." The polemical rhetoric offended many Jewish conservatives in particular and threatened to shatter the bonds that had united them. . . . Father Neuhaus played a central role in forging an alliance between evangelical Protestants and Catholics and in bringing conservative Christians into the Republican conservative coalition in the 1980s and 1990s.*

The groups Kreeft, Colson, and Neuhaus had in mind to "bring together" in an ecumenical jihad were alienated Evangelicals, Orthodox Jews, and conservative Roman Catholics, to which Kreeft added Muslims (not that any actually signed on to his program as far as I know). These groups did not share each other's theology, but they had a deeper link: anger at the "victimhood" imposed on them by modernity.

---

*Alexander F. Remington, "Priest, Conservative Richard Neuhaus," *Washington Post*, January 9, 2009, www.washingtonpost.com/wp-dyn/content/article/2009/01/08/AR2009010803685.html.

Kreeft and Neuhaus were calling abortion murder. Thus, the logic of their argument was that of my father's, too: The U.S. government was enabling murder and was thus disparaged as a "regime," even a "counterfeit state," that needed to be overthrown. George and Colson and the others who wrote and then signed the "Manhattan Declaration" (like Kreeft before them) also called for fundamentalists to unite if need be for civil disobedience to stop the U.S. government from passing laws that did not comply with their religious "values" and/or to undermine those laws if they were enacted.

So if the U.S. government legalized gay marriage and thus "compelled" all Americans (including church groups) to recognize gay men and women's civil rights, the government need no longer be obeyed when those laws affected religious people who disagreed with them. The "Manhattan Declaration" called believers to "not comply." And just as Neuhaus dismissed the U.S. government as a "regime"—and my father did the same when saying the government was a "counterfeit state"—George and his cosigners also used dismissive and demeaning language about the U.S. government.

The "Manhattan Declaration" called laws with which its signers disagreed "edicts," thereby conjuring up images of dictators handing down oppressive rules, rather than legitimately elected democratic bodies passing legislation. In other words, when the Right lost in the democratic process, "other means" to undermine the law were encouraged.

Neoconservative intellectuals like Neuhaus helped set the stage for the Quiverfull and Patriarchy Movements. They gave a gloss of intellectual respectability to what was nothing more than a theocratic, Far Right wish list. "Thinkers" like Neuhaus contributed to what I'll call the ideological background noise accompanying the rise of post-*Roe* demagogy.*

Here's how this "contribution" worked: Since the 1960s a vast religious population was seething because of the changes taking place in society. It was led by a group of self-appointed "prophetic voices." This leadership group of pastors, authors, and commentators was made up of a mix of sincere (if deluded) believers and outright charlatans. In turn the most sincere among these leaders looked for some sort of intellectual validation of their belief system. A select group of intellectuals stepped forward to give the "old-time" religion of others some sort of fig leaf of modern respectability. My father was one "fig leaf provider" for the Evangelicals. C. S. Lewis played his part, too.

People like Robert George have (more recently) provided the fig leaf for embattled ultraconservative Roman Catholics. In turn these fig-leaf providers revered an even smaller intellectual class: The high priests of conservative religious/philosophical thought. For instance, George (as we've seen) honored Anscombe. She was of one of the Roman Catholic Church's leading twentieth-century intellectuals, albeit a bizarre woman whose work seemed to plumb the depths of (literal) insanity when she hit on topics such as birth control and other Roman Catholic obsessions.

The point is this: A few smart people allowed a lot of less smart people to *feel smarter* because the few smart people could be claimed as "one of ours." Or as I've heard thousands of people say (something like this) over the years, "I met this guy who had all

---

*This was an updated version of the ideology of 1930s figures like Father Charles Coughlin. (Coughlin was an extremist Roman Catholic priest and one of the first religious leaders to use radio to reach a mass audience.

these tough questions about our faith. It was a good thing I had your dad's books handy to give him!"

There is an indirect but deadly connection between the "intellectual" fig-leaf providers and periodic upheavals like the loony American Right's sometimes-violent reaction to the election of people like Barack Obama. No, your average member of some moronic gun-toting Michigan militia is *not* reading Francis Schaeffer. But it's a question of legitimacy and illegitimacy. What the Religious Right, including the Religious Right's Roman Catholic and Protestant enablers, did was contribute to a climate in which the very legitimacy of our government—was questioned.

It was in the context of delegitimizing our government that actions by domestic terrorists like Timothy McVeigh became thinkable. In 1993 McVeigh told a reporter, "The government is continually growing bigger and more powerful and the people need to prepare to defend themselves against government control."* Change a word or two and his words could have been lifted from my father's book *A Christian Manifesto*, or for that matter from my *A Time for Anger* or, a few decades later, from statements by the so-called Tea Party.

The Far Right intellectual enablers began by questioning abortion rights, gay rights, school prayer rulings, and so forth. What they ended up doing was to help foster a climate in which—in the eyes of a dangerous and growing (mostly white lower class undereducated gun-toting) minority—the very legitimacy of the U.S. government was called into question, sometimes in paranoid generalities, but often with ridiculous specificity: for instance, in the

---

*"Domestic Terrorism 101—Timothy James McVeigh," Eyeonhate.com, http://en.wikipedia.org/wiki/Timothy_McVeigh#cite_note-22.

persistent lie that President Obama was not a citizen or was a Muslim or that the Federal Reserve and/or United Nations were somehow involved in a plot to "take away our freedoms" or that sensible gun control equaled "tyranny."

Not everyone was content to simply believe such lies. Some people took the next step and acted upon them. The night of December 14, 2008, Bruce Turnidge was in handcuffs and sitting next to an FBI agent in Turnidge's farmhouse in Oregon. He was ranting about the "need" for militias and cursing the election of an African American president. Hours earlier, his son, Joshua, had been arrested for allegedly causing a fatal bomb explosion.

"Bruce started talking about the Second Amendment and citizens' rights to carry firearms," said George Chamberlin, the FBI agent. "Bruce talked at length that the government should fear the people and that the people should not fear the government."*

According to press reports, people who knew Turnidge and his son said that they loved their guns, hated President Obama, and fantasized about starting a militia and a tent city in the woods for people who shared their radical beliefs. Prosecutors said that the Turnidges acted on that anger by planting a bomb that blew up inside a small-town bank in 2008, killing two police officers and maiming a third. Turnidge Senior regularly lectured anyone who would listen about the need for citizens to be armed in order to defend their freedom, and he had cheered the Oklahoma City federal building bombing. His son shared similar views. Prosecutor Katie Suver said both men believed the Obama administration

---

*Lynne Terry, "Bombing Defendant Bruce Turnidge Railed About the Government in a House Filled with Weapons," *The Oregonian*, October 7, 2010, www.oregonlive.com/pacific-northwest-news/index.ssf/2010/10/woodburn_bombing_trial.html.

would crack down on their rights to own guns. The attack occurred about a month after Obama was elected.*

In February 2010, a little more than a year after Obama's inauguration, Joseph Stack, a fifty-three-year-old software engineer, piloted a plane into an IRS building in Austin, Texas, and killed one man and injured several others. Before killing himself, Stack posted an online suicide note railing against the federal government and expressing grievances similar to those Neuhaus, Dad, and I had enumerated in our books and articles about the evils of the U.S. government, except without our "pro-life" twist. A Facebook group celebrating Stack had thousands of members sign on almost instantly after he was "martyred for our freedoms," as one contributor called it. The site featured the Gadsden flag (the flag with the logo "Don't Tread On Me") and these words: "Finally an American man took a stand against our tyrannical government that no longer follows the constitution and turned its back on its founding fathers and the beliefs this country was founded on."

In March 2010 the so-called Hutaree Militia, a right-wing, biblically inspired fundamentalist group, was alleged to have hatched a plot to kill police officers. Members of this outfit had planned attacks on police officers as a way of acting out their hatred for the government as well as a way to launch the civil chaos "predicted" in so-called End Times biblical prophecies. The day the plotters were arrested, I checked their online homepage. Here's what I found as their mission statement (misspellings in the original post, which has since been taken down, as has the site):

> As Christians we all are a part of the Souls of the Body of Christ, the one true church of Christ. . . . This is the belief of the Hutaree soldier, as should the belief of all followers in Christ be. We be-

---

*Ibid.

lieve that one day, as prophecy says, there will be an Anti-Christ. All Christians must know this and prepare, just as Christ commanded. . . . Jesus wanted us to be ready to defend ourselves using the sword and stay alive using equipment. The only thing on earth to save the testimony and those who follow it, are the members of the testimony, til the return of Christ in the clouds. . . . The Hutaree will one day see its enemy and meet him on the battlefield if so God wills it. . . . You can find the news we find in some of the places we have in the information sources section. Also you can get gear from some of the choice places we have on gear links.

I clicked on the Hutaree's "gear links" and found the Evangelical fish symbol on a catalog for mail-order weapons that proudly indicated that the company was run by "Bible believers." Then I checked the Hutaree's other links and found Evangelical organizations and other conservative groups, including *Worthy Christian News*, WorldNetDaily, Jack Van Impe Ministries, *Real Truth Magazine*, *Times of Noah—Current Events and Bible Prophecy*, Christian Apologetic Web site.

Following the election of our first black president, the "politics" of the Evangelical, Jewish, Roman Catholic, and Mormon Far Right was not the politics of a loyal opposition, but rather the instigation of revolution, which was first and best expressed by Rush Limbaugh when even before President Obama took office he said, "I hope Obama fails."*

---

*On January 16, 2009, Limbaugh told his listeners that he was asked by "a major American print publication" to offer a four-hundred-word statement explaining his "hope for the Obama presidency." He reported, "So I'm thinking of replying to the guy, 'Okay, I'll send you a response, but I don't need four hundred words; I need four: I hope he fails.'"

Ironically, at the very same time as Evangelicals like Dad, Mary
Pride, and I were thrusting ourselves into bare-knuckle politics,
we were also retreating to what amounted to virtual walled com-
pounds. In other words we lashed out at "godless America" and
demanded political change—say, the reintroduction of prayer
into public schools—and yet *also* urged our followers to pull their
own children out of the public schools and homeschool them.

The rejection of public schools by Evangelical Protestants was
a harbinger of virtual civil war carried on by other means. Protestants had once been the public schools' most ardent defenders.*
For instance, in the 1840s when Roman Catholics asked for tax
relief for their private schools, Protestants said no and stood
against anything they thought might undermine the public
schools that they believed were the backbone of moral virtue,
community spirit, and egalitarian good citizenship.

The Evangelical's abandonment of the country they called
home (while simultaneously demanding change in that society)
went far beyond alternative schools or homeschooling. In the
1970s and 1980s thousands of Christian bookstores opened, countless new Evangelical radio programs flourished, and new TV sta-
tions went on the air.** Even a "Christian Yellow Pages" (a guide
to Evangelical tradesmen) was published advertising "Christ-
centered plumbers," accountants, and the like who "honor Jesus."

New Evangelical universities and even new law schools appeared, seemingly overnight, with a clearly defined mission to "take

---

*See "Moral Education: A Brief History of Moral Education," "The Return of
Character Education," and "Current Approaches to Moral Education," http://
education.stateuniversity.com/pages/2246/Moral-Education.html#ixzz0oef
KiFH7.
**Christian product sales in the Christian Booksellers Association (CBA) alone
grew to $4.63 billion in '06, according to CBA's research. See www.cbaonline
.org/nm/timeline.htm.

back" each and every profession—including law and politics—"for Christ." For instance, Liberty University's Law School was a dream come true for my old friend Jerry Falwell, who (when I was speaking at his school in 1983 to the entire student body for the second time) gleefully told me of his vision for Liberty's programs: "Frank, we're going to train a new generation of judges to change America!" This was the same Jerry Falwell who wrote in *America Can Be Saved*, "I hope I live to see the day when, as in the early days of our country, we won't have any public schools."*

To the old-fashioned conservative mantra "Big government doesn't work," the newly radicalized Evangelicals (and their Roman Catholic and Mormon cobelligerents) added "The U.S. government is evil!" And the very same community—Protestant American Evangelicals—who had once been the bedrock supporters of public education, and voted for such moderate and reasonable men as President Dwight Eisenhower, became the enemies of not only the public schools but also of anything in the (nonmilitary) public sphere "run by the government."

As they opened new institutions (proudly outside the mainstream), the Jesus Victims doing this "reclaiming" cast themselves in the role of persecuted exiles. What they never admitted was that they were *self-banished* from mainstream institutions, not only because the Evangelicals' political views on social issues conflicted with most people's views, but also because Evangelicals (and other conservative religionists) found themselves holding the short end of the intellectual stick.

Science marched forth, demolishing fundamentalist "facts" with dispassionate argument. So science also became an enemy. Rather

---

*Jerry Falwell, *America Can Be Saved* (Murfreesboro, TN: Sword of the Lord Publishers, 1979), 17.

than rethink their beliefs, conservative religionists decided to renounce secular higher education and denounce it as "elitist." Thus, to be *uninformed*, even willfully and proudly stupid, came to be considered a Godly virtue. And since misery loves company, the Evangelicals' quest, for instance when Evangelicals dominated the Texas textbook committees, was to strive to "balance" the teaching of evolution with creationism and damn the facts.

In the minds of Evangelicals, they were recreating the Puritan's self-exile from England by looking for a purer and better place, this time not a geographical "place" but a sanctuary within their minds (and in inward-looking schools and churches) undisturbed by facts. Like the Puritans, the post-*Roe* Evangelicals (and many other conservative Christians) withdrew from the mainstream not because they were forced to but because the society around them was, in their view, fatally sinful and, worse, addicted to facts rather than to faith. And yet having "dropped out" (to use a 1960s phrase), the Evangelicals nevertheless kept on demanding that regarding "moral" and "family" matters the society they'd renounced *nonetheless had to conform to their beliefs.*

In the first decade of the twenty-first century the Evangelical and conservative Roman Catholic (and Mormon) outsider victim "approach" to public policy was perfected on a heretofore-undreamed-of scale by Sarah Palin. She was the ultimate holier-than-thou Evangelical queen bee. What my mother had represented (in her unreconstructed fundamentalist heyday) to a chalet full of young gullible women and later to tens of thousands of readers, Palin became for tens of millions of alienated angry white lower-middle-class men and women convinced that an educated "elite" was out to get them.

Palin was first inflicted on the American public by Senator John McCain, who chose her as his running mate in the 2008 presidential election for *only one reason*: He needed to shore up flagging support from the Evangelical Republican antiabortion base. McCain wanted to prove that he was fully in line with the "social issues" agenda that Dad, Koop, and I had helped foist on our country over thirty years before. Palin lost the election for McCain but "won" her war for fame and fortune and self-appointed "prophetess" status.

She presented herself as called by God and thus cast in the Old Testament mold of Queen Esther, one chosen by God to save her people. Palin perfected the Jesus Victim "art" of Evangelical self-banishment and then took victimhood to new levels of success by cashing in on white lower-middle-class resentment of America's elites. She might as well have run under the slogan "I'm as dumb as you are!"

Brad Greenberg documented a serious movement inside the Evangelical world to hail Palin as the "next Esther":

[Biblical Queen] Esther was selected queen in a beauty contest; Palin was runner-up in the Miss Alaska pageant. So Queen Esther apparently provided the role model for the former beauty queen who went to our own king and asked for earmarks for her people. The Palin/Queen Esther report has sparked a flood of commentary from fundamentalist Christian web sites. One reports that "Sarah Palin, like Esther, was an unlikely choice. Sarah Palin, like Esther, is bold and courageous in the face of fear. Sarah Palin, like Esther, proves you can be loyal and devoted to your family while having a high position. But perhaps, more than anything, . . . we are seeing someone right before our eyes who is capturing the hearts of the American people in a way that defies description— just like the Bible says." And "Esther won the favor of everyone who saw her." Another says, "Every once in a while a woman comes along who is made for the times. Sarah Palin is such a woman. . . . Another woman, Esther, was brought on the scene by God at just the right time. God's timing was perfect for he used Esther to save the Jews."*

Palin made a fortune by *simultaneously* proclaiming her Evangelical faith, denouncing Liberals, *and* claiming that she would help the good God fearing folks out there "take back" their country. This "Esther" lacked seriousness. But born-again insiders knew that the "wisdom of men" wasn't the point. Why should the new Queen Esther bother to actually finish her work governing Alaska? God had chosen her to confound the wise!

So she became a media star *and* quit as governor of Alaska. Then she battled "Them"—the "lamestream media" (as she labeled any media outlets outside of the Far Right subculture)—in the name of standing up for "Real Americans." Palin used the alternative communication network that had its roots deeply embedded in those pioneering 1970s and 1980s Evangelical TV shows and radio shows that I used to be on just about every other day. She did this to avoid being questioned by people who didn't agree with her. By not actually governing or doing the job she'd been elected by Alaskans to do, and by using the alternative media networks as an "outsider"—all the while reacting to and demanding attention from the actual (theoretically hated) media—Palin *also* made buckets of money.

And the greatest irony was that many women in the Evangelical/Roman Catholic/Quiverfull movements were cheering for Palin as a defender of "traditional family values." Yet Palin was the least-"submissive" female imaginable. She misused her children as stage props and reduced her husband to the role of "helpmeet"; indeed, he became the perfect example of a good biblical wife.

---

*Brad A. Greenberg, "Comparing the Lives of Sarah Palin and Queen Esther," September 10, 2008, www.jewishjournal.com/thegodblog/item/comparing_the _lives_of_sarah_palin_and_queen_esther_20080909/.

Speaking of "good biblical wives," in the Palin era the Evangelical Right still liked to pay lip-service to the Puritan community as an ideal to "get back to." Yet the post-*Roe* Evangelicals ignored the Puritans' actual ideas about government's biblically mandated role.

The Puritans' theology of government was formed in the context of an embrace of all Christians' duty to enhance the public good. This was exemplified by such unquestioned well-established concepts as the "king's highway," a *common* road system protected by the crown (government) and a *common* law that applied to all. One's *common* duty to others was accepted as the essential message of Christian civilization. Public spaces were *defended by government* in the early New England settlements, just as they had been in England.

What's so curious is that in this religion-inflicted country of ours, the same Evangelicals, conservative Roman Catholics, and others who had been running around post-*Roe* insisting that America had a "Christian foundation" and demanding a "return to our heritage" (and/or more recently trashing health care reform as "communist") ignored the fact that one historic contribution of Christianity was a commitment to strong central government. For instance, this included church support for state-funded, or *state-church*-funded, charities, including hospitals, as early as the fourth century.

Government was seen as part of God's Plan for creating social justice and defending the common good. Christians were once culture-forming and culture-embracing people. Even the humanism preached by the supposedly "anti-Christian" Enlightenment thinkers of the eighteenth century was, in fact, a Deist/Christian "heresy," with a value system espousing human dignity borrowed wholesale from the Sermon on the Mount.

In the scorched-earth post-*Roe* era of the "health care reform debates" of 2009 and beyond, Evangelicals seemed to believe that Jesus commanded that all hospitals (and everything else) should be run by corporations for profit, just because corporations *weren't the evil government.* The Right even decided that it was "normal" for the state to hand over its age-old public and patriotic duties to private companies—even for military operations ("contractors"), prisons, health care, public transport, and all the rest.

The Religious Right/Far Right et al. favored *private* "facts," too. They claimed that global warming wasn't real. They asserted this because *scientists* (those same agents of Satan who insisted that evolution was real) were the ones who said human actions were changing the climate. Worse, the government said so, too!

"Global warming is a left-wing plot to take away our freedom!"

"Amtrak must make a profit!"

Even the word "infrastructure" lost its respectability when government had a hand in maintaining roads, bridges, and trains.

In denial of the West's civic-minded, government-supporting heritage, Evangelicals (and the rest of the Right) wound up defending *private* oil companies but not God's creation, *private* cars instead of public transport, *private* insurance conglomerates rather than government care of individuals. The price for the Religious Right's wholesale idolatry of *private everything* was that Christ's reputation was tied to a cynical union-busting political party owned by billionaires. It only remained for a Far Right Republican-appointed majority on the Supreme Court to rule in 2010 that *unlimited corporate money* could pour into political campaigns—*anonymously*—in a way that clearly favored corporate America and the superwealthy, who were now the only entities served by the Republican Party.*

---

*On January 21, 2010, a decades-old system of rules that governed the financing of the nation's elections was overturned in the Supreme Court decision *Citizens United v. the Federal Election Commission.* The Supreme Court decision on corporate spending in political races thereby allowed the big corporations to call the shots on these elections (anonymously).

The Evangelical foot soldiers never realized that the logic of their "stand" against government had played into the hands of people who never cared about human lives beyond the fact that people could be sold products. By the twenty-first century, Ma and Pa No-name were still out in the rain holding an "Abortion is Murder!" sign in Peoria and/or standing in line all night in some god-forsaken mall in Kansas City to buy a book by Sarah Palin and have it signed. But it was the denizens of the corner offices at Goldman Sachs, the News Corporation, Koch Industries, Exxon, and Halliburton who were laughing.

CHAPTER 8

"Make *Sure*
You Tell Your
Readers I Changed
My Mind!"

I n 1983 I was the leader of a group of protesters who screamed
abuse at Justice Harry Blackmun and made him beat a hasty retreat back into a college building at the University of Nebraska after he'd just been awarded an honorary degree. In the early 1980s
my daughter Jessica and I—she was twelve—drove into Boston
several times to picket abortion clinics, including one where a few
years later (in 1994) two people were shot dead and five were seriously wounded by "pro-life" activist John Salvi.

Dad agreed to lead several antiabortion demonstrations, too.
He said, "We're telling everyone else to get out there and picket,
and some of our people are getting arrested, so we can't say no to
doing what we're telling others to do."

PHOTO: *Mom speaking in the L'Abri chapel in 1980 or so*

When my parents and I were participating in antiabortion demonstrations, bystanders would do a double take if they saw my mother. At an Atlanta event (in 1983), Mom was dressed as if attending a concert rather than picketing an abortion clinic. She marched wearing a Chanel original and a chic pair of shoes. The other two or three hundred marchers wore their clothes the way we slovenly Americans travel these days: in sweats, jeans, running shoes. Mom seemed cool and comfortable and as out of place as if she'd been picked up by a tornado and lifted from her favorite seat at Carnegie Hall and then dumped on a chewing-gum-blotched pavement in a sketchy part of town. It would have been a brave cop who handcuffed Mom when she was wearing her favorite cocktail dress, cut simply and quite short—as Audrey Hepburn wore in *Breakfast at Tiffany's*—but in Mom's case accessorized with stunning modern Danish silver jewelry rather than pearls.

A few years later domestic terrorist Eric Rudolph confessed to the bombings of an abortion clinic in the Atlanta suburb of Sandy Springs. But the afternoon of Mom's protest march no one was killed. Mom made everyone near her look as if they were not just homely, but also moving in slow motion. Even when she was in her sixties (as she was during various demonstrations, including one in Rochester at one of the hospitals used by the Mayo Clinic because abortions were performed there), Mom looked as if she were forty. She exuded the energy of a rambunctious nineteen-year-old. The teens milling around my mother seemed tired by comparison.

Mom's energy was something like the sun, wonderful—unless you got too close or were her typewriter (I'll explain the typewriter's misfortune). Back when Mom and Dad were still missionaries touring Europe and conducting Bible studies, my sisters (none of whom would have ever led a demonstration in downtown Atlanta if they could help it) loved our mother, but they were just plain exhausted trying to keep up with her, as were all her fellow workers, from the L'Abri staff to her editors, who in later years would stagger out of eighteen-hour meetings about some manuscript looking as if they'd been simultaneously drugged and thrown under a bus.

The word "strong" doesn't come close to describing Edith Schaeffer as she was until her mideighties. When I was a child, my mother occupied a category in my mind right up there with the Alps, God, the sun, and the ocean as representing everything that is permanent, beyond frailty or weakness or even time. Mom was *never sick*. Mom was up *before* anyone else every day. I never once saw my mother asleep. She went to bed last and rose before dawn and made Dad look terribly mortal—he slept! Her very *presence* was an assurance of eternal life: Here was one person death would surely never dare tangle with!

It was the week before Christmas 2010, more than thirty years after I had watched Mom chatting cheerily as she marched in front of a downtown abortion clinic in Atlanta. I sat holding the ninety-six-year-old version of my mother's hand. We were perched on a bench outside on her chalet balcony. It was a perfect winter day; hot sun, flawless blue sky, and crisp white newly fallen snow framed the staggeringly lovely view of the Alps above us. The Swiss "bath lady," as Mom called her, had come and gone. Mom smelled like pine, because of the traces of the bath oil she liked best. The bath lady was provided by the local authorities three times a week to bathe Mom, as happens everywhere in Switzerland. The Swiss provide a full range of what Republicans would call "socialist" services. Those godless Europeans do the oddest things, like care for their elderly, provide trains that can get people to work in minutes instead of hours. . . .

Anyway, my mother stared unseeing at the mountains we both love. She listened to me speak words she'd forget an hour or two after I spoke them, though at the time our exchanges were warm and comfortingly ordinary and she was "all there."

If I fell silent for a few minutes, I felt the gentle pressure of Mom's head as it settled against my arm while she drifted into a sleep interrupted by wakefulness.

Edith Schaeffer sleeps! The French might as well renounce food! Perhaps the British hate their dogs and cats now, too! As a child, I could never have imagined this day, let alone my mother leaning against me, *asleep*. "How are you Mom?" I asked, wanting to wake her because her sleeping was so unsettling.

"I'm old!" she said and grinned.

"John has had a son," I said. "They called him Jack."

"John?" Mom asked with her eyes shut again.

"Your grandson," I reminded her. "Remember, he was in the marines before he went to the University of Chicago."

"Who was a marine?" she asked, opening her eyes but staying put against my shoulder.

"Your grandson," I said.

She said nothing.

"I'm going to call the book I'm working on *Sex, Mom, and God*," I said.

"The one about me?" she asked, perking right up.

"Last time I checked I only have one mother," I said.

Mom laughed.

"Sex, Mom, and God," Mom said, and shook her head in exaggerated mock dismay. "You never change!"

She reached up and patted my cheek.

"I'm going to tell them how you always used to say that the only real necessity in life is a sheer black see-through nightgown."

"Well it is!" said Mom.

My mother remembered Jessica and Francis better than John because they lived with her back in that part of her life that, for
whatever neurological reason, is still fresh. It's as if the older memories were cast in a better sort of concrete than the rest of Mom's
inner "building."

But there were no flies on Mom when she was awake, even at
ninety-six. An attractive young caregiver was living with her during that visit, and anytime we were all in the room together, Mom
pointedly asked, "And *how* is Genie?" and then added, "I just
LOVE Genie!" At other times Mom blurted, "Thank you *so much*
for allowing Genie to go to China with me!"

Mom was talking about a trip she took when Genie was her
companion for five weeks. My mother was eighty years old at the
time. Genie was the person Mom wanted with her.

The reason Mom kept bringing Genie up—right out of the blue
and in the middle of other conversations—was that even though
she was *supposed to be blind*, Mom was still herself in one area: Her
Sexual Attraction Radar was working as well as ever! Mom's caregiver was attractive, young, and sleeping in Mom's little chalet that
I was staying in, too.

"So HOW IS Genie?!" Mom would ask, shooting her kind but
dangerously winsome blond helper a slightly worried look anytime I glanced at the young woman, which I did quite a bit.

One morning we were lounging on Mom's couch, and Mom
reached up and rubbed my neck the way she used to do when we'd
be together for my bedtime stories. Her hand was so frail that I
could barely feel her touch. Her delicate hands were gnarled but
still lovely. Debby made sure Mom got a manicure every month,
and her fingernails were well kept. When I was a child, Mom's
massages were powerful and effective. Her hands were small but *so*
strong! Mom always used to give me back and foot rubs, especially

concentrating on massaging my "bad" leg—the atrophied one wrecked in early childhood by polio.

Those hands! She gardened. And her fingernails always had dirt under them in the summer. I remember the armfuls of broccoli and cabbages glistening with dew that Mom would carry into the house at dawn after she got up to weed, plant, thin, hoe, and pick by first light. To me her hands were instruments of power that expressively "talked" right along with her as she gestured when speaking. They also pounded multiple carbon copies out of her huge old manual typewriter. Spellbound, I'd watch her type, mesmerized by her speed, accuracy, and the deadly beating she gave that typewriter.

Mom typed in a way that should have caused the paper to combust. Passionate content aside, my mother typed with a furious energy because she made six to ten carbon copies of each letter and so had to beat her machine as she pounded the keys.

In those days (for those who don't know) carbon copies were made by putting a layer of carbon paper between each thin airmail paper sheet so that the force of the little hammers—typebars—striking the page would carry through to the sheets underneath, marking them with the carbon from the carbon sheets. Physical pressure was needed to stamp the letters through the many sheets, and the more sheets, the more violence was needed to make the typebars fly and hit the page with a "thwack!" Mom pounded so hard on the keys that the top sheet of paper always had holes in it as if the letters had been fired at the paper by a machine gun.

Mom would make up to ten copies at a time by feeding a thick wad of paper sandwiched with her carbon sheets into her huge old typewriter. She even did this when typing her books, producing multiple copies of even the first draft of manuscripts that later she'd fight editors over.

Mom always looked fierce when her manuscripts came back marked up with "stupid changes" on them. She refused to change a word.

"Those Dreadful People," Mom would say referring to her cowering editors, "just don't understand me because they're used to dealing with all those so-called writers in the American Evangelical world who can barely speak English and are just too spiritual, with all their Jesus blah-blah! I write REAL books!"

To the person reading copy five or six of anything Mom typed, the indistinct carbon-copied words looked like some sort of illustration demonstrating the fuzzy vision endured by cataract sufferers. Since Mom never sent one copy of anything, but always sent copies of every letter (or book) she wrote to her mother, to my sisters, and so forth, any words she wrote were shared by many people. And like Mom herself, every word she wrote seemed permanent and inspired. She treated her own words with the same deference she treated the Bible since God was "speaking" through her, too, and woe betide the cringing editor who did anything more than compliment every last carbon-copied bit of "revelation."

"How dare they change it!" Mom would say if an editor insisted. "They can just jolly well write their own books if they have such great ideas!"

During the visit when I was telling my mother about this book, she asked (repeatedly), "Do you have a good editor, Dear?"

"Yes," I said.

"Well, don't let them change anything, Dear!" said Mom with a flicker of her old fire. "They always wanted my books to be more Evangelical!"

"I don't write Evangelical books. The Evangelicals hate my guts."

"Pay no attention to those Evangelical Idiots," said Mom, and then she dozed off again. A moment later she opened her eyes. "And *don't* let your editor change anything, my Dear!"

This time Mom was asleep in her chair. I reached out from where I was sitting at her feet and patted her knee. Mom opened her eyes.

"Mom, the only reason I'm a writer is because of all the books you read out loud to me. You were a good mother."

"Do you mean that?"

"You opened the doors to everything I love most," I said.

When Mom was ninety-two, she was taken very ill and put in the hospital. My sister Debby called me and told me to fly over right away. "Otherwise they'll kill her," Debby said.

I sat with Mom for a week night and day because the nurses had "tested" Mom and decided that she would be better off dead. They didn't put it that way, of course; they just left her untouched food tray in front of her and made no effort to get her to eat or drink. They medicated her into a stupor.

They had given her some sort of cognitive test made up of questions like "What did you have for breakfast?" or "Who is president of Switzerland?" Good luck with that! They should have asked, "Describe in detail the compound you grew up in when you lived in China." They would have gotten a wonderful answer and decided Mom was a genius.

"Poor dear," said one nurse. "She has no quality of life. She didn't even know she was in a hospital! You should just let her go."

After the nurse walked out of the room—we were in a swanky rehabilitation clinic set in the lovely vineyards above Vevey—Debby said, "See what I mean? They would've made good Nazis!"

These nurses were actually very nice people—if they decided you were worth saving. But they had no old stories to share with

Mom. Nor did they know what would draw her out. And Mom didn't know her nurses. But Debby and I still saw Mom as *Mom*. And because we knew how to talk to her, we had real conversations. Mom ate because we fed her, and she returned to her home fully recovered. The nurses weren't evil, just doing the best they could in a country where suicide is legal and no big deal, what with an outfit called Dignitas just up the road in Zurich that—for $5,000—puts "suicide tourists" out of their misery.*

From Mom's nurses' point of view, our mother was not like them. And age is indeed incurable. Mom even appeared vegetable-like to them. To Debby and I she appeared very much human—in other words, still *like us*.

Appearances, empathy, and emotion count when it comes to ethics. What human life *is*, is a messy, inexact business as soon as you include a spiritual component related to consciousness, memory, and pleasure, let alone the ability to make moral choices.

How ironic that in extreme old age Mom became more her true self than ever, yet was slipping away and so very forgetful. How ironic that those nurses would have let a woman die who still teared up with pleasure when she heard Glenn Gould play Bach or BB King's "Every Day I Have the Blues." And this was the same woman whose most treasured possession—which she wore like beloved jewelry—was the backstage pass BB King gave her after they met.

This meeting took place in the Montreux Palace Hotel. Mom had gone there with my sister Susan for tea just before she got ill.

---

*Dignitas is a Swiss assisted-dying group that helps those with terminal illness and severe physical and mental illnesses to die assisted by "qualified" doctors and nurses. It even provides euthanasia for people with "incurable mental illnesses." Who decides someone is incurable is a good question.

And Mom, *of course,* met BB King since he "looked so interesting, Dear, so I went *right over* to speak to him and sat down at his table." Mom told him which of his songs she always listened to, and King, charmed, sent out his entourage to get tickets and a backstage pass to that night's concert at the Montreux Jazz Festival. There's a picture of Mom and King taken backstage in his dressing room framed on the wall above her bed. . . .

So what *is* human life? The Christian tradition has produced demarcation lines *even after birth* to describe human life's gradual transformation into full personhood, such as the concept of "the age of accountability." The Roman Catholic Church even invented a "destination" for the souls of unbaptized infants—Limbo. This invention (out of thin air) was to help assuage the distraught parents of dead babies, too young to have committed sins but still cursed by "original sin." Saint Augustine said that "such infants as quit the body without being baptized will be involved in the mildest condemnation of all." This "doctrine" was "discovered" in order to cover the not-quite-fully-accountable stage of life and death of babies, such as stillborn infants, who, going strictly by the book in terms of the official fate of the unbaptized sinner, would otherwise have been consigned to burn in Hell. (Dead babies' prospects have been steadily improving. In 1984 Joseph Ratzinger, then a cardinal, said that he rejected the claim that children who died unbaptized could not "attain salvation.")

Absurd theological demarcations aside, just try to apply smug answers pro or con to the life issues in a hospice or the ICU of a major hospital. Talk to the transplant team about to harvest a heart about whether or not to take the donor off life support. See how far purist theological *or* secular rules—or science—will get you when deciding the fate of even just one actual individual sliding into a vegetative state. Talk to a nurse who doesn't know to ask your mother about China or her meeting with BB King and instead asks her what day of the week it is and the names of her grandchildren and then draws a blank.

One factor that is actually more of a constant than anything science or religion provides concerning the "life issues" is what I call our innate sense of aesthetic empathy. Mom's lifelong lament "He had all his fingers and toes!" illustrates what I mean. Aesthetic empathy is that combination of feelings and facts whereby most of us *recognize* ourselves in others who *look like us*. We are moved to compassion when confronted by others when we can relate to them. Notice that big-eyed baby seals get support from people but less cute chickens are slaughtered without compunction, and as for all those frog species disappearing—*fuggedaboutit*!

When we see a six-month-old fetus in a 3-D ultrasound picture, pro-choice absolutist claims that the fetus is "nothing" and that the woman is everything are rudely disconnected from our actual experience. Conversely, if you didn't know what to ask Mom and talked to her in her ninety-six-year-old incarnation, you might think she was gaga.

These days everyone seems to live in separate worlds, as cut off from other people as those nurses were from my mother and for the same reason: We don't see The Other as being like us. The Internet allows us to entertain ourselves with our own private versions of reality. We stick to "our sort."

Even our "facts"—say, that "all Evangelicals are dumb" or that "President Obama is the Antichrist"—are private and need pass no test imposed by actual truth. Our information is as personalized and as "inside" as Mom's memories became in extreme old age.

And Mom's attitude toward her "stupid" editors, opinionated as she was, seems open-minded when compared to today's blogs and the level of "discourse" that's become the language of politics post-*Roe*. The Left, too, has its very own secular fundamentalist versions of Edith Schaeffer. Members of the "open-minded" Left also believe *very literally* in their own various "scriptures" and special "leading," if not by God, then by ever-so-correct progressive thinking. But unlike my mother, today's "true believers" of the Left and Right are not as polite as Mom was and much less compassionate, let alone tolerant.

For instance, consider the poisoning of our shared public space as illustrated by what has befallen the nomination Senate hearings for future Supreme Court justices. "To Bork" entered the American vocabulary as a reference to the way pro-choice Democrats savaged—and lied about—Ronald Reagan's antiabortion (but otherwise qualified) nominee for a seat on the Supreme Court. President Reagan nominated Robert Bork for the Supreme Court on July 1, 1987. Within forty-five minutes of Bork's nomination, Senator Ted Kennedy took to the Senate floor condemning Bork in a nationally televised incendiary speech declaring:

> Robert Bork's America is a land in which women would be forced into back-alley abortions, blacks would sit at segregated lunch counters, rogue police could break down citizens' doors in midnight raids, schoolchildren could not be taught about evolution, writers and artists could be censored at the whim of the Government. . . . President Reagan is still our president but he should not be able to reach out from the muck of Irangate, reach into the muck of Watergate and impose his reactionary vision of the Constitution on the Supreme Court and the next generation of Americans. No justice would be better than this injustice!

Since the Bork "hearings," the whole process of confirmation hearings has become a politicized farce in which candidates for seats on the Court have to say as little as possible of substance. Because of *Roe* and the reaction to it, each new Supreme Court justice begins his or her life as a justice by first being infantilized in front of the whole nation in a Kabuki play of staged hypocrisy. Ironically, *Roe* has kept the debate on abortion alive and well. Since abortion was being legalized state by state *before* 1973, *Roe* and *Bolton*—not the legalization of abortion per se—needlessly set back the progressive movement by poisoning American politics. At a stroke the Supreme Court handed America (and the Left in particular) a time bomb and then walked away. The collateral damage spins into a violence-blighted future with no end in sight.

Had abortion been legalized in a more moderate way and/or on a state-by-state basis—as we've seen was already happening with minimal controversy before *Roe*—there would have been fights, but nothing like the societywide meltdown that followed. And I'm not alone in pointing this out. There are many pro-choice critiques of *Roe* besides the one I'm making. For instance, in a 2007 interview Justice John Paul Stevens said that *Roe* "create[d] a new doctrine that really didn't make sense" and that if Justice Blackmun "could have written a better opinion, that . . . might have avoided some of the criticism."* Justice Ruth Bader Ginsburg criticized the decision for terminating a democratic movement to liberalize abortion laws.**

---

*Jeffrey Rosen, "The Dissenter," *New York Times Magazine*, September 23, 2007. Rosen notes that Stevens is "the oldest and arguably most liberal justice."
**Ruth Ginsburg, "Some Thoughts on Autonomy and Equality in Relation to *Roe v. Wade*," *North Carolina Law Review* 63 (1985): 375: "The political process was moving in the early 1970s, not swiftly enough for advocates of quick, complete change, but majoritarian institutions were listening and acting. Heavy-handed judicial intervention was difficult to justify and appears to have provoked, not resolved, conflict."

Watergate prosecutor Archibald Cox wrote, "[*Roe's*] failure to confront the issue in principled terms leaves the opinion to read like a
set of hospital rules and regulations. . . . Neither historian, nor lay-
man, nor lawyer will be persuaded that all the prescriptions of Justice Blackmun are part of the Constitution."* Professor Laurence
Tribe (a scholar of the Constitution) said, "One of the most curious
things about *Roe* is that, behind its own verbal smokescreen, the
substantive judgment on which it rests is nowhere to be found."**
Law professors Alan Dershowitz, Cass Sunstein, and Kermit Roosevelt also criticized *Roe*.

Abortion—as defined by *Roe* and *Bolton*—remains *the* constant irritant that keeps both the public and Congress polarized.
It does this by elevating policy differences to the level of winner-
take-all hysterical accusations of "murder!" from one side and
"misogyny!" from the other.

Roe set back the prospects of progressives. How would you like
to hitch your fortunes to a story like this?*** And, sure, this horror is not *Roe's* "fault," but a leader who decides to dig in his or
her heels and defend late-term abortions will always be cast as a
villain by events that tend to outrun platitudes:

> While this week's [January 20, 2011] indictment involving a
> grisly abortion mill in Philadelphia has shocked many, the grand

---

*Archibald Cox, *The Role of the Supreme Court in American Government* (Oxford, UK: Oxford University Press, 1976), 113–114.
**Laurence Tribe, "The Supreme Court, 1972 Term—Foreword: Toward a
Model of Roles in the Due Process of Life and Law," *Harvard Law Review* 87,
no. 1 (1973): 7. Quoted in Richard Gregory Morgan, "*Roe v. Wade* and the Les-
son of the Pre-*Roe* Case Law," *Michigan Law Review* 77, no. 7 (1979): 1724–
1748, doi:10.2307/1288040.
***Sabrina Tavernise, "Squalid Abortion Clinic Escaped State Oversight," *New
York Times*, January 22, 2011, www.nytimes.com/2011/01/23/us/23doctor.html.

jury's nearly 300-page report also contains a surprising and little-noted revelation: In the mid-1990s, the administration of Pennsylvania governor Tom Ridge, a pro-choice Republican, ended regular inspections of abortion clinics—a policy that continued until just last year. . . . Pennsylvania health officials deliberately chose not to enforce laws to ensure that abortion clinics provide the same level of care as other medical service providers.

The District Attorney's office this week charged an abortion doctor, Kermit Gosnell, with murder and infanticide. Nine other workers at the abortion clinic, the Women's Medical Society, also face charges. According to the prosecutors, Gosnell and his associates not only broke state law by performing abortions after 24 weeks—they also killed live babies by stabbing them with scissors and cutting their spinal cords. . . .

The Pennsylvania Department of Health abruptly decided, for political reasons, to stop inspecting abortion clinics at all. The politics in question were not anti-abortion, but pro. With the change of administration from Governor Casey to Governor Ridge, officials concluded that inspections would be "putting a barrier up to women" seeking abortions.*

Many Evangelicals and Roman Catholics I know would have long ago been voting for progressive candidates (i.e., Democrats) because these voters (particularly young people) are sick and tired of the Republican Party's slide into the role of Far Right war machine/shill for corporate America. Many religious people have become increasingly sympathetic to gay rights, favor closing the

---

*Marian Wang, "Why a Gruesome Pennsylvania Abortion Clinic Had Not Been Inspected for 17 Years," ProPublica, January 21, 2011, www.propublica.org/blog/item/gruesome-pennsylvania-abortion-clinic-had-not-been-inspected-for-17-years.

gap between rich and poor, and root for policies that foster racial diversity. They want immigration justice. They're for cutting back the bloated defense establishment, and they favor the conservation of the environment. If it weren't for the needlessly sweeping *way* abortion was legalized, as defined by *Roe* and *Bolton*, the Evangelicals and the many Roman Catholics who joined them would not have been manipulated into voting as a Republican Party bloc since 1973.

After the election of 2008, a student poll conducted at Gordon College (an Evangelical school in Massachusetts) found that about 20 percent of the students had voted for Obama. For the first time ever during that year's election, a group of the Evangelical students on campus even opened a student Democratic Party office. And though the powers that be at Gordon knew I was a vocal Obama supporter, I was invited to speak in chapel shortly after the election and talked about why I supported President Obama, "in spite of the abortion issue," as my support was described by the person introducing me.

After my talk many students told me that they had wanted to vote for Obama but could not "because of abortion." When I asked them to elaborate, the students spoke about the horror they felt over late-term abortions, the very extremes (late-term abortion) *Doe v. Bolton* opened the door to by "clarifying" *Roe*'s fuzzy, inexact permissiveness and allowing abortion of babies that—given today's medical advances—might live outside the womb.* It seems that these young Evangelicals were telling me that their "because-of-abortion" reluctance to vote for *any* Democrat Party candidate

---

*According to the Guttmacher Institute, 1.5 percent of abortions are done at twenty-one weeks of gestation or more. That represents about 20,000 abortions a year. "Facts on Induced Abortion in the United States," Guttmacher Institute, January 16, 2011, www.guttmacher.org/pubs/fb_induced_abortion.html. 0.08 percent are performed after 24 weeks, when the fetus is viable.

was less about abortion per se than about the fact that *Bolton* and *Roe* allow abortion at any stage of fetal development.

I think that these students' views were also about something else: that since *Roe* demolished the state-by-state approach, the ruling has remained a perpetual insult to many Americans. This wound won't heal. Abortion rights rulings were not like civil rights rulings wherein there was plenty of biblical material within various religious traditions to move people's hearts to accept men and women of other races as brothers and sisters. There is nothing warm and fuzzy about abortion. "Doing unto others" doesn't translate well into eliminating a fetus.

Evangelicals, most Roman Catholics, and others believe that their right to be heard on abortion was steamrollered by *Roe.* This sense of grievance—maybe as much as their horror over late-term abortions—has kept the debate hot. And the anger has been passed to each successive generation. Hence, many young Evangelicals and Roman Catholics are ready to change their views (and have) about many social issues—but not about abortion. This reminds me of the way many Jewish young people I know are Liberals when it comes to everything *but* their support for the state of Israel. When it comes to "Israel issues," their usual lefty empathy for minorities and oppressed peoples (say, for people just like the Palestinians) goes out the window.

Roe represents a trauma to the psyche of American Evangelical and Roman Catholic communities (among others) that has to have been lived to be understood, something many of my secular friends just don't "get." This wound has been passed down since 1973 with—if public opinion polls mean anything—no end in sight.

The "I-wish-I-could-vote-for-Democrats-but-I-can't-because-of-abortion" conscience-stricken Gordon students I talked to were not alone, nor were they reactionaries, bigots, or misogynists, and most of them were *young educated women.* Typically, students

from top Evangelical colleges have gravitated to organizations that
are working on justice and poverty issues worldwide. Without a
pool of Evangelical leaders, students, and workers, there would be
many fewer people on the front line of charities around the globe,
helping the poor, caring for the sick, and fighting for the restoration of the environment.*

Something else has been lost in the debate: The "sides" aren't clearly
"Left" and "Right" when it comes to *actual people* (especially "ordinary" people as opposed to the talking heads). The notion that
"most Liberals are pro-choice" and that "most Conservatives are antiabortion" is simplistic. Many actual people don't fit such blanket
simplification of their views. For instance, take the paradoxical con-
founding of stereotypes that this amazing (e-mail) letter represents.
The writer is a single mother, educated, bisexual, progressive, and
impossible to "label" neatly when it comes to abortion.

Is she "One Of Us?" Or is she one of "The Evil Other?" Maybe
she's just too thoughtful to see everything in black and white.

> *Fri, Jan 14, 2011, 10:27 am*
> *Dear Mr. Schaeffer,*
> I don't know if you remember me but I was close friends with
> your daughter Jessica back in high school and hope she is doing
> well. Your blog and books are very thought provoking and I want
> to read more. Actually, it's interesting, when I was very young I
> always instinctively believed in God even when my friends and

---

*In an analysis of survey research on American civil life, Hoover Institution
scholar Arthur C. Brooks finds that religious people are 23 percentage points
more likely than secular people to volunteer their time to charities. See Arthur
C. Brooks, "Religious Faith and Charitable Giving," *Policy Review* (October–
November 2003): 17.

family didn't. I could never find a sympathetic ear growing up, as most of my friends were atheists.

Having Jessica as a friend was really wonderful to me because even though our beliefs were often very different, she helped me to form my own ideas and validated my growing belief in God. I decided in high school that abortion was wrong, and even though I still consider myself progressive in most ways, I still, to this day, am informed by that awakening of conscience I experienced. I feel like our equating "freedom" with a woman's right to dissociate with her natural empathy and maternal instincts feels wrong deep inside me. It feels anything but "feminist" to me. This is what led me to choose to have my own daughter, now seven, despite the many adversities I faced at the time—poverty, a brand-new marriage that was already on the rocks, and the disapproval of many well-meaning people in my life.

It hurts me even now to write this but I can't imagine my world without Jeni, even though I am now a struggling single parent of a little girl with some special needs (she has mild Aspergers and ADHD, and is a lot of work but also such a joy). I feel blessed in every way to have listened to my heart, not my mind and logic and my bank account, and welcomed her into the world.

I always had a lot of faith that God provides for every person, and that none of us are "mistakes." But I can't force that belief on others, beyond what science can prove about a child's viability/ sentience (which in itself is already significant). I think the fact that women are willing to go to such lengths to seek abortion when it's not available, says something about women's universal need for control over their reproductive process, and I honor every woman's right to make personal choices about that. But not at the expense of common sense. It's possible to have a dialogue about abortion that includes sympathy, compromise, as well as sober honesty about the process of abortion, free of sugarcoated terms and politically correct rhetoric. It is possible to have this dialogue without engaging fear, guilt and self-righteousness. There IS a middle ground on this issue, and it is a loving and understanding place where we can listen to another person's pain and forgive. I know it exists because I feel it in my own heart. I hope that your work helps to further this synthesis.

I am also bisexual. I knew this from the time I was very young, even in high school. I did everything to try to deny it, including living in an ashram and later marrying someone from a very conservative culture. I am now happily engaged to a very kind and spiritually profound woman who loves my daughter, and quite honestly, I'm living a much more mutually God-conscious, peaceful and emotionally fulfilling life than I ever did while trying to be straight.

I am glad that someone as influential as you is questioning a lot of the homophobia in the Christian Right, and seeing just how much harm this can be causing people. . . . I agree that God created men and women and that's great and I celebrate that. But some of us were also, I believe, born gay, transgender or bisexual, and I don't think God makes mistakes. This is an excellent opportunity for people to learn compassion and going beyond the bodily concept . . . something we need so much and are resisting so much in the world today. In the end, I think we are so much more than just a male or female body. We are souls, and we don't get to keep this "male" or "female" body when we leave it behind. So why so much focus on heterosexuality and homosexuality? . . .

. . . I don't think we will ever heal unless both the right and left learn to empathize and synthesize to some degree. No one is really moving toward the center, the heart. This is one reason why I believe the "abortion issue" and the "gay issue" are so central to this divide, they are both deeply concerned with sexuality and the sexual conscience. There is so much religious sexual shame (as well as guilt about actual misconduct) that is being displaced onto gays, bisexuals, transgenders and lesbians. At the same time, the left is displacing a lot of feelings about personal victimization, etc onto the right, while disconnecting from their own power.

For me, choosing to have my daughter, and OWNING that choice, was the most empowering thing I ever did. Despite the fact that I was working as a cashier when I got pregnant and my daughter's father didn't have a green card yet, I could no more terminate the life of my own child than I could commit suicide. To me it was the same thing. And I think as long as we keep focusing on the rights of women (and their partners) to choose dissociation and cold logic over love and instinct, we will continue to miss the point completely. And as long as conservatives keep denying GLBTQ people the right to have families, and labeling the rights of living children to healthcare, education, housing and basic sustenance as "liberal" priorities, the disconnect intensifies. Until the left and right are able to listen to each other and find common ground, we'll never find peace.

> *Please say hi to Jessica for me!* . . .
> *God bless,*
> *Sarah Noack**

Both sides on the "life issues" remain totally invested in being morally right. Both sides define the "Other" as evil and refuse to admit that people like Sarah Noack even exist. The purists also refuse to admit that most Americans (if public opinion polls are to be believed) occupy a—*sensibly conflicted*—middle ground on "the issue."

A plurality of Americans would like to see stricter limits placed on abortions in the United States. According to a *New York Times/*

---

*Letter and name used by permission.

CBS News poll, only 23 percent of those surveyed called for an end to all abortions. But the split between those who wanted it kept legal without restriction (34 percent)—in other words to maintain the *Roe/Bolton* status quo—and those who would like to see more restrictions (41 percent) was tilted against *Roe*. Thus, almost forty years after *Roe* a whopping 61 percent of the American public (including many who are pro-choice) have negative views about the abortion laws—as they stand.*

But for the ideological purists on both sides of the abortion issue to admit any compromise would be to invalidate their staked-out territory. Pro-choice fundamentalists say that abortion rights could be "taken away" with the stroke of a pen. (Send us that check, *and we will protect your reproductive rights!*) Pro-life fundamentalists say that abortion rights could be taken away with the stroke of a pen if one votes for Republicans, if a "constitutional amendment" banning abortion were passed, or if Supreme Court appointments went to conservatives. (Send us that check, *and we will protect the unborn babies!*)

Less ideologically driven people on both sides admit that if *Roe* were overturned (let alone amended), legal abortion would remain available in America. The Guttmacher Institute—an organization whose research is cited by all sides in the debate—says that only twenty states currently have laws on the books "that could be used to restrict the legal status of abortion" if *Roe* were overturned. And most of those would quickly legalize abortion if the matter were returned to the states. Seven states already have specific laws protecting the right to abortion as completely as does *Roe*.** Abortion

---

*Megan Thee, "Public Opinion on Abortion," *New York Times*, April 19, 2007, http://thecaucus.blogs.nytimes.com/2007/04/19/public-opinion-on-abortion.
**Jess Henig, "What Would Happen if the Supreme Court Overturned Roe v. Wade?" FactCheck.Org, April 6, 2008, www.factcheck.org/askfactcheck/what _would_happen_if_the_supreme_court.html.

rights are here to stay. The morning-after pill is here to stay.* The suction machines tucked away in many a doctor's office are here to stay. And our post-1970s heightened sense of women's rights is a permanent (and blessed) fact of American life.

I predict that *Roe* and *Bolton*—in their present form wherein they permit abortion without restriction and at any age of fetal development—are not going to survive. I also predict that abortion will remain legal but be restricted to more closely reflect the vast majority of the American public's conflicted feelings and beliefs.

The politics of the antiabortion movement became about everything *but* saving babies. Just as Glenn Beck's mentor, Robert George, was misusing abortion as a handy stick with which to beat up on Obama during the 2008 election, so, too, other Far Right Republicans used abortion when they were in power to do everything *but* help women. If the Republicans had wanted to prevent abortions, they would have funded a thorough and mandatory sex education initiative from the earliest grades in all schools and combined it with the distribution of free contraceptives in all high schools, public and private (religious schools included). They would have legislated generous family leave for both mothers and fathers. They would have provided federally funded day care as a national priority. They would have expanded adoption services, including encouraging gay parents to adopt children, and they would have encouraged gay

---

*"Researchers are finding an alternative that is safe, cheap and very difficult for governments to restrict—misoprostol, a medication originally intended to prevent stomach ulcers. This pharmaceutical approach is called 'medical abortion.' In the United States and Europe it typically consists of two sets of 'M' pills. The first is mifepristone, formerly known as RU-486, and then a day or two later the misoprostol. Using the drugs in combination produces a miscarriage more than 95 percent of the time in early pregnancy." Nicholas Kristof, "Another Pill That Could Cause a Revolution," *New York Times*, July 31, 2010.

couples to marry and adopt. They would have provided a generous tax incentive to have children and direct financial assistance and educational opportunities for all families, including single parents. They would have raised taxes to pay for these programs. They would have never equated stem cell research with abortion, much less with murder, thereby making the antiabortion position patently ridiculous. Above all, they would have addressed the injustice of the growing gap between the superrich and everyone else and fought to raise the living standards of poor people.

What the Republicans did instead was misuse abortion—again and again and again—as a polarizing issue to energize their base. But so did the Left.

The semi-"official" spokespersons for the pro-choice side have consistently cast the debate in dishonest terms. They have acted as if *Roe* were somehow a foundation (if not *the* foundation) of the entire progressive agenda, rather than a needless impediment to it. And the pro-*Roe* absolutists have masked the facts about abortion with propaganda, for instance, by depicting all abortions in the "light" of dramatic hard cases when in fact 22 percent of all pregnancies in America end in abortion and they are not all hard cases.*

---

*"Facts on Induced Abortion." Nearly 50 percent of pregnancies among American women are unintended, and 40 percent of these are terminated by abortion. Twenty-two percent of all pregnancies (excluding miscarriages) end in abortion. Forty percent of pregnancies among white women, 69 percent among blacks, and 54 percent among Hispanics are unintended. In 2008, 1.21 million abortions were performed, down from 1.31 million in 2000. However, between 2005 and 2008 the long-term decline in abortions stalled. From 1973 through 2008, nearly 50 million legal abortions occurred. Each year, 2 percent of women aged fifteen to forty-four have an abortion; 50 percent have had at least one previous abortion. At least 50 percent of American women will experience an unintended pregnancy by age forty-five, and at current rates about 33 percent will have had an abortion.

(And as I mentioned in New York City 40 percent of pregnancies end in abortion.)*

Here's a quote from a study (cited by the Guttmacher Institute) on the statistics of repeat abortions that you won't find quoted in the literature produced by the professionals running pro-choice lobbying groups: "The proportion of women having abortions who were undergoing a repeat procedure increased rapidly following the legalization of abortion, more than doubling between 1974 and 1979 (from 15% to 32%). Levels of repeat abortion increased at a slower pace between 1979 and 1993 (from 32% to 47%) and have remained stable since then."**

In other words almost half of all abortions in the United States are repeat abortions. The statistics on repeat abortions are hardly conducive to accepting the claim that abortion is *always* an agonizing choice that one must never question. Nevertheless, the absolutists on the pro-*Roe* side have cast anyone who doubts their version of abortion "facts" as evil and woman-hating. In that sense they are the mirror image of the Far Right and are misusing abortion as a polarizing issue to energize their base for political as well as fund-raising purposes. Moreover, the idea that somehow abortion is always beyond question has led to the lack of inspection of facilities, for instance in Pennsylvania, that has resulted in disasters for some women.

And here's a point *no one* wants to talk about: Forty-two percent of women obtaining abortions have incomes below 100 percent of

---

*"The annual figure has averaged 90,000 in recent years, or about 40 percent of all pregnancies, twice the national rate." "Religious Leaders Call for New Efforts to Lower the City's 'Chilling' Abortion Rate," *New York Times*, January 6, 2011.
**Rachel K. Jones, Susheela Singh, Lawrence B. Finer, and Lori F. Frohwirth, "Repeat Abortion in the United States," Occasional Report No. 29, November 2006, Guttmacher Institute, www.guttmacher.org/pubs/2006/11/21/or29.pdf.

the federal poverty level ($10,830 for a single woman with no children).* The people on the pro-*Roe* side seem to have sided with the Right in that they settled on access to abortion rather than economic justice as one "solution" for poverty. Maybe it's just cheaper to kill the poor. One hears less from organizations like Planned Parenthood and NARAL about economic justice—say, raising taxes on the wealthy—than about the right to abortion for poor women.

The Right and Left seem agreed on one thing: Fighting over *Roe* is easier than struggling for education rights and tax and social reform to help the poor women who are the people who have most of the abortions.

As Sarah Noack writes, "Until the left and right are able to listen to each other and find common ground, we'll never find peace." Such listening has to move past "facts" that are used only to make political arguments. It's time for honest people who actually care about the future of America to consider that they may need to change their minds about the policies and legal tactics they pursue. And the discussion should be about abortion *as it is,* not about talking points for sound bites.

In the spirit of listening and trying to tell the truth (as I see it), where do I stand?

I was wrong when I was an antiabortion activist. I changed my mind.

Today, I am *pro-choice.*

Today, I'm decidedly *not proabortion.*

I think abortion must be legal because women have a need to determine their individual futures, because many women find themselves pregnant without the support of a loving community and in horrible circumstances, because women have been picked

---

*"Facts on Induced Abortion."

on and kicked around throughout history as a result of religious beliefs related to "family values" that turn out to be anything but. I believe all this *because* of my aesthetic empathy for the women in my life, the women I love spanning a generational arc from my mother to my granddaughters.

When I was a young man (and sure about everything), like many of my fellow "pro-life" activists, my original and deeply felt moral qualms about abortion were soon subsumed by the adrenaline rush of the chase for headlines and power over other people's lives, not to mention buried by the hubris that comes with being acclaimed as a folk hero by an army of dedicated followers.

Today, as I said, I'm pro-choice—but with a caveat that will not please the professional activists dug in on either side. I am pro-choice, but not pro-*Roe* and -*Bolton*. In other words I think it's time to put out the fire at the heart of the American culture wars or at least damp it down. And this fire—for the vast "middle"—is not caused by abortion per se but the extremes of *Roe* and *Bolton*.

I think that abortion should be legal only up to an early stage of pregnancy, say up to the twelfth week (cases of fetal deformity, rape, incest, and/or threat to the mother's life excepted). This would leave the majority of women seeking abortion in America unaffected. According to the Guttmacher Institute, 88 percent of abortions occur in the first twelve weeks of pregnancy.* Such a change would also make the law conform to what opinion polls show is the majority position of most Americans on abortion: Keep it legal, but make the law less gut-wrenchingly permissive than *Roe*.

The idea of keeping abortion legal but restricting it to earlier stages of pregnancy isn't original with me, let alone ideal. Worst of all—from a heartland American perspective—it's French!

---

*"Facts on Induced Abortion."

In self-consciously secular France (where many progressive American say they'd love to live and where the reputation of the French is not to be "hung up" over Sex), abortion is legal on request only in the first twelve weeks of pregnancy.* After the first trimester, two doctors must certify that the abortion is necessary to prevent serious permanent injury to the physical or mental health of the pregnant woman, to remove a risk to the life of the pregnant woman, or to end the suffering of a fetus with a severe incurable illness. And, sure, the French law is a face-saving device to help people accept some sort of moral fig leaf to cover their feelings about what abortion *is*. So, yes, the way the French legalized abortion *is* "typically French"—emotional more than logical. But perception matters. Feelings matter. Aesthetics matter. Empathy matters. Otherwise, the abortion controversy wouldn't have remained terminally divisive.

There is a real-world political issue related to the sustainability of *Roe* and *Bolton*: public opinion. In what may someday be cited as a classic example of hubris and ego producing unintended consequences, the loudest defenders of *Roe* may eventually set back abortion rights in a way the Religious Right never could have achieved. Bluntly: *Roe* and *Bolton* allow abortion for any reason up to twenty-four weeks. Welcome to the world of perpetually defending abortion in the shadow cast by news stories about doctors severing spinal cords of living viable (or almost viable) babies. With "friends" like *Roe* and *Bolton*, abortion rights do not need any enemies. A midcourse correction to American law along the lines of how the French legalized abortion might help preserve abortion rights.

Whatever you think about the issue of abortion, here's a fact: We Evangelicals in the early 1970s weren't politicized (at least in the cur-

---

*Abortion was decriminalized with the passage of the Veil Law in 1975.

rent meaning of the word) until after *Roe v. Wade* and *Doe v. Bolton*. Here's another fact: Almost forty years after helping to launch the Evangelical wing of the antiabortion movement, I am filled with deep regret for the antigovernment and ultimately anti-American, not to say murderous, consequences Dad and I helped unleash.

In marked contrast to the steady liberalizing of opinion on other culture war issues, such as premarital sex and gay rights, the younger generation in America is increasingly antiabortion. I'm not just talking about Evangelical or Roman Catholic young people. If the early-twenty-first-century tracking polls of young people's views on abortion are any indication, the 1960s generation that pushed for *Roe* and *Bolton* is losing the national debate.

According to a Gallup Poll (April 2010), the percentage of college-educated people who favor legal abortion under any cir-cumstances has been dropping since the early 1990s. As an article in the *New York Times* (that cited this poll) noted, "There is a long-range trend of public opposition coming from unexpected quarters."* And even though the largest overall drop in support for abortion rights was among men over sixty-five, it was closely followed by a drop among women under thirty.

And it's not just young people who (according to the polls) are ambivalent about abortion. There is a another question looming: Which lives in our brave new world—at any "stage" of life or development—will be given the full protection of the law and rated as "fully human"?

Consider movies and television. Films like *Blade Runner, Brazil,* or *District 9* or the *Battlestar Galactica* TV series, not to mention

---

*Charles M. Blow, "Abortion's New Battle Lines," *New York Times*, May 1, 2010. The Gallup Poll is available at www.gallup.com/poll/127559/Education-Trumps -Gender-Predicting-Support-Abortion.aspx.

comedies like *Waitress, Juno,* and *Knocked Up* (even some hilarious Monty Python skits about unwilling transplant "donors") are
hardly the work of "pro-lifers." And yet these films and series have
raised philosophical, moral, aesthetic, and political questions related to issues of personhood that, taken together, seem to fly in the
face of the facile "it's just tissue" ethic of *Roe,* let alone equating out-
fits like Dignitas with a good future or an enlightened outlook.

The advances of the mid-1970s made it possible to *visualize* the
fetus throughout gestation and to monitor its development. Tests
of fetal well-being were invented post-*Roe* and led to fetal therapy.
By the mid-1970s, an unborn child had become a patient, and ob-
stetrics had become a complicated specialty—so much so that in
1974 the first board-certification examination was given in the
subspecialty of maternal-fetal medicine. As the *New England Journal of Medicine* noted in 2001, "Obstetricians now care for two pa-
tients, the pregnant woman and her fetus, and are expected to
diagnose abnormalities accurately and to provide therapy appropriate to both."* By the end of the first decade of the twenty-first
century, the science that was available in the early 1970s related to
fetology seemed to be from the Stone Age. That fact may doom
Roe—and whatever political party or special interest group hitches
its wagon to that particular means of guaranteeing abortion rights.

The tyranny of reproductive reality *and* the fabulous beauty of
children collide with my sense of aesthetic empathy for women
and for babies—born, to be born, and unborn. This paradox can't
be resolved but only recognized and mediated as best we can in

---

*Katherine D. Wenstrom, M.D., "Massachusetts Medical Society in a review of
Fetology" by Diana Bianchi (Author), Timothy Crombleholme (Author), Mary
D' Alton (Author), Fergal Malone (Author)," *New England Journal of Medicine*
23 (2001): 47.

ways that will always be heartwrenching. The *context* of any given pregnancy is everything.

The tension between the beauty of life-giving and the slavery of some unwanted pregnancies can't be resolved by a one-size-fits-all law or moral teaching. But science, aesthetics, emotions, evidence, and the collective wisdom and compassion that exist in religious teachings about loving thy neighbor must be given their due when we're trying to figure out *how* to reconcile the irreconcilable as best we can.

"As best we can" is not perfect. And that is where both sides in the abortion debate fail when they seem willing to tear our culture apart (not to mention constantly derail the whole progressive agenda and set it back decades) in order to stick to their fundamentalist purity on "the issue." One side sweeps the fetus under a "rug" of moral platitudes about female empowerment, and the other does the same to women with platitudes about the sacredness of life.

CHAPTER 9

"Strange Women"

E sther arrived each day a little breathless, hair tied back with a black velvet ribbon to stop it from going "frizzy," as she called it. From the way she gulped the mug of coffee that I brought her, I knew that it was her first of the day, that Esther had probably been asleep twenty minutes before. A moment after arriving, she kicked off her shoes, slipped on the sandals that she kept under the console, and got to work. As soon as Esther was settled, I rolled my chair close to hers under the pretense of needing a better look at the monitor. I sat breathing in Esther's fresh morning scent of warm bathed skin, blissful as a child face down in new-mown hay.

I was the director of an "industrial"—a corporate series of videos. Esther (not her real name) was my video editor, assigned to me by a nearby video postproduction facility. She was also one of several women I've had a powerful crush on since marrying Genie.

Esther and I worked together for over a year. Esther was bright, kind, articulate and good company. She was also twenty-eight years old and looked younger. When we went out for a drink after work, Esther got carded. This was in the early 1990s, soon after I'd fled the Evangelical scene for parts unknown. By the time I met

PHOTO: *Mom sailing with one of her friends in the early 1990s*

Esther, I'd directed four Hollywood features that I wouldn't have paid to see.* I supplemented my income for two or three years (before I began to earn my living as a writer) producing and/or directing industrials, commercials, and this particular Esther-saturated corporate video series.

Mom had warned me about "Strange Women" like Esther. My mother often said that Strange Women lead Believers to destruction. This topic was usually broached when Mom and my sisters would be gossiping in lurid detail about this or that former L'Abri student who had "married a non-Christian" and how this now "unequally yoked" backslider's heart had "grown cold toward the Things Of The Lord." Which brings me back to the Strange Women, like Esther, who I can imagine a happy life with and from time to time fall in love with: in other words, the talented and warm females who remind me most of Genie. They're not necessarily physically similar to Genie, but they, like her, are relaxed, kind, intelligent, and graceful. They are dangerous to my marriage.

Mom taught me that The Battle Of The Heavenlies touches down to earth more often than not through "the sort of Male Temptation that Fran suffers from." And Dad provided lots of examples of that "sort" of temptation. Mom made sure that I noticed Dad's failings, all the better to "grow up spiritually stronger than your poor father."

Men were a source of danger to women. But women, too, according to Mom, could be dangerous, less to my body than to my soul.

---

*Here they are in reverse order: *Baby on Board* (1992), slapstick comedy starring Judge Reinhold and Carol Kane; *Rebel Storm* (1990), futuristic action film starring Zach Galligan and June Chadwick; *Headhunter* (1989), occult horror film starring John Fatooh, June Chadwick, and Steve Kanaly; and *Wired to Kill* (1986), postapocalyptic action film starring Emily Longstreath, Devin Hoelscher, and Merritt Butrick.

Or as Dad put it in a sermon: "Turn with me to Proverbs Chapter Five," Dad said. "King David's talking to his son Solomon. He's teaching Solomon about the Good Women and the Strange Women in the world. We read, 'My son, attend unto my wisdom and bow thine ear.'" Dad looked up from his Bible and peered over his reading glasses at about thirty of us in tight-packed rows of dining room chairs (especially brought downstairs for the Sunday service) in our chalet living room/church. Dad fixed his stern gaze on us and then added, "or literally '*submit*' is what this word 'attend' means here."

Dad started reading again, "'Bow thine ear to my understanding; that thou mayest regard discretion, and that thy lips may keep knowledge.'" Dad glared at us. "Notice it's the *Word* that gives children discretion. When a person has the Bible he'll be able to discriminate between right and wrong. Verse Three continues, 'For the lips of a strange woman drip as an honeycomb, and her mouth is smoother than oil.' David's warning Solomon. David tells us, 'For the lips of the Strange Woman drip as an honeycomb.' Verse Five says, 'Her feet go down to death; her steps take hold on hell.' You might think you're having 'fun,' but the Strange Woman's ultimate destination for you will be an 'affair' with death." Dad paused, took a deep breath, and then yelled at the top of his lungs, "*The seeds of this degeneration were sown by Solomon himself because he didn't heed his own warning!*"

Two recently "saved" former Roman Catholics jumped when Dad screamed. Mom winced. Dad lowered his voice back to a normal speaking volume. "Now turn with me to First Kings Chapter Eleven, Verses One and Two: 'But King Solomon loved many strange women, together with the daughters of Pharaoh, women of the Moabites, Ammonites, Edomites, Zidonians, and Hittites; of the nations concerning which the Lord said unto the children of Israel, Ye shall not go into them, neither shall they come in unto you.'"

Dad got ready to yell again. I could always tell when one of his high-pitched godly howls was on the way by the extra deep breath he took. He'd also move his Bible to one side of the back of the big red leather barrel pulpit chair, a sure sign he was about to "spontaneously" pound his chair-pulpit. "This is a"—Dad's voice shot up an octave to his most screechy prophetic shriek—"*Direct Command*!" FIST POUND!

I feared Dad's preaching yells more than I feared any Strange Women I'd ever met, at least when I was eight. Dad's yelling in church scared me when I was young and later embarrassed me when I learned to read the expression on the faces of newly arrived visitors. Students from "non-Christian backgrounds," say Jews who weren't Complete yet and therefore unused to the instant pretend-anger of Evangelicals "fired up for the Lord," always looked stunned the first time Dad got really wound up in his manufactured outbursts of Godly "rage." Dad's yelling also reminded me of his voice when he screamed at Mom, and the veins stood out on his neck as he'd screech through a wide open mouth until his face turned red.

When Dad preach-yelled, Mom squeezed her hands together and nervously crossed and recrossed her legs. She sat up even straighter, but she also lowered her head and stared at the floor, as if she just couldn't abide looking at him. When I asked Mom why Dad yelled when he preached, she answered, "My father was a wonderful preacher, and he *never once* raised his voice when preaching *or* to my mother." Once Mom said, right out of the blue and without specifically mentioning Dad, "Of course, my dear father was a *real* scholar. I don't care for overly theatrical screaming preachers yelling and giving the appearance that they're angry. Preachers who think that they can't be a preacher without their feigned indignation are mistaken. Perhaps they yell to cover their ignorance." Another time Mom said, "Fran yells most when he's addressing his own temptations. No one needs his sermons more than *he* does."

Anyway, Mom would have been thrilled with Esther and would have worked to turn Esther into a Completed Jew. Esther seemed ripe to hear the Gospel because she was rediscovering her Judaism or Yiddish or something, and Mom loved to try to save Jews (she even wrote a book called *Christianity Is Jewish*). I always thought of Mom's preoccupation with Jews as "Mom's Jew Stuff," when she carried on and on and *on* about a Jew she'd just met and the "great conversation we had about Passover's true meaning" or whatever. Mom would have urged me to find ways to talk to Esther about Old Testament prophecies being fulfilled as a way to "open a door."

Esther's first Jew Stuff "proverb"—as I thought of her little sayings she shared after booting up the computer each morning—was *"Di yugnt iz a feler, di menlekhe yorn a kamf, un der elter a kharote,"* which means "Youth is a mistake, middle age a battle, and old age a regret" (or at least that's what Esther said it meant as per her grandmother's instructions). This particular proverb was sighed more than spoken, usually with a shrug. (The Yiddish was all about Esther's recent "I'm-spiritual-but-not-religious" interest in what she called "rediscovering my Jewish roots.")

While Esther used her mouse and keyboard to log the timeline of our digitized show, I logged the daylight filtering through the window blinds as it caressed her pale cheek. As Esther cut together close-ups, establishing shots, pans, created dissolves, cued music, and this and that graphic, I memorized the curve of her slender back. Esther studied the music lists. I studied the winsome nape of her neck by the light of the blue-gray effects menu on the left-hand screen. Esther shifted, crossed and uncrossed her legs, leaned forward and back during the hours she spent fishing for my project's redemption in the graphics bin. I shifted this way and that to study Esther as if the salvation of my soul depended on memorizing her measurements, neck to chin and thigh to knee. I also lectured myself.

"You're crazy," I told myself. "You've made it through twenty-plus years of marriage, only to piss away your marriage *that's been the only thing that's lasted and* . . . you LOVE Genie!"

My internal arguments—or should I say "our" internal arguments—continued something like this:

"I blame your mother! We were brainwashed!" moaned My Penis. "We never had a chance! And you know what?"

"What?" I asked.

"Those way too *few* Girls we *did* explore before Genie annexed our lives were *wasted* on us! Neither of us knew what we were doing! You barely looked at their delectable bodies because you were in such a *hurry* to climb on top of the ones who let us, and I freely admit that I was a bit hasty, too." Then My Penis shrieked, "Those were *very* short excursions we took into their loamy loins! We didn't even pause to enjoy the scenery!"

"La! La! La! I can't hear you," I sang to drown out My Penis's incessant blather.

"Esther's a wholesome, Meg Ryan type," My Penis whispered.

"Genie's classically beautiful!" I yelled. "You said yourself that she's—and I think I'm quoting you word for word—'a Sophia Loren type with brains and good taste *and* limitless kindness.'"

"Yes, but we've always *liked* those wholesome types," My Penis retorted. "Maybe Genie is *too* beautiful!"

"Now you're just being stupid," I snorted.

"Don't you see that there must be something *wrong* with a woman *that beautiful* and *smart* going for a twerp like you? There's something to be said for the 'girl-next-door' type." My Penis lowered his voice to a conspiratorial whisper, "Esther reminds us of that nice little French Girl Who Let Us!"

"The French Girl didn't let *you* near her," I snapped.

"Now if only we'd savored several thousand Vaginas, we'd have a respectable, some might even say *scientific*, point of reference. As it is, how do we know what we've missed?"

For fifteen months or so, on the days I wasn't on location with the camera crew shooting interviews with executives on their product lines and companies, I sat a couple of feet to the right and slightly behind Esther while she edited the dull footage. The edit suite was about ten by fifteen feet. Six linked hard drives, a U-shaped edit console, and two chairs and a small couch filled the space. What was left over was a phone-booth-sized patch of floor that forced Esther and me to sit so close together that it would have been rude anywhere else but in a subway at rush hour.

One day Esther brought some family photos to the edit suite. I happened to mention that Genie and I had twenty-three photo albums, one for each year we'd been married at that time. Esther begged me to bring the albums to work. Genie said that as long as I remembered to return them, and only took two or three at a time, she didn't mind.

Genie also said she thought it sweet of Esther to take such an interest in our family. I thought that the albums would provide a good excuse to sit next to Esther, thigh to thigh on the client couch, as we turned the pages.

Once I started to bring the albums, Esther lingered over everything in them, from faded snapshots of our daughter Jessica's birth to last year's Christmas dinner photos, fresh and glossy as the day we had picked up the double prints. As Esther looked at the albums, she asked questions related to marriage, babies, and parenthood as if they were geographical locations she hoped to soon visit.

During one of our midmorning coffee breaks, Esther told me that she'd had a steady boyfriend from her junior year in high school until a couple of years after college. I'll call him Charles. Reading between the lines, I figured that she'd had sex only with this one young man. So on top of everything else—Esther's warmth, shared confidences, and solid-citizen recognition of what life is really all about (Love and Family)—it turned out that when it came to old-fashioned values, she was very much like the Girls I'd been raised around at L'Abri. That fact plugged my feelings for Esther into a powerful current of longing-drenched nostalgia. It was as if I'd time-traveled back to meet one of The Girls who had always been so unavailable because I was a child and they were grown-ups and (mostly) born-again, Jesus-Following virgins.

"We're still friends," Esther said. "I always keep my friends."

"How can you be friends after turning him down?" I asked.

"At about every other lunch I have to turn poor Charles down *again*!"

"Does he keep asking?"

"Charles just looks the question. I shake my head no; then we talk about other things. It's almost like some kind of ritual."

"If you like him so much, why not marry him?"

Esther brooded over her coffee. She looked up and grinned.

"He asked me to marry him all through senior year in high school and in college, too. I kept saying, 'Don't ask me until you mean it,' and that I didn't feel done yet."

"'Done?'"

"You know grown up. I wanted to have a life, like, be my own person, not like my mother. She just got married and had children and went out to lunch, that Jewish thing," said Esther, and then she frowned. "I'm afraid I really hurt his feelings," Esther said, then sighed and tucked a foot under her trim thigh and stretched her other leg out in the space between us. "I'm waiting to meet someone older, somebody who has done some living. You know my mother married my dad when he was much older than her. They were very happy."

Esther and gave me a warm and direct look. Was I imagining it, or was that "look" an invitation to the "older man" sitting next to her?

A hard drive crashed, and Esther had to reboot. So we didn't join the others in the dining area that afternoon. We split a bottle of wine and shared a porcini and smoked mozzarella pizza in the edit suite. While we picked at the food, Esther turned the pages of the albums. We sat close together on the client couch—*exactly* as I had pictured us doing.

Those pictures depressed me as I reflected on life's passage. I saw the birthdays and Christmases and vacations fly past. In 1983 the Schaeffer family sat in front of a Christmas tree mounded with gifts. Dad looked inscrutable as moonlit water. He had a swollen lymph node, a small cherry of warning on his neck. Creeping, nesting in his resentful body, the spreading cancer silently invaded.

Year to year the thread of aging flesh screamed mortality one picture at a time. My chest lost tone. On sunny beaches Genie's breasts got heavier and began their journey to middle age. Lines deepened in the glare of the sun. Jessica moved far away and sent photos of her first child, Amanda, that seemed to come from another planet and left me feeling cheated by the fact that Amanda's "other grandparents" got to see her every day. Nor did I enjoy leafing through production stills from my movie shoots in Hollywood.

Esther turned a page to snapshots of Genie so very gorgeously pregnant with John. Esther turned another page and tapped a photograph of me standing on Hollywood Boulevard in front of the Roosevelt Hotel.

"That's the day I did the *Wired to Kill* distribution deal," I mumbled.

Esther nodded and pointed to photographs of Genie's and my furnished-by-week-or-by-month apartment at the Oakwood complex in Burbank; of Jessica, Francis, and John in the pool; and of the one-room production office in the unfashionable industrial part of the Valley. Casting, props, a production meeting, the first day of the shoot . . .

Esther tapped the pictures with a perfectly manicured fingernail. I longed to slide unseen and guilt-free from that fingernail to Esther's pink cuticle. From there I wanted to creep to her delicate knuckle, and from delicate knuckle to slender wrist, and from wrist up creamy forearm, past her elbow to Esther's shoulders and pale neck. I dreamed of paving a passionate path up that smooth column with surreptitious kisses until I reached Esther's lips and once there, to kiss Esther.

"Genie always said the script was awful," I said.

"Was it?" asked Esther.

"Yes. But I wasn't going to admit it, not then."

What a dreadful summer that had been, not to mention that in my *Wired to Kill* year Genie was starting to have problems with bleeding that would lead to that terrible night in the emergency room. I'd been in Lust with my nineteen-year-old star and distracted by flirting.

I said nothing to Esther about all that but "heard" echoes of conversations with Genie that made my cheeks burn with shame.

These "conversations" (like most fights at that time) were really about something else: my sense of failure at having made a film I already knew would be a bust.

"You don't understand the business," I mutter. "If you put your name on this, you'll regret it later," says Genie. "We're staying in LA. Find a school here," I say. "We should wait and see how the movie does before we pull Jessica out of school in Massachusetts," Genie says. "No!" I shout. "If I'm not out here, I'll never succeed. I have to be here. This is where it's happening. I have to be where it's at. We're staying!" "For what we'd get for the house, we couldn't buy a shack here," says Genie. "They resent it if you're not here; don't make the LA commitment," I say. Genie folds a T-shirt and quietly asks, "Commitment to what?" "A commitment to the business!" I yell. "You mean you want to invite 'The Business' into your heart as your Personal Savior?" asks Genie with a friendly smile. I don't acknowledge the peace-offering smile and decide to keep fighting. "Why are you dragging me down by shoving Mother in my face?" I scream. "Your per-diem stops next week. What do we live on while you re-cut?" Genie calmly asks. "I'm in a fucking first-dollar position after the Limited Partners!" I bellow. Genie stands up, then glances down. The hem of her dress is crimson. "Shit, I'm bleeding again," Genie says very matter-of-factly.

What is so ironic is that my wannabe affair with Esther was *invaded* by Mom! First, my mother's good example and instructions regarding Monogamy *and* Continuity held sway, but—and here's the amusing perversity of the situation—even when I was chatting Esther up and being titillated by some of our racier talks, I'd slip in a little moralizing. Once a Schaeffer, always a Schaeffer, I guess.

"Why don't you date more?" I asked during one of our lunches.

"Jesus, Frank, why not ask a *personal* question?" Esther said and laughed.

"I mean since Charles. What do you mean 'Mr. Right' has to be 'different'?"

"Older and wiser, I told you."

"I thought you didn't date because you refuse to sleep around like your friends down on the Cape?"

"You remember everything!" Esther said and laughed. "I should *never* have told you that."

I rubbed my hands in mock glee.

"Give me the juicy details," I said.

Esther leaned back and turned her face to the sun. It was a freakishly hot day for late November, almost seventy degrees. We were sitting on a bench in the parking lot eating our lunch surrounded by mounds of dirty melting snow.

"Mmmmm! That sun feels *soooo* good!" said Esther.

"Move to Florida."

"Yuck!"

"Jessica would be jealous," I said squinting up at the sun.

"Why?"

"It's dark for twenty hours a day in Finland at this time of year."

"I thought Scandinavia was so nice and all," said Esther.

"Please," I asked, holding up my hands in a prayerful begging gesture, "*please give me the juicy details!*"

Esther smiled and adjusted her dress. The turquoise ribbon of her bra strap that I'd been fixated on for the last half-hour vanished. My heart sank. I was enjoying that strap mightily.

"Okay. We just go down and rent the house for two weeks, okay? Some of us stay the whole time."

"How long have you done this?" I asked.

"Each summer since college, I go down for two long weekends a year."

"You said they have sex. Tell me about *sex*!"

Esther laughed.

"*I'm* not telling *you* about the private lives of my friends. I should never have said anything about it."

"*P-p-p-p-please!*" I said doing my best Roger Rabbit imitation.

Esther laughed.

"They, we, go to this bar."

"A *singles* bar?" I asked in mock horror.

"*Nothing* like that. It's a regular place, clam chowder, you know oars nailed to the ceiling, all that ye old, ye old. Some of the other girls maybe meet someone at the bar. In the morning I see the men they bring home. End of story."

"Where?"

"Do I have to spell it out? Jesus!"

"What's the point if you're not specific?"

Esther laughed and shifted to face the sun. The turquoise strap reappeared.

"I'm not listening through walls," said Esther. "The first I know anything is in the morning; you know, you'll see the guy leaving or something."

"Is that awkward?"

"It is if he hangs around, wants coffee or something."

"So these are one-night stands?"

"I guess."

"Sluts!"

Esther gave me a playful shove.

"Don't you *dare* talk about my friends that way."

"Sluts!"

"They are not!"

Esther shoved me again. As she swiveled, her dress was pulled a little askew. Esther's bra strap stood off her collarbone, accentuating her small-boned shoulder.

"If it's not sluttish, why won't you do it?" I asked.

"I don't, that's all."

"But they do?"

"That's their choice."

"And you're saying you don't judge them?"

"Of course not."

"But in your heart you're calling them sluts, aren't you?"

"No."

"The fact you don't fuck around implies some kind of moral value judgment," I said, more or less parroting one of my father's favorite discussion lines—minus the word "fuck" of course.

"It's just what a person's comfortable with."

"Say I'm 'comfortable' with rape?" I said, while groaning inwardly at the fact that I seemed destined to forever slide back into old territory. I was doing my best to both flirt *and* "push Esther to the logic of her presuppositions," as Mom would have called it.

Esther glared at me.

"*Consenting* adults, Frank."

"So between 'consenting adults' there is no behavior you disapprove of?"

"That's right."

"Ever?"

"Right."

"Frozen gerbils up the ass?" I said, going well beyond what would have been in the script that Mom or Dad used when trying to "push a nonbeliever to consider that, just maybe, God has given each of us an innate sense of Right and Wrong," as Mom often said.

"No problem, though I believe we should respect animals' rights, too."

"Having an affair with a married man?"

Was that an extra beat before she answered? I hoped so! And then with a sense of disappointment, I realized she'd only paused because she was chewing and had to swallow before answering.

"He should keep his commitments, but I mean if his marriage is coming apart, what can I do?"

The midlife-crises version of me sighed. Esther had just come close to inviting me to say that my marriage was failing. It wasn't. And the rush of Love I'd felt (Love and Guilt) as I looked at those pictures of Genie pregnant rose up, wagging a finger in my face.

"Kiss her!" screamed My Penis, sensing an opportunity slipping away.

Mom placed roadblocks in my brain of a kind that have prevented me from traveling down a path that would have inexorably led away, and possibly prevented me, from arriving at the stage of life where I now live in peace two doors down the street from my beloved Lucy and Jack. You see, what I learned about monogamy from my mother wasn't found in Bible verses but in her life.

My mother wanted her life to be replete with drama, sweep, and poetry. The Swiss Alps, the craggy coast of Liguria, New York City, and Big Sur were Mom's favorite places. All through my childhood she talked about "the Big Sur redwoods and majestic hills cascading down to the ever-rolling foamy Pacific crashing again and again onto that amazing rocky coast." People, too, had to be "amazing" to interest Mom. Though she was kind to everyone, she favored people imbued with poetry, drama, and/or tragedy. She didn't care about measuring people by wealth or what she'd call "worldly accomplishment." Sure, my mother liked meeting wealthy people because they could write a check to L'Abri for that new chalet Mom "just knew" God was leading her to buy so that couples coming to L'Abri would have a place to stay or for whatever else she'd decided L'Abri needed. That didn't mean she *liked* that person personally, which brings me to my mother's almost-affair.

The individuals my mother admired most were what she called "artistic types." *Creativity* was Mom's favorite word, followed closely by *Continuity*. Those two words, or should I say the meaning my mother gave them, came into conflict when my mother fell in love.

I'll call him Noel. He was a poet, an "artistic type" par excellence, *and* wealthy (he'd inherited a fortune). Noel also was kind, well traveled, young (about thirty), and sensitive, *and* he owned a ranch in California on the Pacific coast. In fact, *he owned a chunk of Big Sur*, with many acres of redwoods, enough moss, bark, rock, sand, sun, and water to provide a lifetime's supply of materials for my mother's flower arrangements.

Noel bought my mother expensive Japanese ceramic bowls for her floral creations. He wrote her poetry. He was tall. He looked pleasingly pale, thin, and ascetic. Noel's skin had that delicate, almost translucent quality that most men possess only in the crook of their arms, where veins run close to the surface.

Noel took walks with my mother. He wore sandals he'd made himself and had pictures of a log-cabin-style home he'd built on his ranch, "with his own hands!" as Mom never tired of telling me. And Noel traveled the world intermittently between visits to L'Abri that stretched over a three-year period. I was about ten years old when he'd first arrived, and Mom was in her early fifties and looked as if she were in her thirties. Mom was also married to a man who left the dancer, poet, lover-of-Chinese-art in her unfulfilled. And Dad hit my mother. If anyone had an excuse, Mom did.

Noel used to bring me interesting curios from his journeys, including a snakeskin and several exotic South Sea seashells for my collection. Meanwhile, Mom treated Noel to many extra prayer meetings, and Noel made it very clear he loved my mother. Years later Mom told me he asked her to marry him several times.

Noel was my mother's second (and last) chance to enter into the poetic and free life she'd craved, free of her parents' theology at last, free of her youthful latching on to Dad (they'd met when Mom was eighteen), free of L'Abri and cooking meals for thirty to forty people a day, free of *being* Edith Schaeffer. Noel was Mom's chance to start over as Mei Fuh (beautiful happiness), the wistful little girl who had left China with a world waiting to discover her.

I vividly remember the trouble Noel caused. I was home for the three-month summer vacation from boarding school when all hell broke loose. I remember that period of our lives, 1963 or there-abouts, as a time when there were more fights than usual between Mom and Dad. Mom was very frank about what was happening, both on the phone and in letters (I was in boarding school), not to mention when I was home for vacations. Later Mom referred to this patch of our family history as "That Difficult Time." She even somewhat managed to sanctify it as part of God's Plan inasmuch as Mom pointed out, "Satan must have known that Fran and I were about to write our books and take The Truth to a huge new group of very needy people because Satan was doing everything he could to ruin L'Abri before that happened! No wonder we had such a struggle!"

In other words, Noel wasn't all her fault since her temptation was part of some vast spiritual struggle. But Mom's label of That Difficult Time hardly covers it. Dad threw a heavy brass vase at my mother one Sunday afternoon after church. He'd been screaming at her for over an hour, and she was (untypically) screaming back. Mom rushed into my bedroom with a deep cut on her shin and slammed and locked my door behind her. She asked me to call a taxi (we had no car) and not to tell anyone. When I got back to the room after making the call in the downstairs hall, Mom sent me to the bathroom for bandages. There was blood pooling on my cracked linoleum floor.

I accompanied my mother to Dr. Clerc in Villars, the ski resort on the mountainside above our village. I remember watching as the doctor trimmed a sliver of yellow fat protruding from the inch-long, to-the-bone gash just below Mom's knee and then put in five stitches. Mom told me to tell anyone who might ask about the bandage that she'd tripped on the front-door steps and fallen on the boot scraper.

That night I sat on the edge of my bed clutching the souvenir Zulu spear my sister Sue and her husband, Ranald, had recently brought me as a gift from their South African honeymoon. I swore to myself that if I heard Dad yelling at Mom or hitting her one more time, I'd kill him. But that accident—and it was an accident because, as Mom explained, "your father *did* mean to throw something, but *didn't* mean for it to hit me on the shin because I leapt the wrong way into the arc of the projectile"—sobered Dad up. For several months the so-called Difficult Time eased up. And soon Mom's special sensitive friend left L'Abri, never to return.

Whatever Mom and Dad were or weren't doing with the men and women they very obviously had crushes on from time to time— Dad clearly favored certain young women over others—they did their best to set their children on a monogamous path. They extolled the virtues of family life and, above all, of Continuity. Of course, they added a needless theological gloss to what I think is a commonsense biological/psychological fact: Humans are programmed to be jealous nest-makers who (usually) don't like to live alone or be cheated on.

I think that my parents were right about the benefits of monogamy because I think that their beliefs happened to tap into the larger reality of evolutionary psychology. I don't agree with Mom and Dad's God-Will-Hate-You-If-You-Sleep-Around theology of monogamy, but speaking in practical terms (and with apologies to Winston Churchill), I *do* believe that monogamy is the worst form of all sexual relationships, except for everything else that has been tried. Brain, Penis, Vagina, and Heart may bicker among themselves, but I think that kindness and common sense should win the genitals-versus-brain debate whenever possible. Hurting your partner's feelings is stupid.

When I was fifteen, I decided to have it out with both my parents. I confronted Dad about hitting Mom. On another day soon after telling Dad just what I thought of him, I confronted Mom over my memories about Noel.

"You're a hypocrite," I said. "You talk to everyone about family and almost ran off with Noel!"

Mom answered calmly. "I never lied to you," she said. "And I *didn't* run off. I was in love, though."

The way my mother said the words "in love" was so forlorn that all the teen hubris was knocked out of me at a stroke. I looked her in the face—I'd been staring at the floor when I made my accusation—and I saw the tears in her eyes. I started to cry, too.

I'd wanted to cast her "sins" in her teeth in my snotty, fifteen-year-old incarnation. Instead, I rediscovered my mother and had my first grown-up conversation with her.

"I didn't go with him because it would have hurt you," Mom said. "Continuity *is* important."

"Why?" I asked.

"Because if our memories are cut off from time and place, then they wash away. I wanted you to have a family. And it wasn't the right thing to do."

"But Dad was hitting you."

"There's two sides to everything."

"Were you sleeping with Noel?"

"No."

"Did Dad think you were?"

"No, he believed me because I was telling the truth. What hurt Fran so deeply was that he knew that I loved Noel in a way I'd never love him. Remember how Noel always would go for walks and hunt for things to bring me for my arrangements?"

"Yes."

"Well, Dear, your father wouldn't have even known what to look for. Noel understood. I could have had a life with him." Mom wiped away her tears. Then with a smile she added, "He even prayed better than poor Fran! Fran just has all those little lists of people's names. Noel used to pray like I do, really *talk* to God, for hours. And he danced with me, too, in the woods once."

We sat in silence together for a long time.

"You should have gone with him," I said at last.

"No, Dear, I should *not* have gone with him," said Mom. "To destroy a family, you have to have a real reason. Fran is a good husband as far as he's able to be, and I love him. You know that I do, in spite of everything. Also, you were too young to go through that. I love you."

"I know," I said. "I love you, too."

Noel was the embodiment of Creativity.

My mother's family was the embodiment of Continuity.

Mom chose Continuity. There was one small happy ending, besides Mom defending her children by not leaving Dad: Years later Mom told Genie that after I'd confronted Dad, he never hit her again.

CHAPTER 10

Godly Sexual Dysfunction, Hope, and Love

Had I been the person I am now when I first met Genie—as well as grandfather to my beloved ones, Genie's lover, a man who long since left his fundamentalist religion behind—I would have warned her. I love Genie, and I would have begged her to avoid that damaged young man.

By the time I met Genie, L'Abri had evolved into a community where absurd fundamentalist theology was masked by a hippie "with-it" exterior. Rules had become lax. By 1969 we were (as I've mentioned) trolling for the Unsaved by using modern culture and "what's happening now" as bait. Under that benign exterior the heart of unreconstructed fundamentalism still beat steadily, just as even after my father grew a goatee, let his hair grow, quoted Woody Allen and Bob Dylan, gave lectures on art and sermons on love, was acclaimed by an eclectic group of groupies and visited by the likes of Timothy Leary (not to mention most

PHOTO: *Mom at age 96 during my Christmas visit in 2010*

Evangelical leaders), my father still hit Mom—until Dad's and my talk, that is.

Worse, if you had pressed him, Dad (like Mom) would have said he still believed the Bible was all literally true. Thus, anyone "saved" at L'Abri who then bought into the Schaeffer package was saddled with trying to live by a book that—if taken at face value—demands a descent into madness.

The word "artist" and the words "Jesus Victim" and "Bronze-Age Thug" seem to be contradictions. But I managed to combine them in my young self. Inside my bosom the heart of a Leviticus-saturated male asshole beat out its angry, domineering rhythm. I harbored a woman-controlling mean streak that would have done Moses and/or any Saudi prince proud. But when it came to girl-attracting bait, along with that new Beatles album, I had a studio full of my paintings. They were just the sort of paintings—of the naked human body—that my soon-to-be "friends" on the Religious Right would have burned.*

A very few years later I was about to dump my painting vocation in favor of a fast-buck, fast-paced life and access to power by becoming my father's sidekick. In that sense the contradiction within L'Abri of a "with it" art-loving commune and a bastion of fundamentalism was lived out in me. When push came to shove, I pulled my own "Franklin Graham" by veering back onto the "straight and narrow" and dumping art for Far Right activism, not to mention money.

---

*My paintings of that period were somewhat in the *Rouault* manner, with heavy dark outlines and vivid blocks of color. I had early successes in my art career with a one-man show near Geneva at the Chante Pier gallery, in London at Criteria Arts, and in New York at the Frisch Gallery, where Mrs. David Rockefeller purchased a painting. I gave up painting in 1974 after I went full-time into producing my dad's movies, hit the road, etc. In 2006 I took out my old paints and resumed painting, now in a different style and for my own pleasure.

By then Genie was stuck. I was no longer the artist she *thought* she'd married. I was wearing a creepy three-piece (dreadful 1970s) suit and sometimes flying around in Jerry Falwell's borrowed jet, raising millions of dollars from Nancy DeMoss, Rich DeVos, Howard Ahmanson, Mary Crowley, the Hunt brothers, and the other many financiers of the emerging Far Right/Religious Right. I was regularly appearing on the *700 Club* with Pat Robertson, was a guest (several times) on Dobson's *Focus on the Family* radio show, and was selling hundreds of thousands of copies of my Far Right screeds *while also* being an agent-instigator by discovering the likes of Mary Pride and unleashing their updated Bronze-Age tribal mythology on a new generation. I was a favorite of conservative "pro-life" Roman Catholics like Archbishop Fulton Sheen (of New York) and also (then) Archbishop Bernard Law of Boston. I was appearing on platforms with Law at antiabortion fundraising events. Neither Genie nor I saw this bizarre future on the horizon in 1969.

Genie slept with an artist and woke up married to a Religious Right nut. I'm not sure why Genie stuck it out. She says it's because she loved me and took her wedding vows seriously.

We've been married for forty years and are happy. Nevertheless, if I were an unselfish person (I'm not) and could warn Genie *before* she walked through that chalet door, I just might send her this letter.

Dearest Genie,
This is a message from the future from someone who loves you. You are about to meet your husband. Don't!

He—rather I, because I'm afraid this is me we're talking about—grew up helping to hide my father's violence against my mother. Violence seems "normal" to the young angry thug you are about to meet.

There were two ANGRY MALES in our house, Dad and our Jewish/Christian "God." I grew up trying to do the best I could to hide The-God-Of-The-Bible's and Dad's true character from myself and from their followers *and* help my parents convert people to believing in this "God" by pretending that our "Deity" was nicer than He is.

You and I are "foreordained" (stick around my parents, and you'll learn what that word means) to have three lovely babies— Jessica, Francis, and John—*if* you walk through the chalet Les Mélèzes door. So there's that. But . . . in a few years after we meet (by the way, I'm going to get you pregnant before we marry, so don't you believe me when I say, "I'll pull out"), I'll do my best to hide the fact that I slap our daughter and pull her hair when I lose my temper just as I did my best to hide the fact that Dad hit Mom.

No one in our Evangelical circle will think that "spanking" our children is wicked (let alone criminal) because they, too, will be following our dreadful, vengeful little God, Who "inspired" pro-torture child-smashing garbage such as Proverbs 13:24: "He that spareth his rod hateth his son: but he that loveth him chasteneth him betimes (diligently)." And Proverbs 19:18: "Chasten thy son while there is hope, and let not thy soul spare for his crying." Or take Proverbs 23:13: "Withhold not correction from the child: for if thou beatest him with the rod, he shall not die."

The "God" Who "said" these things—because we believe God "inspired" (i.e., virtually dictated) the Bible—wants us to beat our children *so severely that a reasonable parent might worry that the child would die.* I never even came close to doing that because, like most people, I am much nicer than the so-called God-Of-The-Bible, but that's not saying much.

In case you're wondering, here's what I was taught *by example* about how to treat women: I lay in my bed at night listening to

Dad's voice screaming at Mom and hoping he would keep yelling because when his voice fell silent, sometimes the next sound I heard was the thud of his fist.

And here's a passage (there are sickeningly more like it) from the Bible about how to "treat" women. I was raised on shit like this story from Deuteronomy (22:16–21): "The girl's father will say to the elders, 'I gave my daughter in marriage to this man, but he dislikes her. Now he has slandered her and said, "I did not find your daughter to be a virgin." But here is the proof of my daughter's virginity.' Then her parents shall display the cloth [that the girl bled into when she lost her virginity] before the elders of the town, and the elders shall take the man and punish him. They shall fine him a hundred shekels of silver and give them to the girl's father, because this man has given an Israelite virgin a bad name. She shall continue to be his wife; he must not divorce her as long as he lives. If, however, the charge is true and no proof of the girl's virginity can be found, she shall be brought to the door of her father's house and there the men of her town shall stone her to death. She has done a disgraceful thing in Israel by being promiscuous while still in her father's house. You must purge the evil from among you."

After learning what sane humanity looks like from you, I'll eventually leave the Evangelical/Jewish/Jesus Victim netherworld and *slowly* change for the better. I'll even grow kinder as I decide that no matter what the Bible says about itself, it is an unreliable book and that if there is an actual God—say, one Who made loving, lovely, strong, intelligent, and forgiving (and sexy) females like you and endowed them with levels of common sense, altruism, and mercy beyond description—He, She, or It *must* want us to use our brains to discern barbaric lies from truth.

If you do stick with me, it will be *your* sanity, *your* kindness, and *your* love that will save me. But you can do better than to undertake a remedial marriage with someone who will spend the first third or so of our marriage trying to escape the Bronze Age.

Run, Darling!

With All My Love,
Frank

Genie, too, was no stranger to The-God-Of-The-Bible's crippling ideas. She was raised Roman Catholic in the 1950s and 1960s. And until she was sixteen, Genie was "trained" (read temporarily frozen) in parochial schools. The nuns warned Genie about her Temptress Body. They told her to use a facecloth to wash with so that "your hand never touches yourself down there." They warned her not to use tampons, lest she defile her virginity. And boys were The Enemy.

Though by age sixteen Genie had rejected her religion intellectually, fled Catholic school, and become a supposedly liberated San Francisco hippie princess (who took drugs, hung out at the old Fillmore West, had Sex, saw the Beatles and Rolling Stones in concert—twice), the nuns had successfully manipulated her into viewing her body as The Enemy. According to Genie, to be a good Catholic girl in those days was to "pretend you were a doll with nothing but smooth plastic between your legs."

So we two traveled our bumpy learning path—from angry and horny fornicating Jesus Victim and Enemy Body to happy husband and wife. While we completed growing up in each other's arms, I gradually learned that Genie's gratification was the most powerful aphrodisiac I could imbibe and that the ultimate means of attaining pleasure is selflessness—at least in bed. I also discovered that Mom was right: If you stick out the bad patches of life, fight to make them better, and hang on to what counts, one day you may wake up to discover that the best gift is a grandchild.

The sexual dysfunction of the Evangelical and Roman Catholic communities that Genie and I grew up in is evident in the larger world as surely as that dysfunction was built into both Genie's and my childhoods. The moralistic denial of healthy heterosexual and homosexual sexuality has also unhinged the Evangelical leadership as much as it long ago unhinged the Roman Catholic "celibate" popes and bishops and those body-fearing nuns who "instructed" Genie.

The sexual dysfunction that unleashed the culture wars sprung from the heart of the Bible. Put another way: Either Jesus was oddly preoccupied with self-castration or the person who made up this deranged pro-celibacy and antimarriage story was.

According to the author of Matthew, Jesus said, "'And I say unto you, Whosoever shall put away his wife, except it be for fornication, and shall marry another, committeth adultery: and whoso marrieth her which is put away doth commit adultery.' His disciples said unto him, 'If the case of the man be so with his wife, it is not good to marry.' But he said unto them, 'All men cannot receive this saying, save they to whom it is given. For there are some eunuchs, which were so born from their mother's womb: and there are some eunuchs, which were made eunuchs of men: and there be eunuchs, which have made themselves eunuchs for the kingdom of heaven's sake. He that is able to receive it, let him receive it'" (Matthew 19:9–12).

I get it. As someone who has argued with his Penis in a "down boy!" manner, I've sometimes been reduced to threatening my (close but pesky friend) with some Matthew 18:8 logic. "If your hand or your foot causes you to sin, cut it off. . . . It is better for you to enter [heaven] maimed . . . than to have two hands or two feet and be thrown into eternal fire."

When delivering her Talks, Mom read the antimarriage "he that is able to receive it, let him receive it" passages in a bored voice of the kind she usually reserved for the hurried incantation of the dreary biblical genealogies. When pressed to explain just *why* Jesus and Paul seemed antisex and elevated celibacy to a nutty status where Jesus actually urged those "able to receive it" to castrate themselves, Mom had a way of discounting the inconvenient passages.

"Well," Mom would say, "given how marriage is presented in the Bible between God and Israel, Christ and the Church, why do both Jesus and Apostle Paul *seem* to sanction celibacy as better than marriage in First Corinthians, Matthew, and Revelation? Well, *they don't!* Jesus just *seems* to have told the disciples when they questioned His condemnation of easy divorce laws that 'there are eunuchs for the sake of the kingdom of heaven. He who is able to receive this, let him receive it,' but Paul, in First Corinthians, makes it clear that yes, indeed, those who aren't able to receive his teaching on celibacy *aren't* sinning when they marry to avoid burning with passion. You see, what Paul and Jesus *really mean* is that because some married people are more divided in their interests between serving God and other things than compared to some single men or women, maybe those easily distracted people should just stick with being missionaries and not marry. So you see *that* doesn't apply to all Christians at all times! It applied *only* to those *easily distracted Corinthians* Paul was writing to. *I* can do a lot more than one thing at once, Dear! Being married to Fran doesn't stop *me* from witnessing! Helping him is *part of* my ministry, not an impediment to it. Anyway, Jesus had to exaggerate sometimes, Dear, to get people's attention."

Mom's best efforts to rehabilitate The-God-Of-The-Bible's sexual dysfunction failed. The sexual sickness that cripples The-God-Of-The-Bible is catching. Worshipping a "God" who sniffs around women's menstrual cycles, hands virgins to warriors to be raped as a reward, worries about who ejaculates where, wants unmarried women who lose their virginity (premarriage) stoned to death, recommends castration so that men can become eunuchs for the sake of the kingdom of heaven, is the sort of "God" who winds up attracting the worst sorts of nuts to His "cause." And those born into that cause imbibe deeply from a well of sexual dysfunction before they make any choices of their own. They—we—are marked for life.

Lurking in the heart of the Jewish/Christian/Muslim communities—the people of the book—is a strange take on Sex that keeps exploding into public view. It's easy to sit in the "enlightened" West and shake our heads over Afghan tribesmen raping little boys en masse (as reported in the *San Francisco Chronicle* article I cited earlier), but how are we of the enlightened West doing?

The Roman Catholic Church, as it has tried to make "eunuchs which have made themselves eunuchs for the kingdom of heaven's sake" via a celibate priesthood, has had its sexual "ethics" discredited ever since Giovanni Boccaccio called the Church's bluff when he wrote the *Decameron* in the fourteenth century. Nothing has changed since. Boccaccio's wonderfully ribald satire at the expense of the Roman Catholic Church's gross sexual hypocrisy is as apt today as ever. And the Evangelicals find themselves in the same mess, from the sexual-scandal-mired Evangelical leadership to the nefarious enablers like the so-called Family and its C Street enclave of congressional adulterers (of which more in a moment).*

If there is one thing *all Christians* should have learned by now, it's that we—*of all people*—should never, ever cast aspersions on anyone else's sex life. When it comes to pointing the finger over

*The Family was founded in 1935 and is known for its long history of friendly dealings with dictators worldwide as well as for its clearly defined aim to infiltrate the U.S. government with Far Right Evangelicals who will, in turn, carry out a Reconstructionist-type of campaign to "reclaim" the country and world for a politicized "Jesus."

sexual "sin," the worldwide Christian community—from the halls of the Vatican and many a Greek, Russian, or Arab Orthodox bishop's palace, to an Evangelical "home church" established in somebody's basement two minutes ago—is in the morally compromised position of a violent habitual rapist criticizing a shoplifter for stealing a candy bar.

We're talking not about "a few bad apples" but about the whole edifice of religion top to bottom. An impartial inquiry into child abuse at Roman Catholic institutions in Ireland found that the top Church leaders *knew* that sexual abuse was endemic in boys and girls institutions. A nine-year government inquiry investigated a *sixty-year period* when more than 35,000 children were placed in a network of "reformatories," "industrial schools," and "workhouses." The children suffered physical and/or sexual abuse that more than two thousand witnesses confirmed to the commission.*

Church authorities in league with government enablers were placing children in these camps until the 1980s. Physical and emotional abuse was a built-in *deliberate feature* of these "homes" for young men and women. The inquiry proved that child rape defines Irish Catholicism as surely as the sign of the cross once did. The state-ordered investigation into cover-ups by the Dublin Archdiocese revealed that church officials had shielded scores of priests from criminal investigation over several decades and did not report *any* crimes to the police until the mid-1990s.**

This was much the same behavior as happened in the United States: The Church's leaders spent much more time protecting their institution than their flock, let alone children. For instance, an ac-

---

*See BBC News, May 20, 2009, http://news.bbc.co.uk/2/hi/8059826.stm.
**"Vatican Shielded Dublin Priest Until He Raped Boy," Associated Press, December 17, 2010.

quaintance of mine in the Boston area, Cardinal Bernard Law, with whom I'd worked on various Massachusetts "pro-life" initiatives and fund-raising efforts, left Boston for Rome "in a hurry" after he was being investigated for enabling child-molesting priests to remain in ministry.

I have a photograph of the two of us (back when Law was a mere archbishop), with Law sitting next to me at the head table at a banquet held by Massachusetts Citizens for Life, where we both spoke. Law was a hand-on-your-forearm political operative. He possessed the sort of smoothness that is achieved only after years of deftly "handling" people in a climb to power. Those sorts of political instincts depend on the practitioner being perceived as a "good guy" and had transformed Law into a glad-handing, remember-everyone's-first-name shell of jovial bonhomie.

After his "fall" Law was whisked off to the Vatican and "reassigned." Then Pope John Paul *kept him on as a cardinal*! In what has to be one of the strangest (and unintentionally revealing) "defenses" of Cardinal Law, according to a report by National Public Radio, Deal Hudson (a conservative Roman Catholic activist) tried to somewhat exonerate Law by saying that, after all, what Law did wasn't so unusual! National Public Radio's Boston station (WBUR) filed this report: "'There is a particular animus being manifested toward Cardinal Law,' said Deal Hudson, president of Catholic Advocate and director of InsideCatholic.com, two conservative Catholic Web sites. 'When you stand back and look across the United States at all the dioceses and the way this scenario was repeated in so many dioceses and in some cases with even higher levels of abuse cases, I don't think that animus is fair.'"*

---

*Deborah Becker, "Irish Catholics Call for Cardinal Law's Resignation, Following Clergy Abuse Report," WBUR.org, February 10, 2010, www.wbur.org/2010/02/10/irish-priests-followup.

After rescuing Law from his American accusers, Pope John Paul II made Cardinal Law a member of the so-called Pontifical Council for the Family! According to the *Boston Globe*, the pope's new "family expert" had, under questioning by the Boston police, admitted that when a priest committed a sex crime, his practice was to only seek the analysis of "therapists" in residential treatment centers before deciding whether to *return a priest accused of sexually abusing a child to the pulpit*. According to countless media reports from the *Boston Globe* to WBUR, Cardinal Law became the first bishop in America shown to have actively participated in the cover-up of child molestation.* Despite substantial amounts of documentation that demonstrated his deep involvement with covering up the molestation of thousands of children, Law refused to step down as archbishop of Boston. After he left Boston, there remained a significant number of undisclosed priests in the Boston area who had confessed to molesting children and who—as I write this—*continue to work as priests*. Law declined to disclose the names of these "shepherds."**

And *this* is the church that "conservative" bishops and priests in the Anglican and Episcopal communions in the United States and the United Kingdom have since been joining in droves because the Roman Catholic Church has preserved "pure" doctrine that condemns homosexuality as a sin! So "breakaway" Anglicans and Episcopalians (and not a few Evangelicals, too) are received into the "true church" by popes and bishops eager to swell their ranks with laypeople and priests who just *can't abide* having homosexual marriages between monogamous, law-abiding gay men and

---

*The *Boston Globe* archive of coverage of clergy sexual abuse is listed in chronological order online. Use the links at right to see articles from previous months, dating back to January 2002, www.boston.com/globe/spotlight/abuse/chronological.htm.

**Becker, "Irish Catholics Call for Cardinal Law's Resignation."

women blessed in their churches but are happy to throw their hats
and/or miters into the ring alongside the miters of the leaders of a
worldwide network of pedophiles and their enablers.

Go figure.

I remember my reaction when back in the mid-1980s I heard the
first rumblings about the Boston Diocese's sex abuses before the
scandals broke wide open. At that time I had several friends who
had recently converted or were about to convert (in good faith) to
the Roman Catholic Church because they (like me) were becoming increasingly disillusioned with the merger of the Evangelical
world and the entertainment business and the celebrity culture of
personality cults. Conditioned by years of poor-little-Us Evangelical victim-think, I assumed that somehow the priests and bishops
were being "badmouthed" and had been set up by "Them." This
must be another wicked plot by the Liberal elite, I thought, and the
other enemies of the pro-life movement!

I remember talking over my sense of the bishops having been
"set up" with my friend Thom Howard, a well-known Protestant
author and convert to the Roman Catholic Church. (He lost his
job teaching at Protestant Gordon College because he became a
Roman Catholic.) What neither of us asked each other at the time
was *why* both communities—Evangelical and Roman Catholic—
were continually mired in sexual scandal and (as was even then
becoming evident) so much criminal behavior. Nor did I wish to
ask myself *why* I thought that conservative religionists like me
had a right to "speak out" on so-called moral sexual issues, such as
gay rights, given that my own Christian community *was* rotten to
its core.

The hypocrisy I participated in continues. Roman Catholic bishops in North America have led the "moral" crusade against gay

marriage and stem cell research with no sense of irony. And much of the abuse of children that took place worldwide was on Pope John Paul II's watch. And he did all he could to cover up Cardinal Law's activities and even rewarded him with a plum assignment in Rome. Notwithstanding, a Vatican ceremony (early in 2011) moved John Paul II one step closer to "sainthood!" Meanwhile Roman Catholic bishops—while presiding over the bankrupting of the church from lawsuits and *while* fighting off prison sentences for themselves and/or their priests—found time to denounce President Obama's health care reform, which aimed at helping 34 million uninsured poor people, as "proabortion."

And how were those moral "family values" Old Testament Jews (Mom so idealized) doing in their modern Levitical incarnation? According to National Public Radio (to cite just one of scores of reports), in 2009 four ultra-Orthodox rabbis in Brooklyn were sued and/or arrested for abusing boys. As NPR reported, "That's a tiny fraction of the actual abuse, says Hella Winston, author of *Unchosen: The Hidden Lives of Hasidic Rebels.* She says that in researching her book, she encountered dozens of alleged victims who told her sexual abuse is an open secret in the Hasidic community. But the community is so insulated and the rabbis are so powerful that few dare to come forward."*

And according to the same story:

> Brooklyn District Attorney Charles Hynes says he has 10 active sexual abuse cases involving Orthodox Jews—including a school principal. . . . And Hynes says there could be many more.

---

*Barbara Bradley Hagerty, "Abuse Scandal Plagues Hasidic Jews in Brooklyn," NPR, February 2, 2009, www.npr.org/templates/story/story.php?storyId=99913807.

Yeshivas are private schools, which means they don't have to report accusations of sexual abuse to civil authorities. "I've got no way to know if there's a pattern of concealing the conduct," he says. Hynes says the Jewish leaders—like Catholic bishops—try to handle these affairs internally, through a rabbinical court. It's a practice that infuriates him. "You have no business taking these cases to religious tribunals," Hynes says. "They are either civil or criminal in nature, or both. Your obligation is to bring these allegations to us and let us conduct the investigation."*

And how are women treated by these most "observant" of "Real Believing Jews," as Mom called them? Esther Rachel Russell's 2006 documentary about domestic abuse in the Orthodox Jewish community, *Shame, Shanda, and Silence*, reveals a sad fact: Orthodox Jewish women tend to stay with violent abusive partners. And abuse is rampant in this biblically patriarchal enclave of devotion to God.**

As for the "moral authority" of the North American Evangelicals, one of their leading organizations and the organizers of the annual presidential prayer breakfast, the Family (or the Fellowship), ran a residential "ministry" for many years before it drew unwelcome media scrutiny in 2009 and 2010. The Family specialized in housing and indoctrinating members of Congress in its Washington, D.C., C Street residence in order to "take back" the world

---

*Ibid.
**Yaelle Frohlich, "Shame, Shanda, and Silence: Domestic Abuse in the Orthodox Community," *The Observer*, May 5, 2009, www.yuobserver.com/home/index.cfm?event=displayArticlePrinterFriendly&uStory_id=eef70b04–0736–4fd8–9953–6afade58ad25.

for Jesus. The Family also had worked actively for years to influence both American politics and foreign leaders and had done so with great "success."

Several leading Family members—Senator John Ensign of Nevada, governor of South Carolina Mark Sanford, and former representative Chip Pickering of Mississippi—were all found guilty of adultery. This would be meaningless to anyone but their wives except for that all three defined their political careers by *loudly advertising their so-called Christian family values.* Sanford admitted to an affair with a woman in Argentina. Ensign admitted that his family had paid $96,000 in hush money to his former mistress and her family. Pickering is said to have conducted his adulterous affair within the walls of the Family's C Street complex.

Then there was George Rekers, who played an important role in many of the most extreme Evangelical assaults on gay people's rights. His career started in 1982 with his publishing a homophobic "textbook," *Growing Up Straight: What Families Should Know About Homosexuality.* Rekers was a cofounder with James Dobson of the gay-bashing Family Research Council. In 2010 Rekers was found to be "in a class by himself" when it came to sexual hypocrisy (as *New York Times* columnist Frank Rich noted). A Baptist minister with a bent for "curing" homosexuality, sixty-year-old Rekers was caught by a *Miami New Times* reporter with a twenty-year-old male escort at Miami International Airport. The "couple" was returning from a ten-day trip to London. Rekers's only mistake, he told *Christianity Today* magazine, was to hire a "travel assistant" without proper vetting. Rekers said, "[My assistant] did let me share the gospel of Jesus Christ with him, with many Scriptures in three extended conversations."*

---

*Frank Rich, "A Heaven-Sent Rent Boy," *New York Times,* May 14, 2010.

Sex scandals seem to be the only actual interdenominational ecumenism that exists; perversity unites many Christian groups, as does their propensity to judge others. We've arrived the point where I think I may (only half-jokingly) safely say that *all* Evangelical antigay activists and *all* conservative Roman Catholic bishops are probably closeted gays hiding behind their loud antigay public proclamations and/or that *all* these same "traditional family values" leaders will eventually be shown to have committed adultery and/or enabled child molesters—when not calling press conferences to denounce "godless Liberals," gay rights, and stem cell research!

There is an attending level of smarmy hypocrisy expressed as "we hate the sin, but love the sinner" that is as ludicrous as it is two-faced. For instance, in 2010 top Evangelical leaders participated (as I mentioned before, they have clamored to do each year for decades) in the Washington schmooze-fest "prayer breakfast" organized by the Family. At *that very moment* the Family was also hock deep in yet another scandal, this time in Uganda.

The story of the Ugandan legislation to kill gays *for being gay* was intertwined with the Family and also with representatives of the wider "respectable" American Evangelical community. According to many press reports, the genesis of the antihomosexual Ugandan bill may be traced to a three-day seminar in Kampala in March 2009 called "Exposing the Truth Behind Homosexuality and the Homosexual Agenda."* This seminar was led by Evangelical leader and hero to the Religious Right Scott Lively. He is best known for his Holocaust revisionist book *The Pink Swastika*, which claims

---

*Jody May-Chang, "Exporting Homophobia: American Far-Right Conservative Churches Establish Influence on Anti-Gay Policy in Africa; Gay Ugandans Face Daily Fear for Their Lives," *Boise Weekly*, September 8, 2010, www.boiseweekly .com/boise/exporting-homophobia-american-far-right-conservative-churches-establish-influence-on-anti-gay-policy-in-africa/Content?oid=1767227.

homosexuals founded the Nazi party and were responsible for death camp atrocities.

According to sources who attended the conference (and who were later widely quoted in the press), Lively told his Kampala audience, "I know more about this [homosexuality] than almost anyone in the world. . . . The gay movement is an evil institution. The goal of the gay movement is to defeat the marriage-based society and replace it with a culture of sexual promiscuity."* The results of the seminar were dramatic. "The community has become very hostile now," Frank Mugisha, executive director of Sexual Minorities Uganda, said in an interview. "We have to watch our backs very much more than before because the community thinks if the Ugandan government is not passing the law, they will deal with [gay] people on their own."**

For decades Evangelical leaders have jockeyed for good tables at the Family-run "prayer breakfast." (My father, to his credit, always called the Family a "fascist cult" and "evil," long before its bizarre actions came to anyone else's attention. He refused all the many invitations to attend the prayer breakfast, let alone speak at it, as he was asked to do several times.)

After the Family was reported to be hock deep in the Uganda scandal, Evangelical leaders still turned up in droves anyway! They did this even though David Bahati, the man behind the kill-the-gays legislation, was deeply involved in the Family's work in Uganda at that time, and a minister in the government of Uganda and *was also helping to organize the Family's National Prayer Breakfast.****

---

*R. W. Johnson, "West Turns Africa into Gay Battlefield; Western Evangelists and Gay Rights Groups Are Stoking Africa's Bitter Rows over Homosexuality," *Sunday Times*, January 17, 2010.
**May-Chang, "Exporting Homophobia."
***See Jeff Sharlet, *The Family: The Secret Fundamentalism at the Heart of American Power* (New York: Harper Perennial, 2009); and Jeff Sharlet, *C Street: The Fundamentalist Threat to American Democracy* (New York: Little, Brown, 2010).

A day before this "prayer" farce, I participated in a press conference held at the National Press Club in Washington, D.C., sponsored by the Human Rights Campaign. I did so to call attention to the antigay activities of the Family. "Prayer is a good thing, and Americans ought to gather to pray, but we better be careful what we pray for," said one of our presenters, Gene Robinson (the first openly gay bishop in the Episcopal Church). "I call upon our president to make himself known to be in opposition . . . to this violation of human rights for all of God's children in Uganda and beyond," Robinson concluded.

At our press conference a gay Ugandan who was seeking asylum in the United States gave a detailed account of the harassment he withstood "from my fellow Christians in Uganda." Given the multiplying death threats he was receiving for speaking out, Moses (not his real name) addressed reporters with a paper bag over his head to conceal his identity. He described in detail how "one would rather die than come out of the closet" in religiously conservative Uganda. He also spoke about how American Evangelicals had egged on the Ugandan authorities with the American Evangelical-propagated pseudoscientific myth that homosexuality is a "chosen lifestyle" that can be "cured" by Jesus and/or therapy and that therefore people who remain gay do so out of choice.

When Moses spoke at our press conference, his hands gripped the Press Club lectern, and when he released that grip, they trembled. He had every reason to be fearful.

As the *New York Times* later noted in a news story (January 2011) the dire influence of the Evangelical "leadership" on gay issues in Uganda continued to have its effect:

> David Kato knew he was a marked man. As the most outspoken
> gay rights advocate in Uganda, a country where homophobia is so

severe that Parliament is considering a bill to execute gay people, he had received a stream of death threats. . . . A few months ago, a Ugandan newspaper ran an anti-gay diatribe with Mr. Kato's picture on the front page under a banner urging, "Hang Them." On January 26, 2011, Mr. Kato was beaten to death with a hammer . . . "David's death is a result of the hatred planted in Uganda by U.S. Evangelicals in 2009," said Val Kalende, the chairperson of one of Uganda's gay rights groups, in a statement. "The Ugandan Government and the so-called U.S. Evangelicals must take responsibility for David's blood." Mrs. Kalende was referring to visits in March 2009 by a group of American evangelicals, who held rallies and workshops in Uganda discussing how to make gay people straight, how gay men sodomized teenage boys and how "the gay movement is an evil institution" intended to "defeat the marriage-based society."*

I hugged Moses after he concluded his remarks and discovered that his back was drenched in sweat even in that ice-cold air-conditioned room. I spoke next, and I felt ashamed to be holding forth at so little personal cost. I could speak from that podium without risk of more than a few e-mails from people who wrote things like "You fucking fag lover" and "Your father would be ashamed of you" while Moses faced death for standing up against the religion-led lynch mob. Nevertheless, I know a little about what he was enduring because I'm used to certain types of "correspondence," like this e-mail (typos in the original) that I happened to receive when working on this chapter.

---

*Jeffrey Gettleman, "Ugandan Gay Rights Activist Is Beaten to Death," *New York Times,* January 27, 2011.

From: D—Date: Mon, Sep 27, 2010 10:27 am
I just read what you wrote in support of our Muslim Marxist, Lying SOB POTUS. He is a shill for the NWO and wants to bring
the USA down to 3rd world status. He refuses to show his long-
form birth certificate, and tha means he is hiding something, like
he is not constitutionally eligible to be in the position that he
findshimself in. A LIAR is what he amounts to, and that kind of
person does not represent me or mine. You are a jaded idoit. . . . I
work for a living, you should try doing the same thing, cause
your ideology and your writing sucks. . . . Do not reply . . . You
must be a communist also, you look like one. . . . RATFINK!

Moses faced daily threats for being who he was. But I *chose* to leave
the Evangelical fold and also *chose* to support candidate and then
President Obama, knowing full well that I'd attract the attention of
the many people gleefully wallowing in the subterranean river of
sewage that flows wide and deep just under the surface of American life. Moses hadn't chosen anything. He was hated for merely
trying to fulfill the natural longings he was born with and that I
was allowed to indulge on that far-off sweet-flower-strewn mountainside with my French *petit amie.*

When I got Genie pregnant, I was deemed normal within the
Evangelical ghetto in which I was raised. I could sleep with my
sweetheart fearing no more than a reprimand for doing something
"too soon" and "before marriage." I might have been called a sinner,
but I never would have been castigated as a deviant and told to
change my inner sexual self. My "sins" left me respectably accepted
within the camp of the righteous and still categorized as fully
human.

Moses was condemned by "moral" people as a "freak" *for being
born who he is* and for possessing *normal* homosexual sexuality.

And so he stood there next to me facing death threats for having done no more than experience the same God-given emotions I had experienced when I met Genie.

No wonder Far Right American Evangelicals, Mormons, Orthodox Jews, Muslims, and Roman Catholics et al. slander gay men and women and *also* have an affinity for certain repressive religion-saturated countries like gay-bashing Uganda. Maybe it's because the Ugandans proposed to do to gay men and women "over there" what many Evangelicals and conservative Roman Catholics would love to do here—if they could carry out what might be called the Reconstructionist solution and get away with it.

As we've seen, a bedrock article of faith in the American Religious Right is that America had "Christian origins" and that today America must be "restored" to its "religious heritage." The "Puritan heritage" of America is cited as evidence for our need to return to our biblical roots and/or to work internationally, as does the Family, to get others to follow our "holy" path.

Antigay Evangelicals are just carrying on the tradition of persecuting people in the name of God begun in the Bay State. Puritans, too, believed that they were defending authentic Christianity. They said that they were on a divine mission, even calling themselves "The New Israel" and a "city set upon a hill." John Winthrop transferred the idea of "nationhood" in biblical Israel to the Massachusetts Bay Company. Puritans said the Bible confirmed their status as the New Israel. And since the Puritans claimed they were God's "Chosen People," they said that they had the right to take land from the "heathen." These were the American Indians whom the Puritans thought of as the "new Canaanites," to be slaughtered with God's blessing and, in the case of the Pequot Indians, burned alive.

Anne Hutchinson was a seventeenth-century settler in Massachusetts and an "unauthorized" Bible teacher in a dissident church group who, in the words of the state of Massachusetts monument honoring her, was a "courageous exponent of civil liberty and religious toleration." Hutchinson was also a student of the Bible, which she interpreted by the light of what she termed her own "divine inspiration."

In other words, Hutchinson came to believe that in order to remain *both* a Christian *and* a sane and decent being, she had to *pick and choose* what she believed in her tradition. Hutchinson was banished from the colony for her stand. And Hutchinson, like all people of goodwill informed by the love-your-neighbor ethic, carried within her *evolving* ethical self the ability to "listen" for the Lord's "prophetical office" to "open scripture" (as she called it).

Hutchinson seems to have concluded that religious believers should worship God, not the books *about* God. Another way to state her case is that God does not reveal Himself, Herself, or Themselves through books but through the heart and the "prophetical office" of the heart.

Our hearts connect to a truth larger than ourselves: Love of others in the context of community.

That is the only value of formal religion. It provides the place and time for the liturgies through which we may unite with others heart-to-heart to seek out those mysterious truths that words can't describe but that the *doing of ritual* helps us to tap into.

And this idea isn't some modern-era "Liberal" view or even original with the "heretic" Anne Hutchinson. A thread of open interpretation of the Scriptures and religious tradition goes back to the beginnings of the Christian era and coexists with the narrower, harsher view of God. That "thread" teaches that we do not find God through dogma but through stillness of the soul. In that quiet place we may be given the gift of encountering something bigger and more beautiful than ourselves.

First-century Church Father Tertullian summed up this more enlightened view, exhorting the faithful, "That which is infinite is known only to itself. This it is which gives some notion of God, while yet beyond all our conceptions—our very incapacity of fully grasping Him affords us the idea of what He really is. He is presented to our minds in His transcendent greatness, as at once known and unknown."*

A whole antifundamentalist, antitheology thread in church history came to be called apophatic theology, or the theology of *not* knowing. This merciful and open tradition takes a mystical approach (similar to Hutchison's) related to individual experiences of the Divine, which are given by God as a gift, not acquired or demanded.

Apophatic theology teaches that the Divine is ineffable, something that can be recognized only when it is felt after it is given. All we can "do" is shut up, listen, and wait. This ancient tradition, this humane thread, flies in the face of today's Evangelical myths about an "inerrant," let alone literal, Bible.

I think that if she were alive today, Hutchinson might agree with me when I observe that the world will not find peace until people wanting to build a Jewish synagogue in Mecca or a Unitarian church in Medina may do so as easily as they could in Chicago; that the world will never be safe until a gay couple may kiss openly and without fear on any street in Tulsa, Islamabad, Lagos, or Kansas City; that America won't find sanity until Utah and South Carolina are no more defined by any one religion than Central

---

*Tertullian, *Apologeticus*, 17.

Park is; and that Americans will keep dying for nothing but stupid theology and fear-filled xenophobic ignorance until the very idea of a "Christian country," "Islamic republic," "atheist people's paradise," or a "Jewish state" is about as credible as a flat-earth theory.

To be true to what I hope is the heart of the best of the universal religious message, I want to say that redemption through selflessness, hope, and Love necessitates a new and *fearless* repudiation of the parts of holy books and traditions—be they Jewish, Christian, Muslim (or other)—that bring us messages of hate, exclusion, racism, ignorance, misogyny, homophobia, tribalism, and fear. To find any spiritual truth within any religion's holy books, we must mentally edit them by the light God has placed in each of us. As Anne Hutchinson put it at her trial, "The Lord knows that I could not open scripture; he must by his prophetical office open it unto me."*

Those who wish to live as Christians, Jews, Muslims, agnostics, or atheists by following the humble apophatic thread, as opposed to those who wish to *force others to be like them* by *using* Christianity, Judaism, Islam, or doctrinaire secularism as a weapon, must shift from unquestioning faith in the Bible, Quran, Torah, or science to a life-affirming message of transcendence.

There is a way to live comforted by faith without being part of the evil that constitutes so much of religion. This way of faith is symbolized for me by a certain annual Greek Orthodox service Genie and I love: the Service of Forgiveness. (And no, this is *not* a pitch for my religion, just a sharing with you of what Genie and I happen to do in our little community, where we encounter a church

---

*"Religious Freedom: The Trial of Anne Hutchinson," PBSkids.org, http://pbs kids.org/wayback/civilrights/features_hutchison.html.

tradition that, like all other church traditions, is far from perfect, not *the* way but *a* way that we happen to love.)

After prayers are read, this service ends with each person in our local Greek Orthodox community walking to the front of our sanctuary, kissing the icon of Jesus, then bowing in front of our priest. "Forgive me," we say. "I forgive you," answers our priest, as does each member of the congregation. We embrace and then together we say, "God forgives us both."

After that exchange, each person takes his or her place next to the priest in a line that—after we've all stepped up and taken our places—stretches around the interior perimeter of the church. Each of us repeats the action and then moves down the line repeating the "forgive me" ritual with everyone in the congregation until we've all asked each other for forgiveness. We bow before children and old people, middle-aged parishioners and giggling children. We ask forgiveness from the people we love and from the people we don't like. Everyone from the priest to the youngest infant in her mother's arms is an equal in this ritual.

When I get to the place in the line where Genie is standing, there's a fraught history in my "Forgive me." We hug just as we've hugged everyone else, but in Genie's embrace is the healing gift of reconciliation. My wife of forty years says "I forgive you" with such warmth and sincerity that I feel that life is not a *step* to a "Better Place" but is that better place—*now*.

EPILOGUE

One recent morning I happened to be riding a full Greyhound bus from Boston to New York. The advice I gave The Probably Unsaved Asian Young Woman, as I'll call the person I met on that bus, was pretty good (though maybe since I was still labeling people, I was less cured of my fundamentalism than I thought).

The seat next to me was open. The only other empty seat was across the aisle next to a heavyset girl in her early twenties. She was talking loudly on her cell phone and sniffing compulsively while brushing her lank sandy blonde hair away from her pudgy white face. Her sniffing and the incessant dragging of her fingers through her hair seemed to be connected; one action accompanied the other. Had my mother been there—not as she is now at the very sweet and forgetful age of ninety-six, but as she was when she was fifty, vibrant, young, beautiful, and energetically opinionated—she would have described the cell phone talker as "a young woman who clearly *doesn't* know the Lord."

If This Unfortunate Young Woman, as Mom would have called her (and as I instantly labeled her) had been happier looking, speaking in a less-petulant tone, and carried on a quieter, more intelligent series of cell phone conversations or if she'd worn something besides too-tight, too-short shorts hugging her bulging dimpled thighs, she might have been attractive. Sniffing, those Unfortunate Shorts, her hair-sweeping, and her head-tossing might have been forgiven. But The Unfortunate Young Woman's face was set in a terminal pout, and her side of successive phone conversations (which she conducted one after the other, like a chain smoker lighting each cigarette off the butt of the last) consisted of bad-mouthing her friends to other friends, combined with an unforgivable "where-I'm-like-at-right-now" travelogue.

If the driver on the Boston to New York run is a smoker, he pulls over at a rest stop near Hartford under the pretense of letting his or her passengers stretch their legs. Almost everyone buys something to eat at the Roy Rogers/Pizza Hut while the driver stands by the bus feverishly consuming two cigarettes. He or she sucks the air through those cigarettes with such nicotine-deprived desperation that each drag creates a quarter to half an inch of ash, and you can hear the tobacco sizzle. Some of the passengers also smoke while others ferry food onto the bus.

For the rest of the way, the air in the bus is redolent of french fries and glopped-up, too-thick Americanized "pizza," not to mention the smoke smell clinging to the smokers' clothes. Weirdly, instead of these odors being nauseating, they combine to foster a mood of friendly domesticity that always makes me feel as if our bus-riding collection of strangers is forming into some sort of community that would, in the event of a terrorist attack, flat tire, or alien invasion from outer space, stick together and share food.

Even without an alien invasion, I've had fellow passengers who hadn't said a word to me before the rest stop offer me french fries soon after we've climbed back onboard. I once shared several chicken nuggets with a Polish tourist. Something about disembarking together and then ten minutes later trooping back onto the bus—with everyone obeying the unwritten rule that you go back to your former seat—makes for bonding.

That said, our driver wasn't a smoker. There was to be no rest stop. And so I never did develop any community feeling toward The Unfortunate Young Woman, especially since ten minutes out of Boston, after the driver announced that we were stopping in Newton for more passengers, the sniffer arranged herself—*on purpose*—in such a way as to claim both seats on her side of our row. She spread out like a stranded jellyfish melting on hot sand.

I didn't even have a briefcase to protect my open seat. Nor, given that I mow my lawn and cut and stack firewood (and don't have a sweet tooth), do I have any extra body mass to spread out when it's most needed. So, short of feigning a particularly severe Tourette-syndrome-type of outburst and/or off-putting Pentecostal-style speaking in tongues, I was defenseless.

The new passenger, a short young Asian woman with a studious intelligent face that was a bit scrunched looking—everything compressed, flatter, and wider than optimal—was timidly glancing back and forth at the two open seats. I tried not to make eye contact. She looked from the open seat next to me to the one across from me being smothered by The Unfortunate Young Woman's flaccid right thigh. I was too cowardly to contort my face, twitch uncontrollably, or scream "Praise Jesus!" so instead—something like Sir Alec Guinness playing Obi-Wan Kenobi in *Star Wars* and instructing the storm troopers to let Luke and him pass unmolested—I projected several telepathic thoughts: Sit next to the big girl! *Please, sit next to the big girl!* Ask her to move over! *Ask!*

The Probably Unsaved Asian Young Woman looked my way again, then back at The Unfortunate Young Woman's open seat. As the bus left Newton, The Probably Unsaved Asian Young Woman peered at the rows behind us. I knew that nothing was open back there. Still undecided and still standing, she held onto the back of a seat as we rounded the bend out of the parking lot and headed for the Mass Pike. I knew that the decent thing to do was to offer to move so that she could step to the open window seat next to me. I'm ashamed to say that instead of moving, I decided to take a last stab at projecting more telepathic thoughts: "No right-minded twenty-something woman *chooses* to sit next to a fifty-eight-year-old man!" I thought as hard as I could. "Sit next to the nice, albeit extra-large girl your age! She's made herself look far bigger than she really is! It's the oldest trick in the book! Ask her to move! There's plenty of room for you both! You can lower the armrest and contain her! The large ones fall asleep, so you'll have a nice quiet ride. *Sit there*! SIT T-H-E-R-E!"

"May I sit here?" The Probably Unsaved Asian Young Woman asked me so quietly that she was almost whispering.

"Of course," I muttered, given that my mother had a "special burden" for the Chinese and that I'm the product of British boys boarding schools from back in the day when politeness counted. I usually play the part of a gentleman by habit, if not by inclination. I smiled as if I'd just noticed her and swung my legs around into the aisle, making room for her to step to the window seat. It was the right thing to do, and besides I've arrived at the F-you stage of life.

Once you're old enough to know that the accomplishments and possessions you once craved aren't what they're cracked up to be, and once you spend enough time on your hands and knees crawling around with your ten-month-old granddaughter finding everything she does deeply fascinating—say, taking boxes of raisins and cornmeal out of a kitchen cupboard again and again—then everything else in your life begins to be fascinating again, too.

Each grandchild Genie and I have been blessed with is something like cataract surgery: The misty veil lifts, and I see more clearly, not that I've ever had cataracts. The F-you stage sounds antisocial. It's not at all; it is just my way of saying that these days I'm content to let the chips fall where they may. The point is that the F-you stage isn't directed against anyone, just against the Virus of False Certainty that is threatening to destroy us. The F-you stage is a state of mind that I fell into after hitting my fifties, wherein I say what I think because almost nothing much embarrasses me these days, except my own past false certainties. Knowing you could and probably are wrong about most of what you say is freeing. There is a peaceful sort of "knowing" in admitting unknowing once you accept the basic human Paradox: The evolution of our species is a journey, not a destination, and we are only just at the very beginning.

In my grandchild-rejuvenated, F-you frame of mind, I talk to strangers as if they were old friends. People respond to self-revealing, even self-flaying transparency. So strangers talk to me. They tell me surprisingly intimate details about themselves. I'm a good listener. I also give outrageously forward personal advice. For instance, while flying to Los Angeles, after hearing one divorced and unhappy middle-aged guy's life story, I told him to track down his high school sweetheart and start over. On a train to Washington, D.C., I told a young Harvard Business School graduate who said he didn't find his career rewarding to forget his fancy job on Wall Street and join the Marines while he was still young enough to "do something useful." I advised a businesswoman I met on a flight to London, who (in return for me telling her about how I got Genie pregnant when we were teens) told me about her struggle to "balance career and family," to go ahead and *have* a third child if she wanted to, and "damn the career consequences!" I've told atheist

Jews that they need Jesus, and Evangelicals that the best thing they could do is never set foot in a church again, that they should become secular Jews. I'm sure I've had next-to-no effect on most people, besides making this or that bus or plane ride interesting and/or intolerable; I may have helped one or two people and probably ruined a few lives. I enjoy the conversations nonetheless and get a strange adrenaline rush from offering unsolicited advice.

Before we were off the Mass Pike, The Unfortunate Young Woman was blessedly asleep, and once she stopped talking, I was able to shift my mood from dyspeptic brooding to my usual look-out-the-window I-84 daze. The Probably Unsaved Asian Young Woman next to me had her laptop open, and when she typed, her elbow protruded across the armrest. I wasn't wishing The Probably Unsaved Asian Young Woman ill. I was merely passing the time by visually measuring the airspace her elbow was poking into between our seats. My eyes were tired from editing a draft of this book, so I'd decided not to read. And looking out the window wasn't that interesting because I know every inch of I-84 as it winds through Connecticut. Thus, I was just killing time by measuring my seatmate's elbow intrusion.

Glancing at my seatmate's laptop, I saw that she was writing something about education. Did I have a right to read what was on her screen? Sure I did. She wasn't angling the screen for privacy, and since I was contributing a portion of *my airspace* to *her* elbow and thus allowing her to type and read her notes at the same time, I was helping her. Typing with one hand and holding papers with the other didn't work out very well. There were gaps in the typing action. The Probably Unsaved Asian Young Woman interrupted her work several times by reaching down to her backpack to extract various snacks in the form of Power Bars. When she bent down to scrabble around in the backpack for the third or fourth time (she'd placed it at her feet), my seatmate's T-shirt pulled up from her jeans and I glimpsed the base of her flawless ivory-colored lower back and the top couple of inches of her panties.

They were made of a black and expensive-looking gossamer material. Silk, I guessed. There was exceedingly delicate olive green and pink embroidery featuring a Roman vine motif something like the work one sees framing frescos at Pompeii. If I had to place a bet, I'd say that those panties were handmade in Italy.

From this brief glimpse I deduced not just that my seatmate had good taste in lingerie, but also that there was probably money in her family. This was no made-in-China-five-pairs-for-$10 piece of underwear. I'd say there was $155 worth of La Perla lingerie tucked under those mundane jeans. The panty glimpse also gave me insight into The Probably Unsaved Asian Young Woman's love life. A woman doesn't wear black gossamer silk panties with hand-embroidered Roman-derived motifs unless there's someone in her life to wear them for.

When she sat up, I volunteered to hold her papers. This had nothing to do with The Probably Unsaved Asian Young Woman's lingerie. Miserable cynics may scoff in disbelief; trust me when I say that my consideration of her underwear was fleeting, academic, and passionless! I only offered to hold her papers because from what I'd read on her laptop, her writing seemed to be serious and typing with one hand while holding papers with the other is tough.

"Put your papers on my knees; then you can look at them and type with both hands," I said.

"Oh no, that's fine," The Probably Unsaved Asian Young Woman said while looking somewhat startled.

"Don't worry; I don't mind," I said.

"Really?" she asked.

I nodded and she handed me her sheaf of papers.

"There's no fold-down tray, so that's the best we can do," I said.

After that The Probably Unsaved Asian Young Woman typed faster, but also (it seemed to me) was shooting me worried glances while trying to figure out if I was going to be a nuisance. Also, I think that she felt awkward repeatedly glancing down at my knees and keenly aware that I was perhaps reading her notes. Plus, I had to actually hold the papers since otherwise they would have slipped off my lap. The whole help-my-neighbor gesture was turning out to be far more cumbersome than I'd imagined.

I could sense her growing discomfort. Was my kindness a prelude to murder? Maybe she'd read about that crazy man in Canada who killed—then beheaded—the man riding next to him on a bus. That was also on a Greyhound. Maybe he'd started out on the trip being nice, too, before things turned mean-spirited.

"I'm sleepy," said the exquisitely lingeried, though otherwise plain Probably Unsaved Asian Young Woman. "I think I'll take a nap."

Maybe my offer to hold her papers had embarrassed her and she'd only let me hold them to be polite. Maybe she really was tired and wanted a nap. Whatever her motivation, The Probably Unsaved Asian Young Woman retrieved her papers, then closed her eyes, and a few moments later her jaw relaxed, and unless she was a brilliant actress, she really did fall deeply asleep. The Probably Unsaved Asian Young Woman's head sank forward, then jerked back up again several times, and then her mouth fell slightly open.

About fifteen minutes later when The Probably Unsaved Asian Young Woman awoke, I asked her what she'd been writing. This was something like telling God your troubles: He knows them all already but apparently likes to be asked and voluntarily kept in the loop. I'd been reading her paper, so I knew the phrases she'd been typing. She confirmed that it was a dissertation on education and women or, rather, "on Asian women and educational opportunities." Speaking about her subject—with lots of boilerplate phrases like "Gender diversities and technology, achieving economic, political, and social equality"—my seatmate seemed bored. So we moved on to more personal topics.

Early in the postnap conversation, I mentioned Genie as in "My wife, Genie, loves walking in Central Park." After that my seatmate seemed to relax—given that men don't usually speak warmly about their wives if they intend to hit on strangers. Once the what's-this-guy-really-want factor was taken out of the equation, I learned that The Probably Unsaved Asian Young Woman was getting her PhD at Columbia, that she didn't like New York City "because at night I can't see the stars," that she was a year from being done with her PhD, that she was Chinese, or rather of Chinese extract: Her grandmother had lived in Taiwan then emigrated, her Chinese father and mother had been born Beijing but lived in America since they were toddlers, and her father was a professor at one of the best of the Boston-area colleges. She told me that her mother was also an academic and, like her father, also an international business consultant. Then she told me that she had a boyfriend in New York City.

"He's a black man," she said, while giving me a glance of defiance.

No one in her family approved of her boyfriend, The Probably Unsaved Asian Young Woman said, "even though he went to Yale and started his own electronics business." Her grandmother was an "out-and-out racist," she said, and didn't even pretend otherwise. So was her mother, though she pretended she wasn't. The Probably Unsaved Asian Young Woman's dad hadn't expressed an opinion about the black boyfriend but was deferring to the women in the family.

"My grandmother just hates the idea of me marrying a black man," she said.

"What about your mother?" I asked.

"She says she wants me to be happy, then makes snide comments about how mixed-race couples are always a 'problem,' and once even said, 'Studies show that I'd find it so much easier to love grandchildren who look like me.'"

"She said that?!"

"Yes."

"Did you get on with your family before you met your boyfriend?"

"Yes. We're incredibly close; or rather, we used to be. My grandmother cooks for us every Sunday, and we all spend the afternoon at her house eating together. She's a great cook and cooks all week to prepare. There's never been a problem in our family, until now. It's breaking my heart. How could I have known? My parents are so liberal about everything else."

Once we got onto the subject of family, marriage, Chinese bigotry against other races, men, children, her sister—who had married a Chinese American and thus served as a "why-can't-you-be-like-your-sister" example her grandmother harped on—my seatmate talked to me the way you talk only to a complete stranger when there are two or three hours of a bus ride to kill, or the way a granddaughter might talk to a grandfather when she's feeling desperate. I spoke to her the way a writer—who's willing to tell his secrets in return for confidences while he's fishing for good material—talks.

Whatever the sophistication of the consciousness-raising, postfeminist qualities of my seatmate's dissertation, our conversation could have taken place at any time in history without even a nod to modernity. We talked about her boyfriend, love, and family troubles. Shakespeare would have understood the dialogue perfectly.

The Probably Unsaved Asian Young Woman was thirty and wanted children. Her boyfriend was thirty-two. He wanted to marry and start a family immediately. She didn't want to "rush," but she also knew that she was at the age where biology starts to matter and that if she waited a few more years, then added another year or two for career considerations, then had any trouble getting pregnant, she'd be closer to forty than to thirty when she gave birth. And if she wanted more than one child and wanted to space them, then the second child would be conceived on the cusp of her midforties. And, The Probably Unsaved Asian Young Woman added with a sigh, "midforty is old."

"I got my wife—before she was my wife—pregnant when I was seventeen," I said. "That was forty years ago. We're still together."

"That's how it should be," my seatmate replied, somewhat to my surprise. "We have too many options today. My friends and me all say that when we talk. Sometimes I think arranged marriages aren't such a bad thing."

So we'd traveled from a respectable consciousness-raising dissertation on educational opportunity for Asian women, to a Chinese family of academics (in self-consciously progressive Boston, no less) who were unrepentant racists, to issues of childbearing and marriage, passed through the 1950s as it were, and now were headed smack dab back to feudal China and arranged marriages.

"I know you want to please your family and somehow make all this work, too, but you have to make choices." I said. "Right now the people that really count aren't here to defend themselves."

"What do you mean?" she asked.

"Once you meet your children and grandchildren, it will be impossible to imagine the world without them. Right now they can't speak for themselves, but if they could, they'd tell you to marry the man you love, whatever your grandmother thinks about black people. Is he kind?

"Yes."

"Does he work at making your relationship work?"

"Yes. He listens when I talk. He gives me flowers. He even buys me lingerie."

"Ha!" I exclaimed, as the panty mystery was solved.

"Excuse me?" The Probably Unsaved Asian Young Woman said, looking a bit surprised at my vehement "Ha!"

"I mean," I said, "that's great! He sounds like the right man. Would you like him to be the father of your children?"

"Yes. He'd be a wonderful father. I met his dad, and he's a lovely man, too, spent his working life in the army and was a good father. He likes me, and hopes I'll marry his son."

"That's all you can know. Being married will change who you both are anyway. So all you can know is if he's kind. The rest is guesswork. When you're married, the relationship changes you. So there are things you can't learn until you *are* married, and waiting around won't tell you anything more about what it'll really be like after you make a commitment. That's one reason that just living with a person doesn't prepare you to be married. Everything changes after making a real commitment."

"I'm afraid my grandmother will never speak to me again."

"Your grandmother will come around—or she won't—but once you meet your children, you'll never think about a 'what if' question when it comes to their existence. If they were here, they'd be telling you to marry their father."

I could see from the bemused expression on her face that my seatmate thought she'd either run into a nut or maybe a very forward and slightly demented guardian angel sent to nudge her to woman up and marry her black man. But I had launched. And at the F-you stage, when it comes to spewing wisdom (real or imagined), it's something like having that second martini; there will be a third.

"I've done some interesting things in life, but nothing comes close—on any scale—to my children and my grandchildren," I said. "Yes, it's a cliché. And it's true. Because I got Genie pregnant so young, I wasn't even a good father, at first anyway. I don't even remember who those two kids were who raised my children. We all grew up together, and yet looking back, there's nothing I'd change but my meanness because you can't get here from there by any path than the one you're on. You don't choose anything important. It just happens. The only choice you have is if you'll make life's accidents work."

When the bus ride ended, my new acquaintance thanked me for the advice and said she was going to call her boyfriend and tell him that maybe she was ready to defy her family. Somewhere in the midst of our conversation my seatmate said, "We have too many options." Then we talked about the fact that in most cultures (and in most of history) the big moments in life related to marriage, childbearing, and child-raising. Career was called work, and work was about survival; it was not a form of self-fulfillment, much less expected to be fun, let alone entertaining.

If you were lucky, you married someone kind. Kind or not, you were stuck with the choices you, or maybe your parents, made about who your partner would be, where you lived, what you did for a job, the social class you were born into, and the shape of your life. Cutting and running wasn't an option. If you were lucky, you lived. If you were unlucky, you got killed because stupid people were sure that's what their God wanted them to do to you. The number of children you had, how they were raised, what you taught them about right and wrong, and their expectations were shaped by what would have seemed to be a set of changeless inherited values.

Since the Depression, the invention of labor-saving machines, the liberation of women, the sexualization of our culture from cradle to grave, the invention of "teenagerhood," and college as a rite of passage changed what people expected out of life. What had once seemed like inevitable facts—marriage, children, struggle, work, survival, village, town, community, the faith one was born into—became "choices." So did growing up. In other words, learning to make the most of any situation you're in became optional, just another choice. The concept of freedom was reduced to the soul-shriveling puny right to choose between consumer products. And relationships became mere choices, too, just like buying a car.

So here's the question The Probably Unsaved Asian Young Woman and I hashed out: What *hasn't* changed over time? Here's what we came up with: People still crave Love. So how should we make decisions that take advantage of our new freedoms *and yet* help us to have a shot at happiness related to what never changes and matters most?

While riding the subway uptown after the bus ride, I had time to think, and here's what I came up with in a wish-I'd-thought-of-that-at-the-time way: It strikes me that our American society, from kindergarten through old age, while talking about how great families are (especially when selling worried young mothers and fathers "parenting" products that they don't need) might as well have been designed to destroy family happiness. That's because *both* the religious fundamentalist *and* the higher-education-worshipping consumer/choice models of existence and everything that goes with both "dogmas" fly in the face of the reality of what we fundamentally *are*: tribal, communal, and family-seeking animals craving Unconditional Love *and* Continuity *and* Creativity.

We human animals seek out meaning that transcends the sum of our physical parts. I know only one thing: that any worldview—be it religious or secular—that doesn't start and end with the recognition of Paradox will become a tyranny. So I have rejected many of my past certainties and embraced the meaning I find in loving, raising, protecting, and praying for my children and grandchildren. I also feel that in some inexplicable way my mother's prayers for her family have—and are being—answered every time Lucy says, "I love you, Ba."

That subway ride took me to Genie. Genie and I love to visit New York City. We stay in a small hotel on the Upper West Side. We often walk to the Metropolitan Museum of Art. By the time we're on the jogging path in Central Park, walking briskly around the reservoir, I feel the way I used to feel when I was eight and on my way to Italy riding on the train to our family vacation in Portofino. Our vacations were always as wonderful as I imagined they would be, even back when Mom brought along her Gospel Walnut.

The Metropolitan Museum of Art is like some perfect childhood memory, except it's not beyond reach. It is "about" watching wide-eyed children gathered in front of a painting with sketchbooks, making their own drawings. It is about taking my older grandchildren, Amanda and Benjamin, on pilgrimages to give them something lasting to hang on to, even though they sometimes roll their eyes and sigh when I "suggest" we're going there—*again.*

The day after my bus ride I happened to be at the Met alone. Genie was off buying material at her favorite midtown fabric stores. I slipped away from a Matisse show I'd gone to see. Too many people were talking too loudly about the paintings, so I sought refuge in a place I knew would be quiet. There are very public parts of the Metropolitan Museum of Art. But there are also some corners where it feels as if you've brazenly walked into someone's home. For instance, there are hardly ever any visitors in the dim recesses of the Chinese galleries. People whisper. Everything seems intimate, almost forbidden. Sometimes visitors stumble in from the bigger, brighter parts of the museum and, as their eyes adjust to the cool dim indirect lighting, look around worriedly as if about to ask, "Are we allowed here?" Perhaps it's the subdued light. Perhaps it's the wood floors. But I think that the real reason for the sense that one is intruding is the intimate nature of the objects. Pens, inkpots, writing stands, tablets, finely wrought boxes—they seem as if they belong on a bedside table and are the sorts of things that children are told not to touch, ever.

I'm not "into" Chinese art the way Genie is and as my mother was, and so I'm ignorant about it. Unless Genie is with me to explain what I'm looking at, I rarely go to the Chinese galleries. But that day several ancient jade carvings "broke through." They seemed so impossible. I thought, there's no way anyone could carve so intricately without modern tools.

I started really looking. Maybe it had something to do with having talked to my Chinese seatmate the day before on the bus. Anyway, I forgot that I only wanted to spend a few quiet moments before heading back to take another look at a particular painting in that thronged Matisse show. I stood hunched over the glass case almost forgetting to breathe and peering through my reading glasses at microscopic gnarled pine trees and rocky paths cut out of green and gray semi-opaque rock, miniature worlds that drew me in as surely as those Bible stories that Mom read out loud used to enthrall me.

Looking at those jade landscapes, I felt as if I had been hiking with Mom and Dad through some alpine valley and the fog had unexpectedly lifted to reveal a heart-stopping view. I was also reminded of the evenings the previous winter when I had bundled

Lucy up in my down parka and put on her hat and mittens and we'd go out into the garden to look at the stars.

I held Lucy clasped against my chest, and we stared up. Lucy gazed at the sliver of the universe we could see, and I stared down at my angel made of, and lit by, stardust. When she first looked upward at the vast glittering sprinkle of stars, Lucy's breathing quickened, and then her breathing slowed along with mine as we both sank into a stunned reverie.

It was very much like the reverie I was gripped by when tumbling into those distant jade miniature worlds. Gazing at those jade universes, I connected powerfully with my mother's enigmatic self as she was revealed in the sacrament of her flower arrangements. They were made of long-gone twig, moss, and leaf, but the liturgy they celebrated has survived in me. In the silence it struck me that Mom and I are very much alike: We each have spent most of our lives rescuing ourselves—from ourselves.

For my mother, Edith

INDEX